Japan, 1868–1945

From Isolation to Occupation

Japan, 1868–1945

From Isolation to Occupation

John Benson and Takao Matsumura

An imprint of **Pearson Education**

Harlow, England · London · New York · Reading, Massachusetts · San Francisco · Toronto · Don Mills, Ontario · Sydney
Tokyo · Singapore · Hong Kong · Seoul · Taipei · Cape Town · Madrid · Mexico City · Amsterdam · Munich · Paris · Milan

Pearson Education Limited

Edinburgh Gate
Harlow
Essex CM20 2JE
United Kingdom

and Associated Companies throughout the world

Visit us on the World Wide Web at
www.pearsoneduc.com

First published in Great Britain in 2001

© Pearson Education Limited 2001

ISBN 0-582-30813-5 PPR

British Library Cataloguing in Publication Data
A CIP catalogue record for this book can be obtained from the British Library.

10 9 8 7 6 5 4 3 2 1
05 04 03 02 01 00

Typeset by 35 in 9.5/13.5pt Stone Serif
Produced by Pearson Education Malaysia Sdn. Bhd.
Printed in Malaysia , LSP

Contents

Acknowledgements

We have received a good deal of help in the preparation of this book. We are grateful for the advice of Tom Almond, Paul Henderson, David and Margaret Powell, Paul Rice, Kaoru Sugihara, Carol Volante, Malcolm Wanklyn and Harvey Woolf, and for the financial support of the British Council and the University of Wolverhampton. We are grateful too for the support we have received at Addison Wesley Longman: Andrew MacLennan commissioned the book and commented in detail upon an early draft, Hilary Shaw and John Yates agreed the changes that needed to be made to this draft, and Heather McCallum saw the manuscript through to publication.

We particularly wish to acknowledge the generous assistance of Paula Bartley, Kenichi Tomobe, Naoto Tsuji, Tsuyoshi Nagashima and Maurice Jenkins, all of whom took time from their own work to read, and comment most helpfully upon, the penultimate draft of the manuscript. However, our greatest debt is to Darren Aoki who not only commented on the penultimate version of the manuscript but also contributed enthusiastically and professionally towards the completion of the final version of the text, figures and illustrations as we prepared them for publication.

John Benson
Takao Matsumura

April 2000

A note on sources

We have drawn upon both English-language and Japanese-language sources in writing this book. We believe, however, that it is English-language material that will prove of the greatest use to our readers, and it is this material therefore that we have cited most often in the footnotes, and recommended in the Select Bibliography.

Abbreviations

CH	*Chûô*
CS	*Chûgai Shôgyô*
HS	*Heimin Shimbun*
JS	*Jiji Shimpô*
KS	*Kokumin Shimbun*
OA	*Osaka Asahi*
OM	*Osaka Mainichi*
NN	*Nichi Nichi*
NP	*Nippon*
TA	*Tokyo Asahi*
TM	*Tokyo Mainichi*
YC	*Yorozu Chôhô*

Japan, 1925.

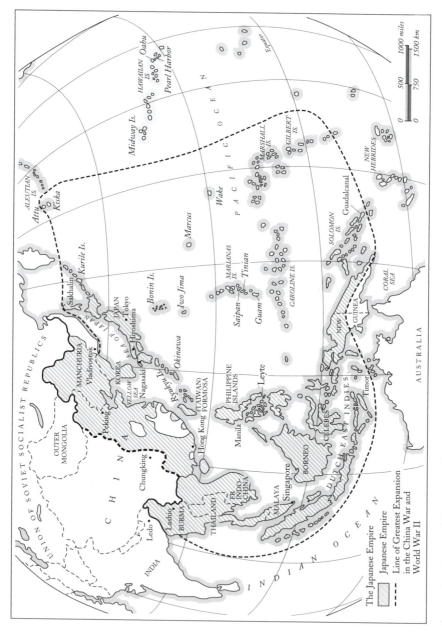

The Japanese Empire

Japanese Empire

Line of Greatest Expansion
in the China War and
World War II

Largest extent of Japanese Empire, early 1942.

Introduction

Japan has the most extraordinary history. In a little more than a century and a quarter, this small group of islands on the edge of Asia has been transformed from an isolated, feudal backwater into a stable democracy and one of the world's leading economic superpowers. During the three-quarters of a century covered by this book, the Japanese abolished the feudal system, established both democratic and authoritarian forms of government, laid the economic, social and cultural foundations of a modern industrial economy, acquired and lost a huge overseas empire, suffered overwhelming defeat at the hands of the Allies, and found their country occupied by the Allied Powers (or rather, the United States of America). It is no exaggeration to suggest, as several commentators have done, that Japan experienced the equivalent of five to six hundred years of European history in the three or four generations between the Meiji Restoration of 1868 and the Allied Occupation of 1945.[1]

'Little men' and 'supermen'

It goes without saying that there were any number of countries that changed, and changed dramatically, between the third quarter of the nineteenth century and the middle of the twentieth century. But few, if any, nations were transformed as rapidly or as profoundly as Japan. When the Meiji regime came to power in 1868, it took over a feudal society that was riven by internal divisions, was still heavily dependent upon a narrow range of agricultural activities, and was only just beginning to emerge, haltingly and uncertainly, from two hundred and fifty years of self-imposed international isolation. Economically constrained, politically weak and diplomatically impotent, the new government faced rebellion at home and challenges abroad. There was little that Japan could do to break the influence of her overmighty neighbour China, not much she could do to restrain the Asian ambitions of the Western imperial powers – and nothing at all she could do to influence what was happening in the rest of the world.[2]

Three-quarters of a century later, Japan had demonstrated beyond any possible doubt her ability to drive forward her domestic agenda, her capacity to destabilise and dominate China, her power to conquer large swathes of Asia – and of course her power to embroil the rest of the world in her political, economic and military ambitions. The leaders of Japan took the country into the Second World War – though not of course out of it – economically successful, politically focused, diplomatically determined and militarily confident. By the late 1930s, Japan possessed the world's third largest merchant fleet, and was self-sufficient in the machinery, power plant and major chemicals that were needed to operate a modern, industrial economy. By the early 1940s, the Japanese empire stretched from the USSR border in the north to the Dutch East Indies in the South, from Burma in the west to the Marshall Islands, thousands of miles to the east in the Pacific Ocean. The racial contempt that so disfigured Western attitudes towards Japan was changed, rather than undermined, by Japanese military successes, with stereotypes of 'little men' and 'supermen' now coexisting uncomfortably in the Anglo-American imagination.[3]

Economic and political transformation

That Japan could achieve so much, wield such influence in imperialist politics, and wreak so much havoc began to fascinate the outside world. There was, as all could see, a great deal to admire in Japan's modern history, but even more perhaps to abhor. Indeed, it was the juxtaposition of industrial development and imperial expansion – alongside economic liberalism and political authoritarianism, cultural aestheticism and military aggression – that seemed somehow to encapsulate the mystery that was the Orient.[4]

As Japan's economic transformation became more widely known, it won her considerable international respect. However, it was respect that was usually tinged, as one might anticipate, with caution, anxiety and hostility. Yet even those commentators who did not subscribe to the view that Japan had somehow discovered the secret of perpetual growth could not fail to be impressed by the country's economic achievements. Between the two world wars, this tiny island, with few natural resources, few natural allies and little or no tradition of industrial development, attained levels of economic growth which were far in excess of anything achieved in advanced industrial countries such as Germany, Great Britain and the United States of America.

Nor was this all. Japan's transformation from a rural backwater to a modern industrial economy was brought about, it seemed, with little of the social and cultural dislocation that accompanied such changes in other parts of the world. What struck most overseas observers particularly forcibly was that despite the pace at which the country industrialised, Japanese society remained united, peaceful and harmonious. There were few strikes, there was little crime, there was very little sign of family dysfunction, there was almost no indication of community breakdown, and there was no evidence at all of the imperial family ever coming in for anything but sporadic and muted criticism. Even the country's most vociferous critics generally conceded that late nineteenth and early twentieth-century Japan produced well-behaved children, amenable adolescents, stable families, valued old people, loyal workers and patriotic citizens.

On the other hand, as Japan's political transformation became more widely known, it brought her little but international criticism and contempt. The opinion of a foreign teacher at Tokyo Imperial University in the early 1890s, as summarised by one contemporary Japanese intellectual – is representative of the kind of scorn that Japan often received:

> Japan's attitude in adopting European culture was problematic in every respect. The Japanese did not try to transplant the roots of the plant, but simply cut off eye-catching flowers. As a result the people who brought the flowers were respected enormously, but the plants that could have produced such blossoms did not come to grow. . . . Despite this, Japanese scholars and prodigies strutted about displaying their knowledge of Western things noisily and proudly. Dr Koeber seemed to feel that that kind of pose and pretension was utterly revolting.[5]

The transformation was a remarkable achievement for all that. Within forty-five years of coming to power, the Meiji regime had brought an end to two-and-a-half centuries of military rule, it had united the country, introduced a 'modern' system of government (complete with constitution, executive and legislature), established a well-respected civil service, and inaugurated a nation-wide system of state education. The new regime showed its military might by defeating China in 1895 and Tsarist Russia ten years later; it began to realise its imperial ambitions by acquiring Taiwan just before the end of the century and by annexing Korea a few years before the outbreak of the First World War.

Thereafter, Japan embarked upon a political roller-coaster. A short period of modest liberal democratic reform was followed, in the early 1930s, by a far better-known period of militarisation and authoritarianism. Military leaders replaced party leaders at the head of government, serious efforts were made to suppress internal criticism, and it seemed at times as if it was the armed forces rather than the cabinet that were determining the direction of government policy. In 1931 Japan seized the north-east

Chinese province of Manchuria, and six years later she invaded China's eastern provinces as far south as Shanghai and Nanking (where at least 20,000 women were raped and more than 200,000 people murdered in what became known as the Rape of Nanking). In 1940, the government established what it called the New Political Order to mobilise domestic support, and what it termed the Greater East Asia Co-Prosperity Sphere to mobilise support across East and South-East Asia. Finally, in December 1941, the imperial air force launched its lethal, surprise attack on the American fleet at anchor at Pearl Harbor, an incident which for many people continues to epitomise all that one needs to know about Japanese culture and the Japanese national character.

What it means to be Japanese

In fact, so extraordinary is the history of Japan that commentators of all nationalities and all ideological persuasions have often felt able to account for what happened only in terms of the distinctiveness of Japanese national culture and the uniqueness of Japanese national character. According to this view, the exceptional nature of Japan's history is to be accounted for primarily, if not exclusively, by the nature of Japanese society which finds no parallel anywhere in the world. There is no doubt that this belief in Japanese uniqueness, whether or not it can be justified empirically, continues to exercise a powerful and pervasive influence upon the ways both in which the Japanese see themselves and in which the Japanese are seen by those in the rest of the world.[6]

It has always been common for the Japanese to point to their uniqueness, to stress the supposed purity, homogeneity and cohesiveness of the society in which they lived. Indeed, it seems to the outsider that they have spent an inordinate amount of time and energy agonising over what it was to be Japanese, the ways in which the Japanese 'race' differed from every other, and the ways in which this uniqueness made them superior to all the other nations with which they came into contact. Nor was this some aberration of the totalitarian 1930s and early 1940s. It has been calculated that between 1946 and 1978 alone, some 700 books were published on 'what it means to be Japanese'.[7]

The belief in Japanese uniqueness continues to manifest itself in many ways. One has only to think, for example, of the popular belief within Japan that theirs is the only country in the world to enjoy four distinct seasons, or of the ways in which Japanese officials have manipulated the idea of national distinctiveness in the furtherance of national economic policy. They excuse limitations on the import of foreign skis by citing the uniqueness of Japanese snow, and justify restrictions on the import of foreign food by underlining the uniqueness not only of Japanese vegetables and rice but of the Japanese digestive system.[8]

It is true, some Japanese concede, that the supposed purity, homogeneity and cohesiveness of Japanese society did not always prove entirely advantageous. According to one school of thought, it was such qualities which encouraged the docility that made it possible, during the 1930s and early 1940s, for a minority of military fanatics to manipulate and dominate the mass of the population. This docility led, it is argued, to the events which culminated in the Second World War, the use of nuclear weapons against Hiroshima and Nagasaki, and occupation by the United States of America.[9]

However, the dominant school of thought takes a very different view. Nearly always, it is maintained, the supposed purity, homogeneity and cohesiveness of Japanese society worked to the advantage of the Japanese people. The Preamble of the Meiji Constitution of 1889 set the tone.

> Having, by virtue of the glories of Our Ancestors, ascended the Throne of a lineal succession unbroken for ages eternal; desiring to promote the welfare of, and to give development to the moral and intellectual faculties of Our beloved subjects, the very same that have been favored with the benevolent care and affectionate vigilance of our Ancestors; and hoping to maintain the prosperity of the State in concert with Our people and with their support, We hereby promulgate . . . a fundamental law of State, to exhibit the principles, by which We are to be guided in Our conduct, and to point out to what Our descendants and Our subjects and their descendants are forever to conform.

In short, the constitution spelled out the fundamental characteristics of the *kokutai*, the 'national principle' or 'national essence' of the Japanese state. Although each country possesses a peculiar 'national principle', Japan's, according to Gluck, was 'by virtue of its immutability . . . more "unique"'.

> By generalizing the living emperor into a timeless series of emperors-in-sequence, *kokutai* seemed to offer the abstract grandeur possessed by such notions as *patrie* or *Vaterland* in the West. *Kokutai* provided a past that was ageless, continuous, and secure in its ancestral tradition. Amuletic and ambiguous, eventually *kokutai* served to identify the nation and separate 'them' from 'us'.

By the late 1930s, 'us' and 'them' as defined by the idea of a 'national principle' had been reduced to racist jingoism. 'There is no such race as the Japanese in the world', claimed the *Japan Times Weekly* in 1939. It is the spirit of the Japanese race which 'sustains them in adversity and spurs them on to the attainment of their objectives. This human strength and hard work compensate the Japanese for their lack of many material resources.'[10]

To be sure, the ideology of the *kokutai* is little mentioned today, being associated with pre-war fanaticism and wartime atrocities. Yet, while many today fervently deny that 'Japaneseness' is based on such untenable myths as an extended family of Japanese united under an imperial lineage extending unbroken to the age of the gods, contemporary ideas of homogeneity and racial/cultural distinction hark, if obliquely, to notions of a 'national essence'. One need only look at the issue of class. Public opinion polls carried out in the 1970s and 1980s, for example, suggested that fully 80–90 per cent of the population considered themselves to be middle class. Regardless of whether or not such beliefs were grounded in empirical evidence, they are of considerable significance. The fact that the vast majority claimed membership of the middle class suggested that, in comparison to other industrial nations, Japanese society was as classless as a society could ever be.[11]

Views from the West

Western opinion, expert and non-expert alike, tends to concur in the view that Japanese national culture and Japanese national character are unique. What has happened, it seems, is that the little which is known about Japan has become transmogrified into a set of widely known, and widely accepted clichés and stereotypes. The Japanese, it is believed, have always tended to forgo private interests for the sake of collective goals and social consensus so that Japanese society has been, if not pure, then most certainly homogeneous, harmonious and co-operative. 'Values and beliefs become mutually compatible over a wide range of work and non-work related issues', claims one management expert. 'Each person's true level of effort and of performance stand out, and the close relationship brings about a high level of subtlety in understanding of each other's needs and plans.'[12]

As might be expected, Western commentators are less agreed than their Japanese counterparts about the consequences of Japan's supposed homogeneity and cohesiveness. When they examine the 1920s and 1930s, what they notice – and what they deplore – is the people's unquestioning obedience, their willingness to work for low wages and, it need hardly be said, their acquiescence in their leaders' military aggression. Inter-war Japan, it appears, can teach the West only what it should try to avoid.[13]

When they examined the post-war years what many Western commentators noticed – and admired – was, for many years, the Japanese people's respect for education, the country's good industrial relations, its high saving rate, its low crime rate and, of course, its so-called economic miracle. Modern Japan, it seemed until the early 1990s, had an enormous amount to teach the West, if only the West was prepared to learn. However, as we all know, such views came in for a great deal of criticism – and were often abandoned – following the economic crisis that struck Asia with such deadly effect during the late 1990s. What had once been presented as economic and social accomplishments were castigated now as barriers to economic and political progress.[14]

Long views and blind spots

How are such views to be reconciled? What is the best way of approaching the history of Japan? Is it possible for those brought up in Japan to free themselves of the values and assumptions with which they have been surrounded? Is it possible for those who are not Japanese ever really to penetrate the country's culture and understand its complex and seemingly contradictory history? As a reviewer in the *Journal of Japanese Studies* remarked some years ago, 'When I read a book on Japanese society I ask myself where the author is sitting as he writes. Each observation post has its long views and blind spots.'[15]

It is the aim of this book to recognise its authors' long views and blind spots, and to provide readers from the English-speaking world with a wide-ranging, accessible and up-to-date interpretation of Japanese history between 1868 and 1945. This is a period which, opening with the Meiji Restoration and ending with the Allied Occupation, is central, we believe, to any understanding of the way in which modern Japan has developed, is developing and is likely to develop in the future.

It is our intention to produce both a narrative and an analysis. We will therefore describe, as fully as possible, the major changes that took place in Japanese political, economic and social life, doing our best to consider the experiences of all major groups in Japanese society. We will also tackle the much more difficult task of attempting to explain, as well as describe, the developments that we have been able to identify. Many of the issues to be discussed remain, of course, exceptionally sensitive and contentious, and we should stress at this point that explanation should not be misinterpreted as exculpation, that trying to understand what happened is not the same as seeking to justify the way that things happened.[16]

Such aims, of course, are a good deal easier to enunciate than they are to achieve. It can be difficult for Japanese scholars to avoid slipping into evasion, exoneration or condemnation when examining the years leading up to the American occupation. It is telling, for example, that there continues to be a number of groups locked in conflict over what sort of history should be presented in school textbooks. In 1996, at precisely the same time that the Society for New History Textbooks was campaigning against the discussion of wartime sex slavery in junior high school texts, the volume *History not Taught in Textbooks* became a national phenomenon, selling 400,000 copies within four months of its publication.[17]

It can be difficult for overseas scholars to avoid adopting racist attitudes, whether overt or covert, and it is even more of a problem to eliminate ethnocentric and 'presentist' assumptions, whereby Japanese history is judged primarily in terms of how nearly it emulated Western aspirations, how closely it conformed to Western developments and how nearly it encapsulated late twentieth-century values. It is a trap into which even the most astute and sensitive of commentators can slip. It is a trap, not surprisingly, into which popular opinion often seems to tumble headlong, with the Japanese compared constantly, and often explicitly, with Western models of what is normal and what is desirable.[18]

Why is it, we ask, that inter-war Japan did not develop into a liberal democracy like those to be found in Europe and the United States of America? Why is it that Japan embarked upon a programme of overseas expansion just as Britain and the United States were beginning to think about decolonisation? Why is it that the Japanese were so much more likely than their Western counterparts to use their disposable income for saving rather than for consumption? Why is it that Japanese families were so much more close-knit than those in the West, and why did they show so much more respect towards the elderly?

So it is that many foreigners look upon Japan with admiration but 'without envy'. They believe that Japanese society displays what has been described as the 'five withouts': the Japanese have wealth without joy, education without creativity, material equality without individual freedom, 'familyism' without genuine family life and great power status without great power leadership. They believe, in other words, that the Japanese should emulate the West in devoting more resources to the social infrastructure and placing less emphasis on harmony and conformity. They should rethink their educational system, alter their work habits and accept the international obligations that economic success brings with it.[19]

Uniqueness, heterogeneity and history

It is hoped that this book will avoid most of these pitfalls. In all events, we are confident that the pairing of a Japanese author with a British author will force us to confront these complications head on. This can only help us, we believe, as we attempt to chart a way between the dangers of evasion and exculpation, of 'presentism' and ethnocentrism, as we undertake our interpretation of modern Japanese history.

We hope, in particular, that our analysis of Japanese history between the Meiji Restoration of 1868 and the Allied Occupation of 1945 will persuade our readers of the truth – and importance – of three major propositions. First, we wish to show that, while there can be no doubting the uniqueness of late nineteenth and early twentieth-century Japanese history, this does not mean – if we may put it like this – that Japan was unique in her uniqueness. Japan – like every other country in the world – developed in her own way, with her own character and her own culture, her own idiosyncrasies and her own sense of herself.

Second, we intend to challenge the view that nineteenth and early twentieth-century Japan was a peculiarly, if not uniquely, homogeneous society. We will find it necessary to stress time and time again during the course of the book that Japan displayed elements both of homogeneity and of heterogeneity. The Japanese people, like virtually any other, were divided – and often divided sharply – by age, gender and ethnicity, by region and geography, by occupational diversity and economic inequality, and of course by ideological predisposition and political affiliation. The homogeneity of Japanese society and culture is, we suggest, a myth, and a dangerous myth at that.

It follows therefore that neither Japanese uniqueness nor Japanese homogeneity can provide a plausible explanation for the way in which Japan developed between 1868 and 1945. We believe that the key to understanding what happened lies not in the uniqueness or homogeneity of Japanese culture and Japanese character but in Japanese history, in the specific political, economic, social and cultural circumstances that pertained in this critical period of Japanese – Asian and world – history. We believe, in other words, that the Japanese, like all of us, made their own history, but not in the circumstances of their own choosing.

Notes

1. **S. Metzer-Court**, 'Towards National Integration: A Comparative Study of Economic Progress in the Prefectures of Wakayama, Okayama and Hiroshima during the Nineteenth Century', in **G. Daniels** (ed.), *Europe Interprets Japan*, Paul Norbury Publications, 1984, pp. 13–14. There are many useful introductions to modern Japanese history including **J.E. Hunter**, *The Emergence of Modern Japan: An Introductory History since 1853*, Longman, 1989; **M.B. Jansen** and **P. Duus** (eds), *The Cambridge History of Japan*, vols 5 and 6, Cambridge University Press, 1989;

W.G. Beasley, *The Rise of Modern Japan: Political, Economic and Social Change since 1850*, Weidenfeld & Nicolson, 1990 (2nd ed., 1995); and A. Waswo, *Modern Japanese Society 1868–1914*, Oxford University Press, 1996.

2. Waswo, *Modern Japanese Society*, p. 1; D.B. Smith, *Japan since 1945: The Rise of an Economic Superpower*, Macmillan, 1995, p. 3.

3. K.D. Brown, *Britain and Japan: A Comparative Economic and Social History since 1900*, Manchester University Press, 1998, p. 74; J. Dower, *Japan in War and Peace: Essays on History, Race and Culture*, HarperCollins, 1995, pp. 269, 292.

4. E.W. Said, *Culture and Imperialism*, Vintage, 1993.

5. Cited in D. Irokawa, *The Culture of the Meiji Period*, M.B. Jansen (ed. and trans.), Princeton University Press, 1985, p. 72.

6. See R. Goodman, 'Sociology of the Japanese State, the State of Japanese Sociology: A Review of the 1980s', *Japan Forum*, 2, 1990; B. Emmott, *The Sun Also Sets: Why Japan will not be Number One*, Simon & Schuster, 1989, p. 25.

7. P. Dale, *The Myth of Japanese Uniqueness*, Croom Helm, 1986; C. Nakane, *Japanese Society*, University of California Press, 1970; T. Doi, *The Anatomy of Dependence*, Kôdansha International, 1981.

8. Emmott, *The Sun Also Sets*, pp. 25–31; E. Behr, *Hirohito: Behind the Myth*, Penguin, 1990, p. 465.

9. See M. Maruyama, *Thought and Behaviour in Modern Japanese Politics*, expanded edition, I. Morris (ed.), Oxford University Press, 1969, first published in 1963; S. Ienaga, *Japan's Last War: World War II and the Japanese, 1931–1945*, Blackwell, 1979; A. Iriye, *The Origins of the Second World War in Asia and the Pacific*, Longman, 1987; Irokawa, *Culture of the Meiji Period*; T. Iritani, *Group Psychology of the Japanese in Wartime*, Kegan Paul International, 1991.

10. *Japan Times Weekly*, 12 January, 23 February 1939; J. Dower, *War Without Mercy: Race and Power in the Pacific War*, Faber & Faber, 1986, ch. 8; C. Gluck, *Japan's Modern Myths: Ideology in the Late Meiji Period*, Princeton University Press, 1985, pp. 145–6.

11. B. Eccleston, *State and Society in Post-War Japan*, Polity Press, 1989, pp. 1, 8–9.

12. Cited J. Woronoff, *Japan As – Anything But – Number One*, Macmillan, 1990, p. 12; Emmott, *The Sun Also Sets*, pp. 26ff.

13. See, for example, R.L. Durgin, 'Japan's Youth Looks Ahead', *Contemporary Japan*, 17, 1948. A systematic and authoritative study of the inculcation of militarism in pre-war Japan is found in R.J. Smethurst, *A Social Basis for Prewar Japanese Militarism: The Army and the Rural Community*, University of California Press, 1974.

14. D. Smith, 'The Asian Tigers Turn Tail', *Sunday Times*, 24 May 1998; W. Keegan, *The Spectre of Capitalism: The Future of the World Economy after the Fall of Communism*, Vintage, 1993, pp. 141–64. See also E.F. Vogel, *Japan as Number One: Lessons for America*, Harvard University Press, 1979.

15. Review by D.W. Plath in *Journal of Japanese Studies*, 12, 1986, p. 156.

16. A. Iriye, *Japan and the Wider World: From the Mid-Nineteenth Century to the Present*, Longman, 1997, p. 13.

17. *Mainichi Daily News*, 30 March 1997; B-A. Shillony, *Politics and Culture in Wartime Japan*, Clarendon Press, 1991, preface; I. Buruma, *The Wages of Guilt: Memories of War in Germany and Japan*, Vintage, 1995, part three.

18. Brown, *Britain and Japan*, p. 5. The notion of modernity as it applies to Japan has been vigorously debated. An interesting chapter which addresses many of the issues

surrounding Japanese modernisation is chapter 1 of **M.B. Jansen** (ed.), *Changing Japanese Attitudes toward Modernisation*, Princeton University Press, 1965.

19. Dower, *Japan in War and Peace*, esp. pp. 266–8, 317–19; **S. Dockrill**, 'The Legacy of the "Pacific War" as Seen from Europe', in **S. Dockrill** (ed.), *From Pearl Harbor to Hiroshima: The Second World War in Asia and the Pacific, 1941–45*, Macmillan, 1994; **E.W. Said**, *Orientalism*, Random House, 1978; **J.J. Clarke**, *Oriental Enlightenment: The Encounter between Asian and Western Thought*, Routledge, 1997.

Politics and political systems

It is not easy to know how best to approach the study of Japanese politics, political systems and political culture. Whoever we are, wherever we come from and whenever our views were formed, we can scarcely avoid bringing to such a large and contentious subject a complex bundle of assumptions, attitudes and expectations. How was it, we ask, that the feudal system was overturned so speedily and successfully in the years after 1868? Why was it, we wonder, that efforts to found a system of liberal democracy floundered so disastrously in the late 1920s? Was it something deep in Japanese culture and character, we reflect, which led to the totalitarianism and dictatorship of the 1930s and early 1940s? Evasion jostles with confrontation, condemnation with exoneration.

But it is not just the answers which depend upon one's point of view. So too do the questions. Was feudalism ever really eradicated? Was Japan ever really a democracy? Was it ever really a dictatorship? It remains exceptionally difficult to know which stance to adopt. For as at least one commentator has pointed out, 'When one realizes how tenuous and frail democracy is elsewhere in the world, and how strong is the tendency towards arbitrary rule, one may conclude by wondering not why democracy failed in Japan, but rather how, despite the undemocratic tradition and the pressures of war, a totalitarian dictatorship did not evolve there.'[1]

It is scarcely surprising therefore that opinions about Japanese political systems and political culture often diverge sharply, especially when considering the years which culminated in the Second World War. There are two broad views. It has been usual to view the 1930s and early 1940s as an aberration, as a 'dark valley' between the democratic promise of the early 1920s and the American-enforced democracy of the late 1940s. According to this interpretation, 'Only after the catharsis of defeat in war and the reforms of the Occupation, which built upon the stymied progress of the 1920s, did Japan get back "on course".' However, in recent years this interpretation has come in for considerable criticism, with a new generation of historians stressing the continuities, rather than the dis-continuities, between the early and middle decades of the century. As one of the proponents of this revisionist school explains, there is now a tendency 'to see the war not as an aberration in Japan's development but as an outcome of that development'. This interpretation, she insists, 'does not amount to an attempt to justify the war, but is an effort to explain it in terms of evolutionary change, rather than of retrogression or breakdown'.[2]

Accordingly, this chapter has two broad, and deceptively simple aims: to describe, and attempt to explain, the course of Japanese domestic politics between 1868 and 1945. However, two points need to be made at the outset. It is important to stress how rapidly politics changed during this period: Japan's feudal regime was brought to an end by the Meiji Restoration of 1868; the regime that came to power in 1868 attempted to establish a 'modern' system of government; the first two decades of the twentieth century saw the system shift towards a form of 'liberal democracy'; and this was followed finally by the imposition of a regime which is often regarded as authoritarian and dictatorial.

It is important to stress too that there was nothing preordained about these developments. The changes which took place were opposed as well as supported, undermined as well as implemented. It will be shown, in other words, that explanations emanating from the supposed unique-ness and homogeneity of Japanese character and culture simply cannot be sustained. It is difficult to see, for example, how a single factor – the homogeneity of Japanese character and culture – can be used to explain two dissimilar developments: the shift first towards 'liberal democracy', and the turn later towards authoritarianism and dictatorship. The key to Japanese political development is to be found, it will be argued, in the particular historical circumstances of the years under examination.

The Meiji Restoration of 1868

A revolution from above

It would be difficult to overestimate the significance of the Meiji Restora-tion. During the third quarter of the nineteenth century, the Meiji re-formers ended 250 years of military dictatorship, restored the emperor to formal power, and laid the foundations for the thorough-going, and remarkably successful, transformation of Japan from a feudal society into a modern, industrial nation. The impetus for change came not, as one might expect, from an emerging middle class, an alienated working class

or a disaffected peasantry. It came rather from three of the most privileged sectors in Japanese society: a group of feudal lords who wished to
strengthen the country's position internationally; a group of 'Restoration
bureaucrats' who wished to modernise the country on Western lines;
and a group of low-ranking warriors from outlying regions who, nominally at least, were members of the very elite which they overthrew. 'It is
rather as if the fox-hunting squierarchy of England, the grandees of the
old Confederate South in America, or the landowning gentry of Russia
had taken up the banner of social revolution and modernization.' Indeed, it has been suggested that the contradictory – some would say
schizophrenic – nature of the Restoration accounts for many, if not
most, aspects of Japan's political development in the years between the
late nineteenth century and the middle of the twentieth century.[3]

Determining the causes and interpreting the events of the Restoration
is a task fraught with immense difficulty particularly as both indigenous
and external factors must be taken into account. On the one hand, the
Restoration was a reaction against two and a half centuries of military
rule* by one of the country's great feudal houses, the *Tokugawa*, which
was headed by a secular ruler known as the *shôgun*. In fact, there were
two rulers at the apex of the Japanese system of feudalism: the *shôgun*
and the emperor. The *shôgun* was the effective ruler. Based in Tokyo (or
Edo as it was known until 1868), he and his subordinates controlled the
major cities and a quarter of all agricultural land, exercised responsibility
for foreign relations, and ruled in the name of the emperor as the 'great,
barbarian-subduing generalissimo'. The emperor himself was a shadowy
and secluded figure whose court was in the ancient city of Kyoto. Although he possessed both large amounts of land and immense spiritual
authority on account of his status as a living God (the direct descendant
of a line which was traced back more than two and a half thousand
years), he exercised little real influence over the running of the country.
In fact, between 1603 and 1868, successive emperors sanctioned the rule
of the most powerful feudal family, the *Tokugawa*, appointing its leaders
to serve as their military deputies, so making them, *de facto*, the rulers of
the country.

Beneath the *shôgun* and the emperor there came 260 great lords (or
daimyô) who controlled the remaining three-quarters of the country. Each
one of them swore an oath of allegiance to the *shôgun*, and in return exercised considerable autonomy over their domains, where they collected
taxes, regulated commerce and dispensed justice among the merchants,

artisans and peasants who made up the overwhelming majority of the population. Both the *shôgun* and the great lords had their own feudal retainers. These warriors (or *samurai*) carried out a wide range of civil and military duties and, by 1868, numbered about two and a half million, a figure equivalent to 6–7 per cent of Japan's total population. However, the position of these retainers was not what it had been in earlier centuries. 'Under the enforced peace of the Tokugawa, the warrior had no obviously important social function to perform. In the meantime, other forms of prestige, based on the wealth of the merchants, were beginning to compete with the martial virtues.' Indeed, it has been suggested that 'the lower ranks of the *samurai* constituted a free-floating source of violence, a "lumpenaristocracy", available for a variety of reactionary purposes but certainly no revolution of the English and French type'.[4]

Matters were brought to a head by developments in the middle of the nineteenth century. For more than two hundred years, the regime had pursued a policy of strict national seclusion, with the few foreigners permitted to stay in the country confined to a small area of Nagasaki, a city which was both under the direct control of the *shôgun* and almost as far away from Tokyo as it was possible to get. It is not surprising therefore that the regime reacted uncertainly when in June 1853 an American squadron of warships commanded by Commodore Matthew Perry arrived in Tokyo Bay, the very centre of the *shôgun*'s power and influence. As an article in *The Times* reported, the purpose of the American mission was to persuade and, if that failed, to coerce Japan into opening itself to the West:

> The empire of Japan has long remained a sealed book to the various nations of the civilized world. The rulers of that rich and populous country have for a long period continued to act on maxims of exclusiveness so complete as to put even the policy of the Court of Pekin to shame. . . . It is a fair question how far any tribe or race of human beings possesses the right of excluding the rest of mankind from all participation in the benefits to be derived from an extensive and beautiful region.
>
> The officers intrusted with the command can have little difficulty in dictating their own terms both at Nangasaki and Jeddo, with such a power at their disposal. . . . The Japanese are undoubtedly a more military nation than the Chinamen; but it is not likely they can offer any effective resistance against the howitzers and rocket-tubes of the United States' squadron.[5]

The *shôgun* had no choice but to consult the emperor and the great lords before deciding what course of action he should adopt (a decision which, of course, involved the emperor in political activity). The Americans returned the following year with gifts which included a telescope, a miniature railway, two boats, a small arsenal of weapons and a telegraph with three miles of line. The *shôgun* agreed eventually to the so-called 'unequal' treaties with the Americans (and later the Europeans) which reversed the country's centuries-old policy of seclusion: these new agreements allowed foreigners to settle in Japan, permitted them to be tried in their own consular courts and prevented the Japanese from imposing protective tariffs on goods imported from overseas.[6]

It proved a grave miscalculation. The regime had opened itself to charges both of weakness and of dereliction of duty: the right of the *shôgun* to rule in the name of the emperor as the 'great barbarian-subduing generalissimo' was revealed to be nothing more than a sham. Emulation, the *shôgun*'s critics felt, would serve better than appeasement: the way to cope with the threat posed by the West was not to negotiate with the interlopers but to strengthen Japanese political, industrial, military and other institutions by reforming them upon Western lines. Some feudal lords around whom the agitation coalesced initiated their own programmes of Western-inspired modernisation, particularly of military institutions. Even the *shôgun* – often portrayed as reactionary – eventually implemented reforms which, with French aid and advice, were substantial and far-reaching: the creation of a modern navy, experimentation with conscription and the liberalisation and/or dismantling of key feudal institutions. In the decade preceding the Restoration, the situation was highly fluid and some have argued that the emergence of an open and modern Japan led by the *Tokugawa* was by no means inconceivable.[7]

In spite of these developments, criticism of the *shôgun* developed eventually into a coherent – and near-revolutionary – programme which involved overthrowing the *shôgun*'s regime and replacing it with a government headed by the emperor, around whom, it was hoped, a renewed sense of national unity would be developed. Opposition coalesced around the imperial court at Kyoto, and was led from the south-west of the country primarily by two of the great rival feudal domains, the *Chôshû* and the *Satsuma*. In the diplomatic manoeuvring and military confrontations which ensued during the following fifteen years, motives were mixed and alliances extremely complicated. Nonetheless, the consequences, if not the course, of the struggle were fundamentally clear-cut. By 1868, the *shôgun* had been defeated, Edo captured (and renamed Tokyo), and the direct rule of the emperor 'restored'. The history of modern Japan was about to begin.[8]

Consolidation and modernisation – the establishment of a 'modern' system of government

It was not clear, of course, which direction the country's history would take. The Restoration was backward-looking as well as forward-looking, the new regime reactionary as well as revolutionary. In fact, one of the keys to understanding political developments following the Restoration is to recognise that the lords, bureaucrats and warriors who seized power in 1868 were perfectly prepared to use reactionary means to push through their reforms. The new leaders exploited and, when it suited them, they invented a particular view of Japanese character, culture and history as a way of driving forward the enormously ambitious programme of reform which they considered necessary to equip Japan to compete successfully with the nations of the West.[9]

The revolutionary nature of the new regime did not take long to reveal itself. Within a year, the important posts in the administration were held by middle-ranking *samurai* from the south-western domains which had played such a large part in the Restoration. In fact, the reign of the new emperor, Emperor Meiji, which lasted from 1868 until 1912, became identified immediately and indissolubly with a sustained, and largely successful assault upon the political, legal, educational and other foundations which had underpinned feudal society. The Charter Oath of 1868 set the tone. The 'Evil customs of the past shall be broken off and everything based upon the just laws of nature', it announced. 'Knowledge shall be sought throughout the world so as to strengthen the foundations of imperial rule.'[10]

The leaders of the new regime were as good as their word. They attacked the country's long tradition of isolationism: in addition to sponsoring a large contingent of individuals to study in Europe and America, they sent abroad the hundred-strong Iwakura Mission in 1871 which, after the failure to secure a revision of the 'unfair treaties', went to learn how best to mobilise the country's political, economic and social resources to meet the demands of the modern age. The impact which the mission had on some of Japan's most important leaders cannot be overestimated:

> The attitudes of the men who took part were profoundly influenced by their experiences. Kido came back a constitutional reformer, Ôkubo was for the rest of his life an advocate of industrialisation. Iwakura, while remaining in most respects a conservative, accepted from that time on that the way forward would have to be in a Western manner.[11]

It was this mission which saw the emergence of the 'civilisation and enlightenment' movement. In its most basic form, all things Western were adulated, adapted and adopted. Although a complex variety of motivations can be discerned behind the Westernisation trends of the 1870s, the 'civilisation and enlightenment' movement nevertheless goes far in helping one to appreciate and describe the mood of Japan's first modern decade. Firstly, there was a reaction to centuries of perceived feudal stagnation. 'Since time immemorial,' wrote Fukuzawa, the pre-eminent 'civilisation and enlightenment' thinker, 'the people of the whole country have suffered under despotic rule which did not allow freedom of expression.'

> They [the feudal authorities] stole security by deception and escaped punishment by telling lies. Fraud and subterfuge thus became necessary tools of life; injustice and insincerity became daily routine. No one felt ashamed and no one asked questions. Honor had fallen to the ground and disappeared with the wind of the times.[12]

In rejecting the past, politicians and intellectuals sought to restructure Japanese society and its political systems according to what were perceived to be the principles governing civilisation – equality, openness, and achievement. Coining the most famous passage of the era, Fukuzawa boldly declared, 'It is said that Heaven does not create one man above or below another man.'

> This means that when men are born from heaven they are all equal. There is no innate distinction between high and low. . . . The distinction between wise and stupid comes down to a matter of education. . . . It is only the person who has studied diligently, so that he has a mastery over things and events, who becomes noble and rich, while his opposite becomes base and poor.[13]

To the modern reader, it may appear that the movement was imbued with a democratic ethos. Although participatory government was debated in the years that followed, one objective defined the drive to become 'civilised and enlightened' more than any other. 'Freedom and independence refer not only to the private self' explained Fukuzawa, 'but to the nation as well.' 'The policies of "national isolation" and "expel the barbarian" are':

> narrow-minded like the proverbial frog in the bottom of the well. . . . We [the nations of the world] should mutually teach and learn from each other, without shame or pride. We should promote each other's interests and pray for each other's happiness. . . . We should associate with one another following the laws of heaven and humanity. Such an attitude implies acknowledging one's guilt even before the black slaves of Africa, because of reason. But it also means not being afraid of even the warships of England and America, because of principle. It further implies that if this nation is disgraced, every Japanese citizen, to the last man, must sacrifice his life to prevent the decline and prestige of her glory. National independence implies all of these things.[14]

Throughout the 1870s, the leaders of Japan attempted to remould the nation comprehensively along the lines of 'civilisation and enlightenment'. At a superficial level, the movement came to be associated somewhat frivolously with such things as electric lights, masquerade balls and the banning of wearing loincloths in public. More profoundly, the Meiji leadership worked to undermine the authority of the great lords and the *samurai* – the very groups from which they themselves were often drawn. In 1869, they declared that feudal castes were abolished and that all groups in society – including the *samurai* – would be treated equally before the law. In 1871, the Meiji government pressed ahead with the most important and far-reaching of its reforms – the abolition of the great lords' domains and their replacement by prefectures. The centuries-old feudal political structure was decisively swept away in one swift stroke. During the early 1870s, the Meiji government introduced compulsory military service, a measure which, though not comprehensive, ended the *samurai*'s monopoly of the right to bear arms, and with it their claim to unchallenged social superiority. It also refused to allow former *samurai* to carry swords (which led to the so-called warriors' war), and commuted the stipends which they received from their feudal lords into lump sums, usually in the form of government bonds.[15]

The abolition of the feudal structure was not of course welcomed without reservation, particularly by those who had the most to lose, the *samurai*. As two leaders of a *samurai* self-help organisation that eventually came to advocate parliamentary government explained, 'At that time, we were samurai in the truest sense of the word. . . . We did not understand very well what [the leader] Itagaki was advocating. Besides, we were privately unhappy about the admonition . . . that we were to conduct affairs of state together with farmers and merchants.'[16]

In a few cases, resentment and fear were transformed into revolt. The most serious of these was the Satsuma Rebellion of 1877 which emanated from the former domain of *Satsuma* (now Kagoshima) south of Nagasaki. Although it was quashed, it was a serious challenge for the newly formed conscript army and momentarily shook the stability of the Meiji leadership since it pitted against each other two of its most influential figures and one-time allies in the battle against the *shôgun*. The victory of the Imperial Army and the Meiji government over this coalition of discontented *samurai*, overtaxed peasants and others opposed to the policy of modernisation and Westernisation was of considerable significance. It eliminated the only force capable of threatening the new regime, it vindicated the government's decision to adopt universal military conscription, and it seemed to confirm the wisdom of its policy of Westernisation and modernisation. It meant that within a decade of seizing power, the Meiji government had dismantled the foundations of feudal society, and laid the basis for the powerful, new nation that it was seeking to create.[17]

If the reactionary threats posed by a disenfranchised military elite momentarily shook the new regime, it was the ideological pressure emanating from almost all sectors of society which had the greatest political and social impact: the People's Rights Movement. In the early 1870s, a number of self-help organisations were formed to aid former *samurai* in adapting to their new circumstances. Within a few years, the movement had become highly political and grown rapidly to include wealthy peasants, urban merchants and intellectuals from across the nation. These organisations, which later coalesced into Japan's first political parties, were devoted to refining the new art of political oratory and the independent drafting of a national constitution. Some of the constitutions, like the one composed by a primary school teacher and discovered hidden away in the walls of a decaying building long after the Second World War, were highly sophisticated, including, for example, references to the political works of Mill and Bentham. More importantly, these groups petitioned the government for the establishment of a national legislative assembly. The comments of one participant reveal something of the mood that characterised the early years of the movement:

> All classes, all ages have joined together to demand a national assembly. Heedless of the costs to themselves, the people are devoting themselves to the movement, giving speeches, rallying supporters and organising local societies and political parties. Each group tries to outdo each other and to make the other struggle to keep up. Enthusiasm is so high that it can be compared with the spirit of the loyalist activists who restored the Emperor and overthrew the *bakufu* at the time of the Restoration-Revolution. Starting in Fukuoka and Okayama, we have presented over fifty petitions, and we are now drafting scores of constitutions. This alone is proof that half of the more than seven million households in Japan support the opening of a national assembly. It is no exaggeration to say that it is the 'public opinion' of the nation.[18]

During the early 1880s, the movement was radicalised with the inclusion of peasants and tenant farmers who suffered under the draconian deflationary policies of the decade. A series of armed insurrections in the mid-1880s was easily quashed by the government and the movement moved once again under the control of moderates who now worked with the government and focused their attention on issues such as treaty revision with the West. Despite a rather prosaic ending to a movement that had revolutionary political (and later social) implications, the movement was remarkable not only for its spontaneity but for its timing. Hardly a decade had passed since the inauguration of the Meiji reformation when suddenly there appeared a popular debate that threatened to steal the momentum of reform from the very leaders who had first advocated and embraced change.[19]

Responding with force when militarily threatened, the leaders of early Meiji Japan nevertheless countenanced and accommodated, albeit begrudgingly, independent forces for change. Through a combination of intelligent reforms, determination, restraint and, of course, luck, they had planted the seeds for a thorough yet remarkably stable transformation of their nation. Indeed, even those least inclined to accept the revolutionary impact of the Restoration agree that it was a major turning point in the course of Japanese history.[20]

The Meiji Constitution

Finally, in 1889, the government promulgated the Imperial Japanese (or Meiji) Constitution which provided the political framework for the country until the Allied Occupation of 1945. It established a system of checks and balances which, drawing on the Prussian model, set in place, alongside the monarchy, an executive and a legislature – the Diet – which convened for the first time in 1890. But this was no Western-style liberal democracy. As Article 3 of the Constitution implied, the basic aim of those drawing up the Meiji Constitution was to retain theoretically absolute (if symbolic) sovereign power in the hands of the emperor, and actual political power in the hands of the ruling elite who acted as his advisors. For as Itô, one of the main architects of the constitution and the first prime minister, explained, 'the onslaught of extremely democratic ideas' had to be resisted, because 'in a country such as ours, it was evident that it would be necessary to compensate for its smallness of size and population by a compact solidity of organisation'. What took precedence was the protection of the rights of the nation rather than those of the people. As Ôkuma, one of the leaders of the People's Rights Movement, reflected in 1907, 'The impetus for the idea that some day Japan must have constitutional government can be ultimately traced to foreign policy.' One of the genrô came more to the point, 'Constitutional government was not created simply to satisfy the desires of the people. Those in the government also believed that it was imperative to create a constitutional regime to expedite the revision of [the unequal] treaties and the restoration of equal rights [between Japan and the West].'[21]

The Constitution was regarded as a gift from the emperor to his people, so that he was bound by it only because he chose to be. It stressed the duties of the subject rather than the rights of the citizen; it gave the emperor, as Article 11 stated, 'supreme command of the army and navy', and afforded him the power both to make war and peace and to appoint the prime minister, cabinet members, military chiefs of staff and other senior officials. Although he was expected to heed the advice of his senior advisers, he retained the right to question the executive, to express his pleasure or displeasure at what he was told, and to make decisions when members of the executive were unable to agree upon their recommenda-tions to him. It was this separation of powers, based on the ideal that 'the emperor stands above the people and apart from every party . . . [to be] fair and impartial', which helped to shape Japanese political develop-ment. It was this separation of powers which accounted, in part, for the controversy which erupted fifty years later over the responsibility to be borne by Emperor Meiji's grandson, Emperor Hirohito, for the behaviour of the Japanese government and the Japanese armed forces during the 1930s and early 1940s.[22]

How then did the separation of powers operate in practice? The sys-tem, it must be stressed, did not consist solely of the monarchy, the executive and the legislature. There were also the privy council, the bureaucracy and the military. The influence of the Privy Council – estab-lished as an advisory body to the emperor – was considerable since its sphere of competence was not clearly defined. Its membership, however, usually included the ruling elites and other conservative bodies includ-ing the House of Peers. Similarly, the bureaucracy and the military were both more powerful than the new constitutional arrangements suggested. The senior members of the bureaucracy comprised a privileged and protected elite whose role as 'servants of the emperor' was to pursue national, rather than sectarian, objectives. The military chiefs of staff were responsible directly to the emperor, and this meant that they were altogether free from executive and legislative control. Indeed, the operational autonomy enjoyed by the Imperial armed forces did not have to be seized by military coup or won by political manipulation. It was enshrined in the Constitution of 1889.[23]

The executive, on the other hand, was less powerful than it appeared. The fact that the prime minister and members of the cabinet – like the chiefs of staff – were appointed by, and reported directly to, the emperor made it difficult for the prime minister to control his colleagues, and gave cabinet ministers a considerable degree of individual autonomy. Moreover, since the Privy Council, the bureaucracy, the military and the House of Peers each represented a discrete centre of power responsible to the emperor, the executive was successful only when it could balance their myriad interests. These highly decentralised constitutional arrange- ments, it will be seen, were of considerable significance in delaying, though not preventing, the emergence of political parties and the estab- lishment of party governments in a form akin to those with which we are familiar today in the West.[24]

The legislature too was weak. The Diet's upper house, the House of Peers, was modelled on the British House of Lords, and consisted of members of the hereditary nobility together with imperial appointees selected from those prominent in fields such as politics and industry. The lower house, the House of Representatives, was elected, but from a severely restricted – and entirely male – franchise. In 1891, two years after the introduction of the new Constitution, barely one per cent of the population was entitled to vote. The two houses of the Diet had the power to pass laws, approve the budget, discuss national policy and question the cabinet. But they had no authority to dismiss the govern- ment – a prerogative which remained, nominally at least, firmly in the hands of the emperor. It is difficult therefore to dissent from the view that, 'With cabinets not responsible to the diet, and their members not selected from among the parties represented in the diet, the legislature appeared on paper to be little more than a talking shop, an outlet for the venting of dissatisfaction (but not subversion).' Yet even a talking shop could have an impact, recent scholarship suggesting that despite their restricted powers, the early Diets helped to set the national agenda, reflected something at least of wider opinion, and provided a public, and well publicised, forum in which dissenting views could be expressed.[25]

However, reassessment must not slip into misrepresentation. The polit- ical system established by the Imperial Japanese Constitution of 1889 remained oligarchic rather than democratic, patriarchal rather than par- ticipatory. A small group of the *samurai* who had been active in the Restoration acquired a leading role in government after the Restoration, and retained their influence until well into the new century. These elder statesmen, or *genrô* as they were known, rotated power among them- selves and their apprentices, providing seven of the nine prime ministers who held office between 1885 (when the post was established) and the

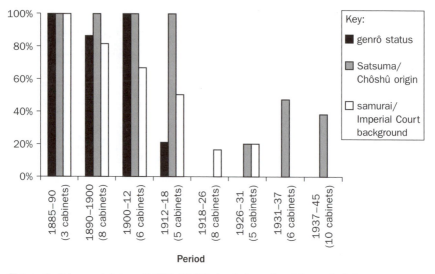

Figure 1: Prime ministers (1885–1945): background, origin and status

end of the First World War (see Figure 1). Itô, for example, served as prime minister from 1885 to 1888, and Yamagata from 1889 to 1891 and again from 1898 to 1900. Whether or not they held office, these men 'were regularly consulted on the conduct of political affairs by emperor, cabinet and the other institutions of government. No major political move was made without first seeking their advice.' These elder statesmen have received a remarkably generous press. They functioned, Barnhart believes, as 'the glue that held the Meiji state together'. He puts it like this. 'The years from 1895 to 1915 were remarkable through most of the West for their extraordinary turbulence as Europe and America adapted to the Industrial Revolution.' However, 'Japan was spared much of this turmoil in these years, primarily because of the mediating influence, conservatism, and wisdom of the *genrô*.' The achievements of the *genrô* were all the more impressive if one considers that they were not necessarily the monolithic entity that subsequent eulogies have implied.

> The description of Japanese political parties as 'exclusive clubs, yet . . . clubs lacking any real unity, torn by violent internal struggles for power which frequently had little or no connection with consideration of public policy' can be said to apply with equal validity to the oligarchy. It should be re-emphasized, however, that strong personal animosities were secondary and in part derived from basic, substantive differences in political philosophies. Any other view, it seems, would be doing an injustice to the intelligence and patriotism of the oligarchs. If the oligarchy, like the opposition, was divided, this does not necessarily compound the causes of the 'failure of democracy in Japan'.[26]

The following extract from Akita's *Foundations of Constitutional Government* gives some idea of how *genrô* politics functioned and 'dysfunctioned'. In it, Itô, who had been contemplating the formation of a government party that would not 'disturb the foundations of the nation' through political factionalism suggests to the other *genrô* in 1898 the formation of a cabinet based on an alliance between the two opposition parties led by Ôkuma and Itagaki.

> He [Itô] said that since he had already determined to resign, he would like to shift the discussion to the matter of a successor cabinet. He was thoroughly satisfied that it would not contravene the true intent of the constitution if he advised the throne to grant the mandate to organize the next cabinet to Ôkuma and Itagaki, the leaders of the new party which had an overwhelming majority in the Lower House. . . . Yamagata and the other *genrô* were 'struck dumb with astonishment'. Yamagata was first to recover. He reiterated his arguments for opposing party cabinets. The other *genrô* also opposed Itô's suggestion. Itô at this point pulled out his trump. He must have enjoyed it when he asked if anyone among those present would step up and assume the responsibility of forming the next cabinet. He took pains to point out to Yamagata that it was properly his task. Yamagata turned aside this thrust with the remark that he saw no reason why he should be singled out. Itô then laughed heartily. Since all the *genrô* washed their hands of the responsibility, there was no other course, he declared, but to ask the leaders of the political party. The meeting was adjourned at this note.[27]

Indeed, despite the *genrô*'s fear that 'the state will eventually collapse when politics are entrusted to the reckless discussions of the people', it is a paradox of Meiji political history that the influence of the *genrô* coincided with, and goes some way to explain, the growth of political parties under a constitution which had been intended specifically to inhibit such a development. It was disagreement among the *genrô* (and later their deaths) which eased the emergence of party-like groupings clustered around leading individuals and personalities. Reischauer explains these developments as clearly and briefly as is probably possible.

> Itagaki in 1874 started the first political party, which quickly burgeoned into the 'people's rights movement', and Ôkuma followed with a second party movement in 1882. From these two sources stemmed the two major traditional party currents. That of Itagaki dominated the early Diets under the name of the Liberal Party (Jiyûtô, which literally means Freedom Party) and then in 1900 joined with Itô's bureaucratic following to form the Seiyûkai (Political Friends Society). . . . The other party had more frequent changes of name, becoming in 1927 the Minseitô (People's Government Party).[28]

In 1895, for example, the *genrô* were unable to agree how to respond to the demand by Russia, Germany and France for Japan to modify the peace terms which had been negotiated at the end of the Sino-Japanese War, a year-long struggle which had been fought over competing interests in Korea. Although the Diet did not have the power to ratify (or refuse to ratify) the revised treaty, it did have the power to block the government's request for increased military spending. Prime minister Itô secured support for his budget but only by making the leader of one of the political parties the home minister in his cabinet. It was the first time that any of the *genrô* had felt it necessary to share power with a party leader, and it encouraged Itô's rivals to develop their own links with Japan's nascent political parties.[29]

Whatever view one takes of the Meiji Constitution, the continuing power of the *genrô* and the gradual emergence of political parties, there is no doubt that they represented a remarkable break with the past. Within thirty years, the new regime had put to rest the formal structures of feudalism, laid the basis for a recognisably 'modern' system of government, and perpetuated an oligarchy which, as intended, allowed those in power to push through the reforms which they felt necessary to strengthen Japan, avoid the fate of China, and permit her to compete effectively on the world stage.

'Enrich the country, strengthen the military'

In the face of the 'unequal treaties' imposed by the West before the Restoration and the West's imperialistic incursions into China, it was the fundamental aim of those who held power between 1868 and 1912 to build a united, prosperous and powerful Japanese nation state. It was an aim which they achieved with remarkable speed and efficiency. However, there was nothing pre-ordained about their success. 'It is true', it has been pointed out, 'that Japan's development in the late nineteenth and early twentieth centuries did not give rise to the massive social and political disruption that occurred in some other modernising societies.' But this, it must be emphasised, was certainly not inevitable. It was the 'outcome of policy and effort'.[30]

It has been seen already that from the earliest years of the Restoration, the leaders of the new regime worked hard to pursue their policy of strengthening and modernising the state. They did their best to undermine isolationism, they put down armed rebellions, and they began to remove the many inequalities which they regarded as inimical to their broader purposes. The Meiji rulers and their officials continued to take a broad view of what needed to be done, but they concentrated their attention upon three central features of national life: the economy, the armed forces and the educational system.

It was essential, they agreed, to 'enrich the country'. Indeed, they saw the strengthening of the economy as the foundation upon which everything else depended – and as too important therefore to be left to the vagaries of the market. So, although Meiji politicians were far from unanimous about the details of economic policy, there was a broad consensus that the state had a role to play in promoting economic development, and that it was economic development which provided the precondition for the achievement of the country's other ambitions.[31]

The state pursued its economic objectives in a number of ways. It will be seen in chapter 3 that, during the first decade or so of the new regime, the government intervened directly in industries which it regarded as strategically important, encouraging the modernisation of its own arsenals, ironworks and shipyards by importing up-to-date technology and significant numbers of expert advisers from overseas. However, a serious financial crisis in 1880 persuaded the government to sell off many of these industries to the private sector, and thereafter the state turned to indirect means of encouraging both the strategic industries and the industrial sector as a whole. The Meiji oligarchs enjoyed close ties with some of the country's leading entrepreneurs, and used subsidies and other forms of support to ease the emergence of the *zaibatsu*, the four great financial and industrial conglomerates – Mitsui, Mitsubishi, Yasuda and Sumitomo – which were to play such a crucial role in the development of the Japanese economy.[32]

The oligarchs also did what they could to strengthen the country's underlying economic infrastructure, making particular efforts to reform public finances and to improve transport and communications. In 1873, for example, they undertook a major reform of the taxation system, and nine years later they established the Bank of Japan as a central bank upon the lines of the Belgian State Bank. They carried out substantial improvements in road transport, developed telegraph communications, oversaw the rapid expansion of the railway network, and in 1906 nationalised the railways in order to provide the country with the more integrated system which they believed was required.[33]

Government efforts to 'enrich the country' were matched by attempts to 'strengthen the military'. The course of international relations and imperial expansion will be considered in proper detail in the following chapter, but it should never be forgotten that domestic politics, military policy, and foreign affairs were entwined in the most intimate fashion. The reform of the public finances made it feasible to increase spending on the armed forces, and increased spending on the armed forces made it easier to contemplate overseas entanglements such as the Sino-Japanese War of 1894–95, the Russo-Japanese War of 1904–05 (and later the long, drawn-out war with China, and the struggle against America and the allies).

In fact, military expenditure was given the highest possible priority, with the result that by the 1890s it accounted for more than thirty per cent of total government spending. The introduction of conscription was consolidated by the use of European military experts, the purchase of foreign warships and the growing availability of domestically pro-duced weapons and uniforms. By 1893 Japan had a standing army of over 20,000, a figure which by 1912 had risen to almost a quarter of a million. Moreover, political, police and military leaders set great store by the dissemination of the martial virtues. At first, the police:

> were armed with a wooden baton, but after 1882, they were given sabres – not the old samurai swords, but European-style weapons. However, the association with the old emblem of the samurai class was strong, and it was reinforced by efforts to coopt certain elements of the samurai code – or more accurately, of an idealised version of the samurai code – for purposes of organizational con-trol, once the actual political threat from the samurai had passed.[34]

Nor were martial values to be exclusive. Tanaka, a career soldier who was to become prime minister in 1927, stressed during the First World War that, 'The outcome of future wars will not be determined by the strong-est army but by the strongest populace.' The strongest populace, he went on to explain, 'is one which has physical strength and spiritual health, one which is richly imbued with loyalty and patriotism, and one which respects cooperation, rules and discipline'.[35]

The inculcation of loyalty and patriotism was the job, of course, of the educational system. From the earliest days of the Restoration, education was seen as the means both of allowing Japan to compete with her rivals in the West and of inculcating unquestioning obedience to the emperor and those who ruled in his name. The Charter Oath of 1868 declared that, 'Knowledge shall be sought throughout the world so as to strengthen the foundations of imperial rule', and these high-minded sentiments were gradually translated into reality. In 1871, a ministry of education was established, and in the following year plans were announced for a hugely ambitious system whereby the country was to be divided into eight districts, each of which was to be served by a university, 32 middle schools and 6,720 elementary schools. In fact, it was not until the early 1880s that the foundations were finally laid for what became known as the Meiji system of education, with all children undergoing four years (and from 1907 six years) of elementary schooling. The Education Ministry's *Explanation of School Matters* pointed out in 1891 that,

> The materials for regular education are provided by our national spirit, customs, prosperity, and strength, and all those who desire the strengthening of the eternal foundation of the nation must be careful to understand correctly our hundred-year plan. In the elementary schools, the first objective – namely the spirit of reverence of the Emperor and patriotism – will be achieved through cultivating morality and practising the Way of Humanity. Children must be encouraged in practical work, disciplined in simplicity, and developed into good and loyal subjects.[36]

This 'undertaking . . . on behalf of the state' could be achieved in remarkably open ways, combining, as one contemporary slogan put it, 'Japanese morals and Western techniques'. One patriotic intellectual put it like this: 'We recognise the excellence of Western civilisation. We value the Western theories of rights, liberty, equality. . . . In some things we have affection for Western customs. Above all, we esteem Western science, economics and industry. These things, however, ought not be adopted because they are Western but only if they can contribute to Japan's welfare.'[37]

How then should one judge the achievements of Meiji Japan? Marxist scholarship views the Meiji Restoration as a stunted bourgeois revolution that resulted in oligarchic absolutism. 'The policy of the Meiji Government,' explains E.H. Norman, 'was to subsidize generously a narrow and comparatively weak merchant-banking class in order to encourage its entry into the field of industry.'

> The reverse side of this policy was marked by a disproportionately heavy tax burden on the agricultural classes, by the stinting of enterprises less vital than those connected with defense, and by a general impatience at any sign of unrest or democratic protest which might precipitate a domestic crisis and so hinder or retard the task of reconstruction. Nevertheless, it was this policy which succeeded in the very speedy creation of industries, a merchant marine, an overseas market, and an efficient navy.[38]

While there is merit to this thesis, it is not without its problems. To be sure, the *genrō* and their colleagues were extraordinarily successful, in an extraordinarily short time, in building the prosperous, patriotic and militarily powerful state which they desired. Yet, it is all too easy to exaggerate the changes which occurred, ascribing too much to those in power after the Restoration and too little to those in power before it.

However, there can be no doubt that by 1912 Japan had undergone a quite remarkable transformation. When the Emperor Meiji came to the throne in 1868 it was still possible for Britain's first permanent diplomatic representative in the country to describe it with amused bewilderment as a 'topsy-turvy' land, where they 'write from top to bottom, from right to left, in perpendicular instead of horizontal lines; and their books begin where ours end, thus furnishing examples of the curious perfection this rule of contraries has attained'. Such a stance became increasingly untenable. By the time the Emperor Meiji died in 1912, the situation, both nationally and internationally, had changed dramatically, and it had become common all over the world to allude to Japan's wealth, power and potential. The *Illustrated London News* put it like this in 1905, in the wake of Japanese successes in the Russo-Japanese War.

> The Western world is trying, in rather dazed ways, to adjust its conventional modes of thinking to the discovery that the Japanese possess heroic virtues, which are not exactly spread broadcast in Christian Europe. They have a conception of public duty, not flagrantly obvious at every corner of other commonwealths; they have a dignity, a reticence, a patient forethought, a self-control. . . . Europe has not recovered from the shock of finding out the Japanese are a great people.[39]

The shift towards 'liberal democracy'

This changed perception is one of the reasons that political developments before and after 1912 tend, even now, to be seen so differently. The years between 1868 and 1912 are revered by those on the right – and respected by many others – as a period during which a wise emperor, experienced oligarchs and disinterested bureaucrats worked together to lay the foundations of the modern Japanese state. By contrast, the years between 1912 and 1926 have long been admired by those on the centre-left as a period during which a new emperor, together with his advisers, politicians and chiefs of staff widened the policy-making process to accommodate the growing pressure for democratic reform. It is perhaps not surprising then that these years have become known as the era of so-called 'Taishô Democracy', an epithet which takes its name from the Emperor Taishô, who succeeded the Emperor Meiji in 1912 and reigned until 1926.[40]

However, no epithet, however memorable or arresting, can possibly encompass the complexities and contradictions embedded within even fifteen years of a nation's history. It follows therefore that the term 'Taishô Democracy' should be employed only with the very greatest caution. This was no seamless transition from oligarchy to liberal democracy, recent historiography stressing that the years between 1912 and 1926 were marked by repression as well as liberation, by the continuing power of the traditional elite alongside the burgeoning influence of new democratic forces.[41]

Enfranchisement, party government and liberalisation

The years between 1912 and 1926 saw significant, albeit easily exaggerated, changes towards a form of 'liberal democracy'. Constitutional thought had evolved beyond the strict interpretation developed by the Meiji oligarchs. In response to growing popular agitation for universal manhood – and for a small minority, female – suffrage, political theorists attempted to define democracy in terms of Japanese political traditions without undermining the primacy of the emperor. Combining Confucian ethics (which stressed the role of a benevolent emperor educating his subjects) and the idea of parliament as an expression of the will of the people, Yoshino, the most prominent theorist of his day, developed a revolutionary and widely-accepted theory best summarised as 'government for and by the people but *not of* the people'. Some politicians and intellectuals went even further and advocated the view of constitutional theorist, Minobe, that the state and not the emperor was sovereign, and that the power of the latter was simply an expression of his role as the highest organ of state.[42]

These new currents of thought coincided with three major developments as those in power sought to balance the competing pressures with which they found themselves confronted: the widening of the franchise, the consolidation of party government and some liberalisation of domestic policy.

By 1920, universal manhood suffrage had come to be viewed as a sort of panacea, conflating as it did the destruction of oligarchic forces in politics and the galvanisation of opposition forces and major sectors of the public. One opposition politician wrote in the journal, *Kaizô* (*Reconstruction*), for example, that

> The significance of universal suffrage resembles somewhat the restoration of power to the emperor by Tokugawa Keiki [the last *shôgun*]. That was the first step in taking special rights from the privileged classes and giving them to the people. However, the restoration of power to the emperor was only the beginning of the Meiji Restoration and not its entirety. In the same way, the goal of universal suffrage – to take from the present governing class those control privileges to give them to all the people – is only the beginning of the Taishô Restoration and not the completion of what has occurred so far.... Without the achievement of universal suffrage, neither will other social reforms by way of parliamentary politics be possible.[43]

Despite the rhetoric of the era, the introduction of universal manhood suffrage in 1925 was much less revolutionary than it might appear. It masked a profound distrust of, if not disdain for, the very people electoral reform was designed to empower. Prime minister Katô, to whom manhood suffrage is attributed, rightly judged that 'the power of the masses [was] increasing' and that there was a need to 'extend to the people as much freedom and as many rights as possible while encouraging in them the notion of duty and the spirit of cooperation'. Nevertheless, as one of the foremost experts on the period put it, Katô

> rarely deigned even to participate in the electoral campaigning of his party's candidates, spoke infrequently in the House of Peers, and hardly ever condescended to address a public audience.

However, the right to vote had been gradually extended since the Meiji Constitution of 1889 with the reduction of the financial qualification in 1900 and again in 1919. The legislation which came into effect in 1928 gave the vote to men over the age of twenty-five – though to no women at all – thereby increasing the electorate from one per cent of the population in 1891 to twenty per cent towards the end of the 1920s. According to at least one commentator, the legislation of 1925 'was in some ways the triumph of Taishô democracy'.[44]

Party government too had been evolving since the 1890s (see Figure 2). In fact, it has been suggested that during the first two and a half decades

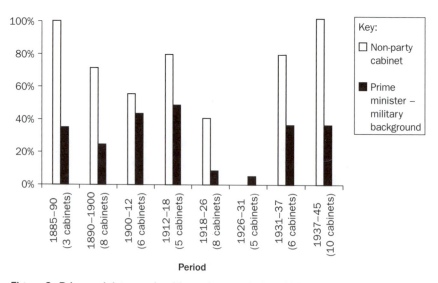

Figure 2: Prime minister and cabinet characteristics (1885–1945)

of the new century, 'the main focus of political conflict was the political parties' attempt to diminish and dislodge the influence of oligarchic-bureaucratic factions'. Only six months after the death of the Meiji Emperor in late December 1912, the increasingly tenuous and fractious arrangement by which the premiership and cabinet was rotated between the oligarchy and the Seiyûkai broke down completely. In response to apparent meddling by the army to bring down the Seiyûkai government and *genrô* manipulation of the imperial house, the Seiyûkai launched an aggressive offensive backed by the liberal press against the evils of 'clique government'. Mobilising its supporters across the nation, the 'Movement to Protect Constitutional Government' quickly developed into a series of popular and sometimes violent demonstrations which harked back to the People's Rights Movement of the 1870s. Between late 1912 and early 1913, politicians, professors and the press declared war against the *genrô* and their control of the bureaucracy, military and political institutions: 'The era of a people's war of independence has dawned. The people must be rescued from their enslavement to clique government.' Some feared for the very survival of modern Japan: 'If we don't bring about the destruction of clique government, I am afraid we will have protected 300 years of inertia. After that, Japan will most certainly enter a state just like that of China.' At the same time as the liberal elite campaigned, a popular martial song called 'Attack Clique [Government]' captured the popular imagination.

> Fluttering banners [declaring] 'Protect Constitutional Government'
> in the fields and the mountains,
> Booming drums beating out 'Destroy Clique Government'
> To the four seas.
>
> The root of all evil – clique government –
> Trampling on the people for forty years
> Will be exterminated and
> the flowers of Constitutional government will bloom;
> the fruit of constitutional government will ripen.
> The time has come . . .
> Now is the chance! Rouse yourselves![45]

The attack on 'clique government' can easily be misconstrued. Not only did the popular movement fade as quickly as it erupted but political patterns returned, initially at least, to compromise albeit between the *genrô* and the parties, an arrangement that increasingly favoured the latter. More importantly, it must be noted that the Seiyûkai, and the Kenseikai a few years later, were not political parties in the modern, Western sense: they were groups which were based more than one might expect upon personality rather than principle. This can be seen in the observations of the *Tokyo Mainichi* on the differences between the Seiyûkai's leaders – Matsuda, the 'man of virtue', and Hara, the 'strategist'.

> Mr Matsuda, while broadminded, does not necessarily make his opinions nor his judgements . . . clear. So, while he is easily accepted by most people, he does not inspire a reliable staff who are willing to lay their lives down for him. In contrast, Mr Hara does not mince his opinions, always clearly indicating approval and disapproval. In addition to his talent and ambition, his effort and manner of taking care [of his followers] are all too manifest with the result that it appears he alone controls the party. Nevertheless, although his supporters whose financial backing motivates his actions increase and a dependable staff multiplies, those who feel antipathy with his ways also grow. . . . Mr Hara is on all things, morally impoverished.[46]

Accordingly to one historian, these groupings 'probably diverged less on stated policy and principles than did parliamentary parties in any other advanced industrial society'. According to another, 'The two main political parties took a generally conservative line and were distinguished more by personal attachment to the leading personalities of each party than by any basic differences in ideology.' If the parties' lack of policies failed to capture the popular imagination, the elevation of personality made for dramatic parliamentary sessions. One address to the Diet by a member of the Kenseikai caused a furore.

> In Japan and in the world today, there are those who still insist on autocratic class rule – in the West is Nicolai Lenin of the radical Russian government; and in the East, there's our own Prime Minister Hara Takashi! . . . Though the classes that raised these men up are different – for Lenin, the working class, and for Hara the capitalists – both classes are void of the great spirit of democracy.[47]

Insofar as there was a struggle between 'oligarchic-bureaucratic factions' and political parties, it was the latter which won, at least in the short-to-medium term. Gradually Hara, Katô (Takaaki), Tanaka, Hamaguchi and the other party leaders managed to enforce the convention that the party with the largest number of seats in the House of Representatives should form the government of the country. Between 1905 and 1918, every government except one enjoyed the support of the majority party, or the majority coalition, in the lower House; between 1918 and 1932, every government except three (in 1921–24) was led by those at the head of the majority party. This new constitutional practice received what seemed like final confirmation in 1924 when, for the first time, a change in the majority party in the House of Representatives led directly to the installation of a new prime minister (Katô) and a new cabinet.[48]

The widening of the franchise and the consolidation of party government was accompanied by a certain liberalisation of policy. Japan was not immune to broader political, economic and intellectual developments, and the defeat of Germany and Austria–Hungary by the liberal democracies in the First World War did a good deal to change expectations among the politically aware. However, the first post-war prime minister, Hara, though not unsympathetic, did little to satisfy this growing demand for reform. Despite the fact that he was the first commoner to become prime minister, and the first prime minister to head a party cabinet, Hara proved cautious and conservative. A natural, some would say brilliant, conciliator facing a turbulent domestic and international situation, he extended the franchise slightly in order to quell the growing popular furore over universal manhood suffrage. He also made minor, if significant, attempts to 'party-ise' and thereby reduce the power of the military, the Upper House and the other unelected groups which continued to wield so much power in inter-war Japan. Such reforms may appear innocuous yet to the political elite of the time, they seemed radical indeed. Yamagata, the most powerful of the *genrô*, complained bitterly to an army general,

> In a day they have destroyed the administrative structure that you and your colleagues directed over the past decades. They have made bureaucrats seem like employees of party politicians. . . . Truly, there is no leadership over the state now. I fear greatly for what the future will bring. . . . The army, too, has been under your direction over these years . . . and even this has been destroyed in a day. Indeed, the lifeblood of a hundred years is like the morning dew.[49]

It was only in 1924, when another party cabinet, led by Katô, came to power, that even the most modest liberal expectations began to be fulfilled. Between 1924 and 1927, the country enjoyed what has sometimes been regarded as a liberal honeymoon: the franchise was extended, the military budget was cut, and the number of civil servants was reduced by 20,000. The Kenseikai led by Katô and then Wakatsuki proved 'as close as the Taishô era came to producing an effective reform-minded cabinet that sought to do more than maintain itself in power or act as a complacent caretaker of national "wealth and strength"'.[50]

Corruption and repression

Although it can be seen, in retrospect, that the Taishô period witnessed the gradual retreat of the oligarchy in politics, it would be asking a great deal of those in power during the first quarter of the twentieth century to expect them to give up their authority in the same way as their predecessors, the feudal aristocracy, fifty years before. Nor did they do so. The shift towards democracy and openness was slow and halting, with the *genrô,* their successors, their supporters – and their opponents – all resorting to corruption, violence and repression in their attempts to retain – or obtain – the power that they wanted.

Corruption was more or less endemic. Regional and village notables controlled the electors' votes, and the party politicians secured their seats through 'ridiculous[ly] extravagant' promises to invest in schemes of local improvement. It was an arrangement that came in for a good deal of criticism.

> How has the Seiyûkai which controls the majority in the Lower House, been able to become the powerful party that it is today? It certainly did not achieve this because its policies were welcomed by the people. It enticed the simple folk of the regions by carrying out needless civil engineering projects under the fancy title: the management of postwar affairs. Consequently, government expenses rose to extreme proportions and the entire financial structure was endangered. During the ten years following the [Russo-Japanese] war, the nation has not been able to recover and there are signs of disaster ahead.

The press was just as critical, lamenting the injustices and inequalities that resulted from such a system.

> Since the Seiyûkai has solidified support in the constituencies of north-eastern Japan, the current [Ôkuma] government [supported by the rival Kenseikai party] has made the gains [to be had in the south-west] its primary focus whilst making light of the north-east. Because of this, there is nothing but ruin [in store for] the north-east should the government continue to pursue this policy.[51]

At the same time that this 'pork barrel' system provided fertile ground for corruption with favours being given and taken, the links between politicians and the *zaibatsu* grew ever more intimate. The four major conglomerates (Mitsui, Mitsubishi, Yasuda and Sumitomo) were perfectly able, and more than willing, to finance the activities of the two major political parties (Seiyûkai and Kenseikai), and they expected, quite naturally, that in return their interests would be protected and promoted. It would be naive, of course, to believe that the convergence of political and economic interests was unknown at other times or in other countries, but there is no doubt that in inter-war Japan the relationship between politicians and big business became exceptionally clear, close and contentious.[52]

Violence and repression were also common, the authorities showing little compunction in putting down what they saw as any direct challenge to their power. In 1911, twelve socialists and anarchists were executed for plotting to assassinate the emperor in what was called the Great Treason Incident of 1910. In 1918, the government dealt with the nationwide Rice Riots by the deployment of more than 100,000 troops, a strategy which resulted in the deaths of more than thirty civilians and in injuries to a great many more. In 1923, the police took advantage of the confusion following the Great Kantô Earthquake (when nearly 150,000 people died and 6,000 Koreans were massacred by vigilante groups in the Tokyo–Yokohama conurbation) to murder two of the country's leading anarchists, Ôsugi and Itô (Noe). In 1926, thirty-seven students were arrested for 'dangerous thought', and in particular for their attempt to contact a Russian workers' delegate as he travelled from Kyoto to Tokyo. The government's opponents could be just as ruthless. In 1921, prime minister Hara, the leader of the country's first party cabinet, was stabbed to death at Tokyo railway station by a young man unhappy with the direction in which he was leading the country. More startling still, on 27 December 1923 another young critic of government policy attempted to assassinate Crown Prince Hirohito as he was on his way to open the Diet.[53]

It was in such an atmosphere that the government passed the Peace Preservation Law of 1925, which significantly, some have argued, coincided with the passage of universal manhood suffrage. Although less explicit in its restrictions than similar legislation enacted at the beginning of the century, it was a fearsome and effective measure. It strengthened the powers of the Special Higher Police in their struggle to control 'dangerous thoughts'. It made illegal the activities of the revolutionary left, and it forbade the discussion, let alone the promotion, of any activity likely to undermine the existing economic and political system – restrictions which could be used to control criticism of the government of the day and were used to eliminate any attack upon the emperor. The Special Higher Police were not averse to using their powers: home ministry figures suggest, for example, that in 1928, 3,426 communists who advocated the overthrow of the 'Emperor System' were arrested (of whom 525 were prosecuted); and that five years later, 14,822 people were arrested, of whom 1,285 were prosecuted.[54]

It is tempting to conclude then that the term 'Taishô Democracy' should be used not just with very great caution, but with almost pathological distaste. Even at the time, the repression and violence that seemed to characterise the era led one opposition politician to ask,

> In our country, to what extent do politicians and educators understand the spirit of the times, and how far are they prepared to adapt to those hopes? Not only do they underrate things like individual rights and freedom of conscience,

but in maintaining feudalistic traditions and past customs, they have no scruples about oppressing the life of the individual and in trampling underfoot the individual character.

Yet this is an overreaction for, despite the corruption and repression that accompanied reform, this era permitted a degree of 'independent civilian thinking which five years later would be inconceivable'.[55]

The shift towards authoritarianism and 'dictatorship'

If the mid-1920s was a honeymoon, it most certainly did not last. The severe financial crisis of 1927 revealed again the fragility of party government and confirmed an apparently ingrained tendency for the leaders of the country to look to the military at times of national emergency. It became clear that the reforms introduced by the Meiji oligarchs and their successors had reshaped, but had by no means destroyed, Japan's deep-seated 'feudal' tradition with its emphasis upon absolute monarchy, aristocratic leadership, military values and popular obedience. It is not difficult to understand why it has been suggested, with some exaggeration that, 'People who were dissatisfied with the economic record or other policies of the party governments and their businessmen supporters yearned for the more patrician and supposedly less self-serving leadership of the past.'[56]

The power of the military

So it was that in 1927, a retired army general, Tanaka, became prime minister. It was a decisive change, laden with significance both political and symbolic. Tanaka's government set about the country's problems by shoring up the banks, exploiting Japan's incursions into China and reinforcing the authorities' control over the population at large. Any form of opposition was regarded as subversive. The Peace Preservation Law was amended to include the death penalty, all outdoor meetings were prohibited, and large numbers of left-wing activists and intellectuals were arrested. According to a British journalist living in the capital, by the summer of 1928, 'every liberal professor had been driven out of the universities'. In the schools too, renewed efforts were made to inculcate acceptable values and promote desirable behaviour: ex-army officers were employed as military instructors, and pupils were required to parade in uniform in front of photographs of the new emperor, Hirohito, which showed him in his uniform as commander-in-chief of the armed forces.[57]

Yet even Tanaka could not contain the military's growing confidence, a confidence which sometimes bordered on insubordination. In fact, he resigned the year after taking office, when the army refused to discipline those responsible for the assassination in June 1928 of Zhang Xueliang (Chang Tso-lin), a recalcitrant warlord in Manchuria, the Chinese province over which the Japanese now exerted widespread control. Tanaka's successors, Hamaguchi and Wakatsuki, faced graver problems still from the military's insubordination, which began to border now on recklessness and operational autonomy. In September 1931, a group of army officers, with the tacit approval of their superiors, staged an incident near the Manchurian capital which provided the pretext for an independent section of the Imperial Army to overrun the whole of the province and set up the puppet state of Manchukuo. Afraid of provoking a *coup d'état* if it attempted to discipline the military, the government eventually acquiesced in what had been done and then attempted to justify it to the rest of the world.[58]

The annexation, which became known as the Manchurian Incident, marked a crucial turning point in Japanese political history – indeed in all aspects of Japan's history. The governments which came to power during the rest of the 1930s and early 1940s were led not by party politicians, though they continued to be elected to the Diet, but by 'national unity' ('ultranationalist' or 'transcendental') cabinets. Dominated by the military, they did their best to reassert a sense of national unity and build up the authority of the state by reversing such trends of the Taishô era as freedom of speech, party politics and the growth of individualism. 'So, Fascism has come to Japan', lamented the liberal intellectual, Yoshino, in 1932.[59]

How did these changes come about? What was it that drove Japan towards militarism, authoritarianism and, some would say, dictatorship? It is a question that is often asked, but is seldom answered to anybody's complete satisfaction. It is a question that cannot be tackled seriously until later in the book, but what can be said even at this early stage is that it is not sufficient simply to point to some supposed flaw – or virtue – embedded deep in Japanese character and culture. The shift towards authoritarianism is to be explained, not by inherent patterns of thought and behaviour, but by the particular circumstances, personalities and events of the 1920s and 1930s. The constitutional arrangements of 1890 gave the service chiefs considerable autonomy, the armed forces enjoyed much greater prestige than parliamentarians, the economic crisis of the late 1920s and early 1930s engendered insecurity and uncertainty, and the opposition was riven by dissension. 'Two Labour parties are almost inevitable at the present stage,' conceded the *Japan Weekly Chronicle* in 1930, 'but five make for complete impotence.'[60]

The military, of course, had good reason to push the country in the direction of militarism and authoritarianism. But in order to understand military attitudes, one must not forget that the armed forces too were divided. There were two different services, many different ranks, and numerous different interests, none of which could be counted on to hold identical views about what was best for the country. The First World War revealed deep divisions between the navy and army that had been festering since the Meiji period. The navy, traditionally dominated by *Satsuma* men, viewed the United States as Japan's main enemy and since this implied a sea war, felt itself to be pre-eminent. In contrast, the army, which until the 1920s was the bastion of the rival feudal domain of *Chôshû*, anticipated hostilities with the Soviet Union, and thus stressed the necessity of securing Japan's position in Manchuria and China. Occasionally, this rivalry had serious repercussions. For example, in 1912, when a Seiyûkai-led government agreed to increase spending on the navy alone, Yamagata commented, 'I feel this is an extremely serious affair that can lead to grave consequences.' His words were prophetic for the government was forced to resign when the army refused to provide a war minister thereby ushering in the political crisis of 1912–13 (which was discussed above).[61]

More prominent still was factionalism within the army. There were ideological divisions and rifts along the lines of generation, class and whether or not one was from *Chôshû*. But broadly there existed two antagonistic groups. The 'Imperial Way Faction' advocated a 'Shôwa Restoration' – the comprehensive internal reconstruction of Japan centred around a mystical reverence and elevation of the emperor. The 'Control Faction', by contrast, concentrated its efforts on preparing the nation practically for total war and allied itself with big business and the bureaucracy. The notes contained in a 1943 study on military factionalism are revealing. The 'Imperial Way Faction' is

> 100 per cent soldier. Hard-boiled sort yet warm-hearted. Ready to sacrifice rules for personal sympathy. Cause of Emperor higher than law of the land. Must make extreme sacrifices today to achieve 'direct rule of Emperor.' Very strongly believes in divine origin of Imperial House and 'manifest destiny.' Bitter foe of communism. In private association hail-fellow-well-met; general associating with private. Battlefield commanders; no peacetime men. Death in battle highest honour that can befall a Japanese. Consider politicians no better than so many 'frogs in a well.' Believes argument useless. 'I will knock him down' type.

No compromise. White or black; no grey. In organisation like steamroller. Very restless. Unhappy in sustained peace. National socialist in their thinking but confused. Not logical. Two and two do not make four.

The notes on the 'Control Faction' presented a very different picture.

Law abiding. Not so 'pious'. Outward observance of national policy, but not fanatical. War Minister type rather than battlefield commanders. Capable administrators, diplomats, suave in manner. Businesslike, possessing relatively clear ideas of figures. Realistic. Watch their step. Lay stress on merit rather than personal sympathy. Respect 'status quo.' Believe in 'evolution' rather than 'revolution.' Pay due consideration to happiness of individual. Individual just as important as State. Present life as important as future. Common-sense sort. Pay due consideration to private property. Believes in wisdom of co-operating important. Two and two make four.[62]

Throughout the remainder of the 1930s, the armed forces played an increasingly prominent role in Japanese politics. With earlier restrictions on political activity abandoned, senior officers campaigned publicly to promote their views on national security, while their more junior colleagues grew bolder in their independence and insubordination. In 1932, a group of young naval officers assassinated prime minister Inukai, and three years later, a lieutenant colonel hacked to death the head of the army's military affairs bureau. It is hard to see how the military's actions could get much more threatening. But they did. In the so-called February 26 Incident of 1936, a group of a thousand and more soldiers, led by junior officers of the 'Imperial Way Faction', murdered the finance minister, the lord keeper of the privy seal and the inspector general of military education, and failed only narrowly in their attempt to kill prime minister Okada. They secured the support of the army minister, seized the centre of Tokyo for two days, and demanded the restoration of direct rule by the emperor. The Incident marked a turning point both in military provocation and in government retaliation. Prime minister Okada and his cabinet put down the rebellion with some determination: Emperor Hirohito made clear that he disapproved of what had been done ostensibly in his name, martial law was declared, and the rebel troops were persuaded that they had no choice but to surrender.[63]

It was a disturbing catalogue of insubordination and violence. Indeed, it remains a fundamental paradox of Japanese political history that, in a country so renowned for its discipline and deference, it was the armed forces, a group that one might have expected to exemplify such qualities, which demonstrated indiscipline, a striking degree of independence, and by the 1930s apparently boundless self-confidence. One must recognise too that however egregious the consequences of the military's involvement in politics, the motives of individual members of the armed forces were not necessarily ignoble. Their contempt for party politicians and the *zaibatsu* derived not only from the belief that government financial policies were holding down the military spending which they thought necessary, but also from the conviction that these policies were aggravating the distress and discontent of those living in the countryside.[64]

War and the new political order

The authorities were not blind to the dangers that they faced. They realised that they could not allow the armed forces to continue unchecked in their attempts to destabilise, and perhaps destroy, the political system under which they already exercised so much influence and power.[65]

However, the governments that came to power after 1936 did more and more to placate the military, by incorporating their leaders into government and by adopting many of their prescriptions for the nation's ills. In 1937, Japan invaded China, and a body known as the Imperial Headquarters and Cabinet Liaison Conference, consisting of the prime minister and foreign minister together with the two chiefs of staff, was established to co-ordinate the war effort. During the next few years, the national government led by Prince Konoe (the next prime minister but two after Okada) did what it could to mobilise the nation's military, economic and 'spiritual' resources. It declared the conflict with China a 'holy war', attempted to raise the nation's morale, called for a 'new order in East Asia' to resist communism and imperialism, and passed a National Mobilisation Law which gave the government unprecedented power to control raw materials, production, labour, wages and prices.[66]

Finally, in the summer of 1940, Konoe launched the New Political Order. The system was designed to mobilise the population behind the government in the war with China – and from 1941 the war with America and its allies. It involved the dissolution, or rather the self-dissolution, of all political parties, the strengthening of the cabinet and the establishment of what was known as the Imperial Rule Assistance Association as a vehicle through which to concentrate political power and exercise control over the population. However, the Association was neither as monolithic nor as successful as one might imagine. Some of the country's leaders wanted it to fail, and it was opposed by the bureaucracy who feared that it might undermine their authority. It is perhaps not altogether surprising therefore that a survey carried out at the end of 1941 revealed that 600 of the 685 people who were polled did not know what the New Order was all about.[67]

The chiefs of staff wanted to use the New Order to mobilise support for the armed forces, and the politicians, who knew how unloved they were, hoped that it would provide them with greater power than they had enjoyed hitherto. They were not entirely disappointed. The dissolution of political parties eliminated party labels, but did not bring an end to political activity or political criticism. One former ambassador, addressing the House of Peers in the spring of 1940, denounced the notion of economic blocs, a central tenet of the New Order ideology, as a 'castle in the air'. One member of the Lower House of the Diet went further, disparaging the war in China as a 'dream' and claiming, contrary to propaganda about a 'sacred war', that Japan's aggression was 'substantively the same as wars waged by Caucasians'. 'The painful endeavors and sacrifices of our military personnel', he continued, were 'meaningless'. Unsurprisingly, his speech was struck from the Diet records and he, himself, was expelled from the Diet. To be sure, such direct attacks on the political order and the war were rare. Nevertheless, criticisms could still be made. When the officially sponsored Diet Members' Imperial Assistance Association was formed, thirty per cent of all members declined to join.[68]

Konoe's successor, general Tôjô, called a general election in 1942 and, despite the government's efforts – both overt and covert – to secure the return of approved 'patriotic candidates', more than six hundred people had the temerity to stand as independents. Some went further still, comparing the country's leaders unfavourably with their Meiji predecessors, praising the United States of America for its humane treatment of prisoners of war, and challenging the authorities when they confiscated electoral literature. In the event, these independent candidates did remarkably well, winning a third of the votes cast, and eighteen per cent of the seats contested in the Diet. Indeed, it has been suggested that the prestige of the lower house probably increased during the war because it now appeared to be a national, rather than a partisan, organisation.[69]

Nonetheless, it was Tôjô who held the reins of power between 1941 and 1944. A man 'of bellicose temperament', it was no accident, claims Dower, that the military group with which he was associated was known as the 'Control Faction'. He was prime minister, army minister, a member of the Imperial Headquarters and the Cabinet Liaison Conference, and later war minister, munitions minister and chief of the general staff. Though not a dictator, and subject to the Japanese tradition of teamwork and collective leadership, he wielded more power than any other twentieth-century prime minister and probably bore more responsibility than any other individual for the way in which the Pacific War was conducted

– and he was, of course, one of the seven Japanese leaders who were executed in 1948 after being found guilty by the International Military Tribunal for the Far East.[70]

For the six months or so following the attack on Pearl Harbor in December 1941, the Tôjô government was enormously successful in its conduct of the war. The Imperial forces cut a swathe throughout eastern Asia, seizing Malaya, Burma, Singapore and Hong Kong from the British, capturing the Dutch East Indies, and driving the American general Douglas MacArthur out of his Philippines stronghold. By the spring of 1942, most of south-east Asia was under Japanese occupation. It was difficult for the rest of the world to comprehend. Winston Churchill recalled his amazement when he learned about the loss of Malaya. 'In all the war I never received a more direct shock. . . . As I turned over and twisted in bed the full horror of the news sank in upon me. . . . Japan was supreme and we everywhere were weak and naked.'[71]

It was not to last. Once the United States began to exploit its immense economic, industrial and technological advantages, the allied troops were able to halt, and then reverse, the Japanese onslaught. The fighting was bitter, the casualties appalling, the contempt chilling and the cruelty almost unspeakable. But slowly the allies moved north towards Japan, 'island-hopping' from one Japanese stronghold to another. Guadalcanal was invaded in August 1942, the Gilbert Islands in November 1943 and Truk in February 1944. Five months later, the allies captured Saipan, an island which, though 1,300 miles from Tokyo, had been designated by the Japanese authorities as a symbol of the nation's determination to resist the allied advance. The capture of the island was a rebuff that could not be endured, and Tôjô had no option but to resign.[72]

Tôjô's successors, general Koiso and admiral Suzuki, were placed in a desperate situation. The allies recaptured the Philippines at the beginning of 1945, and began to use the newly developed B-29 long-range bomber to attack the Japanese mainland. During the spring, attacks were launched not just on the periphery of the Japanese empire but on major, mainland cities such as Kobe, Osaka, Nagoya and Tokyo. In one raid alone on the capital, 80,000 people were killed, and a million more made homeless: it was, claims one Japanese historian, 'the greatest recorded conflagration in the entire history of mankind'. Finally, on 6 August and 9 August 1945, atomic bombs were dropped on the south-western cities of Hiroshima and Nagasaki. It was the end. Prime minister Suzuki called an imperial conference, and Emperor Hirohito was forced to recognise the inevitable. 'My heart aches', he declared, 'as I think of those who have faithfully fulfilled their duties and who now have to bear the disgrace. But this is the time when we must bear the unbearable to restore peace to the nation and to the world.' He announced Japan's unconditional surrender on 15 August 1945.[73]

Judgements on Japan

Victors' justice should always be treated with considerable caution. So it is scarcely surprising that in the aftermath of this bitter and destructive war, the victorious allies should take an exceptionally jaundiced view of Japan's politics, its political systems and its political culture. The so-called 'Emperor System' had an enormous amount to answer for, they believed. Undemocratic, militaristic and aggressive, it had failed the country, in-flicted huge damage on the rest of the world, and stood in need of the most radical root and branch reform. As Dower explains, 'The American overseers of Occupied Japan thought in terms of a civilising mission that would eliminate what was primitive, tribal and ritualistic. . . . They would guide an immature people with backward institutions towards maturity. The Japanese "children" now became pupils in General MacArthur's school of democracy.'[74]

But do such attitudes and judgements stand the test of time? Does the distance of half a century (and half the globe in the case of one of the authors of this book) mean that it is possible to avoid the 'presentism' and ethnocentrism which was inevitable in the aftermath of the war? And if such 'presentism' and ethnocentrism can be avoided, does it demand a new – and more generous – appraisal of Japanese politics, political systems and political culture between 1868 and 1945?

There is no denying that during the 1930s and early 1940s, Japanese politics became undemocratic, militaristic and aggressive, or that those responsible for the running of the country inflicted untold misery on Japan and on all the many millions of people who found themselves caught up in the Pacific War. There is no denying either that the histor-ian has the responsibility to put these arguments as clearly, frequently and forcibly as possible. However, there are several further points that need to be made.

First, it is essential to stress that the political system put in place after 1868 proved to be both highly resilient and remarkably flexible. In 1868, Japan was a feudal society with scarcely the glimmerings of popular accountability; sixty years later, the Japanese people were introduced to manhood suffrage, party government and a degree of liberalisation; and then, during the final fifteen years of the period, the military gained the ascendancy, party government was abandoned and individual liberties were severely curtailed.

Second, it follows that new forms of politics and political culture co-existed alongside – but most certainly did not destroy – more deeply entrenched patterns of thought and behaviour. Liberalism jostled with authoritarianism, party government with military control, democracy with emperor-worship. At times of crisis, there remained a huge temptation, it seemed, to revert to ways of thinking and to traditional forms of leadership established in the Meiji period.

Although the broad thrust of developments from the early to mid-1930s onwards could scarcely be more clear-cut, they have generated a great deal of scholarly controversy. The eclipse of party government, the strengthening of military influence and the assault upon individual liberties represented a break with the era of Taishô Democracy. But did it amount to the imposition of a fascist regime along the lines of that established in Nazi Germany?

Opinions differ sharply. On the one hand, there are those, like Barrington Moore, who suggest that in Japan, as in Germany, 'a form of rightist radicalism emerged out of the plight of the petty bourgeoisie and peasants under advancing capitalism'. This meant, maintain proponents of this view that, by the 1930s, Japan was authoritarian, militaristic and nationalistic, repressive at home and aggressive abroad – the classic symptoms of a fascist regime. By the end of the decade, they believe, Japan displayed, if nothing else, 'the principal external traits of European fascism'.[75]

However, it is more commonly believed that such comparisons misrepresent developments in Japan. The Asian and European versions of 'fascism', it is argued, were quite different. In Japan, unlike Germany, for example, there was no *coup d'état*, no dictator, no single mass party, no independent secret police, no formal change in the constitutional system and nothing comparable to the institutionalised terror and network of concentration camps established by the Nazi regime. The Japanese form of government, concluded a professor from Tokyo Imperial University at the end of the 1930s, was not at all like those in America or in Europe. It was *sui generis*. Japan and Europe were so different, concluded Griffin in his 1991 study of *The Nature of Fascism*, that 'the comforting sense of familiarity that a historian of inter-war Europe might have is quickly dissipated when the period is looked at in terms of the structural forces shaping it.'[76]

Although the debate about whether or not the Japanese state was fascist may seem rather esoteric, it is valuable in that it helps to clarify the nature of Japanese politics and political culture during the 1930s. The conclusion, cautious and colourless though it may seem, must surely be that both major interpretations of the decade possess considerable validity. The Japanese system was authoritarian, militaristic and nationalistic, but it was neither the same as, nor as terrible as, that operating in Hitler's Germany.

These two points lead to the third. The resilience and flexibility of the political system, and the co-existence of the old and the new make it much less easy than it seems to know what stance to adopt when considering Japanese politics between 1868 and 1945. Developments were opposed as well as supported; the 1860s were very different from the 1920s, and the 1920s different again from the early 1940s; and it is only fair to compare what happened in Japan with what happened in other countries at the same time – and not with some ahistorical ideal of what ought to have occurred. When this is done, it becomes less clear whether Japan was a leader or a laggard, an example to be emulated or a pariah to be exorcised. Generalisation remains difficult, and judgement highly subjective.

Notes

1. B-A. Shillony, *Politics and Culture in Wartime Japan*, Clarendon Press, 1981, preface.
2. A. Waswo, *Modern Japanese Society 1868–1914*, Oxford University Press, 1996, p. 96; B. Eccleston, *State and Society in Post-War Japan*, Polity Press, 1989, pp. 8, 15, 23.
3. R. Harvey, *The Undefeated: The Rise, Fall and Rise of Greater Japan*, Macmillan, 1994, p. 43; S.D. Barrington Moore Jnr, *Social Origins of Dictatorship and Democracy: Lord and Peasant in the Making of the Modern World*, Penguin, 1967; J. Macpherson, *The Economic Development of Japan c. 1868–1941*, Macmillan, 1987, p. 14; W.G. Beasley, *The Rise of Modern Japan: Political, Economic and Social Change since 1850*, Weidenfeld and Nicolson, 1990 (2nd ed., 1995), p. 53. Biographical and autobiographical accounts of the most prominent leaders of the Restoration include J. Morris, *Makers of Modern Japan*, Methuen, 1906; M. Iwata, *Ōkubo Toshimichi: The Bismarck of Japan*, University of California Press, 1964; A.M. Craig and D.H. Shively, *Personality in Japanese History*, University of California Press, 1970; R.F. Hackett, *Yamagata Aritomo in the Rise of Modern Japan*, Harvard University Press, 1971; J.C. Lebra, *Ōkuma Shigenobu: Statesman of Meiji Japan*, Australian National University Press, 1973; T. Kido, *The Diary of Kido Takayoshi* (3 vols), S. Devere Brown and A. Hirota (trans.), University of Tokyo Press, 1983; H. Matsukata Reischauer, *Samurai and Silk: A Japanese and American Heritage*, Harvard University Press, 1986; C. Yates, *Saigō Takamori, the Man Behind the Myth*, Kegan Paul, 1995.
4. Barrington Moore, *Social Origins*, pp. 236–7. Also Macpherson, *Economic Development*, p. 24; Waswo, *Japanese Society*, pp. 9–10; G.C. Allen, *A Short Economic History of Modern Japan 1867–1937*, Allen & Unwin, 1946, pp. 14–15; T.C. Smith, 'Japan's Aristocratic Revolution', *Yale Review*, 1961.

5. *The Times*, 26 March 1852.

6. W.G. Beasley, *The Modern History of Japan*, Weidenfeld and Nicolson, 1963, pp. 57–61; G. Wilson, *Patriots and Redeemers in Japan: Motives in the Meiji Restoration*, Chicago University Press, 1992.

7. M.B. Jansen, 'The Meiji Restoration', in M.B. Jansen (ed.), *The Cambridge History of Japan*, vol. 5, *The Nineteenth Century*, Cambridge University Press, 1989, pp. 342–5.

8. In 1864, British, French, Dutch and United States ships bombarded Shimonoseki in retaliation for attacks on foreign shipping by Chôshû. Beasley, *Modern History*, pp. 89–98. Detailed histories of the last years of the feudal era include W.G. Beasley, *The Meiji Restoration*, Stanford University Press, 1973; C. Totman, *The Collapse of the Tokugawa Bakufu, 1862–1868*, University of Hawaii Press, 1980; R.L. Sims, *French Policy towards the Bakufu and Meiji Japan: 1854–1895*, Japan Library, 1998.

9. E.J. Hobsbawm and T. Ranger (eds), *The Invention of Tradition*, Cambridge University Press, 1983; J.E. Hunter, *The Emergence of Modern Japan: An Introductory History since 1853*, Longman, 1989, pp. 8–9; T. Kase, *Eclipse of the Rising Sun*, Cape, 1951, p. 19.

10. R. Tames, *A Traveller's History of Japan*, Windrush Press, 1993, p. 122.

11. Beasley, *Rise of Modern Japan*, pp. 86–7. A detailed discussion of the Iwakura Mission is to be found in I. Nish, *The Iwakura Mission in America and Europe: A New Assessment*, Japan Library, 1998.

12. Y. Fukuzawa, *An Encouragement of Learning*, D.A. Dilworth and U. Hirano (trans.), Sophia University, 1969, p. 23. Other translated works from the 'civilisation and enlightenment' era include Y. Fukuzawa, *An Outline of a Theory of Civilization*, D.A. Dilworth and G.C. Hurst (ed. and trans.), Sophia University, 1973: R. Braisted (ed. and trans.), *Meiroku Zasshi*, Harvard University Press, 1976. See also C. Blacker, *The Japanese Enlightenment*, Cambridge University Press, 1964.

13. Fukuzawa, *Encouragement*, p. 1.

14. Fukuzawa, *Encouragement*, pp. 3–4.

15. In the short term, the establishment of prefectures was less drastic than it appeared because the great lords were often appointed governors. In Iwakura's words, it was a 'welcome miscalculation'. See E. Seidensticker, *Low City, High City: Tokyo from Edo to the Earthquake – How the Shogun's Ancient Capital became a Great Modern City (1867–1923)*, Alfred A. Knopf, 1983, esp. chapter 2. In practice, of course, groups like the *burakumin* were not treated equally before the law (see chapter 6).

16. G. Akita, *Foundations of Constitutional Government in Modern Japan: 1869–1900*, Harvard University Press, 1967, p. 19.

17. E. Baelz, *Awakening Japan: The Diary of a German Doctor*, Indiana University Press, 1974, pp. 20–1; M.B. Jansen (ed.), *The Emergence of Meiji Japan*, Cambridge University Press, 1995, pp. 229–38; Hunter, *Modern Japan*, pp. 324–5; Harvey, *The Undefeated*, pp. 77–9.

18. D. Irokawa, *The Culture of the Meiji Period*, M.B. Jansen (ed. and trans.), Princeton University Press, 1985, p. 106, chapter III *passim*; Rekishigaku kenkyûkai (ed.), *Nihonshi shiryô*, vol. 4, *Kindai*, Iwanami Shoten, 1998, pp. 140–2.

19. K.B. Pyle, 'Meiji Conservatism', in Jansen (ed.), *Cambridge History of Japan*, esp. pp. 674–88. The People's Rights Movement is discussed in N. Ike, *The Beginnings of Political Democracy in Japan*, Johns Hopkins Press, 1950; R.A. Scalopino, *Democracy and the Party Movement in Prewar Japan: The Failure of the First Attempt*, University of California Press, 1953; J. Pittau, *Political Thought in the Early Meiji Period, 1868–*

1889, Harvard University Press, 1967; **R.A. Bowen**, *Rebellion and Democracy in Meiji Japan: A Study of Commoners in the People's Rights Movement*, University of California Press, 1980; **S. Vlastos**, 'Opposition Movements in Early Meiji, 1868–1885', in Jansen (ed.), *Cambridge History of Japan*, pp. 367–431; **R.L. Sims**, *A Political History of Modern Japan, 1868–1952*, Vikas, 1991; **R.H. Mitchell**, *Janus-faced Justice: Political Criminals in Imperial Japan*, University of Hawaii Press, 1992.

20. Jansen, 'The Meiji Restoration', p. 56. For other interpretations of the Meiji Restoration, see **E.H. Norman**, *Japan's Emergence as a Modern State: Political and Economic Problems of the Meiji Period*, Institute of Pacific Relations, 1940; Beasley, *The Meiji Restoration*; **T. Huber**, *The Revolutionary Origins of Modern Japan*, Stanford University Press, 1981; **M.B. Jansen** and **G. Rozman** (eds), *Japan in Transition from Tokugawa to Meiji*, Princeton University Press, 1986.

21. Rekishigaku kenkyûkai (ed.), *Nihonshi shiryô*, vol. 4, p. 209; Beasley, *Rise of Modern Japan*, p. 77; Akita, *Foundations of Constitutional Government*, pp. 12, 207 fn. 49.

22. **W.G. Beasley**, introduction to **T. Kawahara**, *Hirohito and his Times: A Japanese Perspective*, Kôdansha International, 1990; Shillony, *Politics and Culture*, pp. 36–7; **E.O. Reischauer**, *The Japanese Today: Change and Continuity*, Belknap Press, 1988, p. 240; **S.S. Large**, 'The Role of the Emperor', *Insight Japan*, May 1998, p. 6; Rekishigaku kenkyûkai (ed.), *Nihonshi shiryô*, vol. 4, p. 209; Akita, *Foundations of Constitutional Government*, p. 70. There are numerous studies of Emperor Hirohito, in particular, his role in World War II: **P. Manning**, *Hirohito: The War Years*, Dodd, Mead, 1986; **T. Kawahara**, *Hirohito and His Times*; **S.S. Large**, *Emperor Hirohito and Shôwa Japan: A Political Biography*, Routledge, 1992; **P. Wetzler**, *Hirohito and War: Imperial Tradition and Military Decision Making in Prewar Japan*, University of Hawaii Press, 1998. See also **S. Honjo**, *Emperor Hirohito and His Chief Aide-de-Camp*, **M. Hane** (ed. and trans.), University of Tokyo Press, *c.* 1982; **T. Fujitani**, *Splendid Monarchy: Power and Pageantry in Modern Japan*, University of California Press, 1996. An authoritative work on the three modern emperors of Japan is **S.S. Large**, *Emperors of the Rising Sun: Three Biographies*, Kôdansha International, 1997.

23. **R.P.G. Steven**, 'Hybrid Constitutionalism in Prewar Japan', *Journal of Japanese Studies*, 3, 1977, p. 100; Kase, *Eclipse*, p. 21; Reischauer, *Japanese Today*, p. 234; **P. Duus**, Introduction, in **P. Duus** (ed.), *The Cambridge History of Japan*, vol. 6, *The Twentieth Century*, Cambridge University Press, 1988, pp. 39–40.

24. For further discussion on the Meiji Constitution, see Akita, *Foundations of Constitutional Government*; Ike, *Beginnings of Political Democracy*; **J. Banno**, *The Establishment of the Japanese Constitutional System*, **J.A.A. Stockwin** (trans.), Routledge, 1995; **W.G. Beasley**, 'Meiji Political Institutions', in Jansen (ed.), *Cambridge History of Japan*, pp. 618–73; Pittau, *Political Thought*; Scalopino, *Democracy and the Party Movement*.

25. *Japan Times*, 27 March, 7 and 19 April 1897; Hunter, *Modern Japan*, pp. 215–16; **J.E. Thomas**, *Modern Japan: A Social History since 1868*, Longman, 1996, p. 62. See also **L. Connors**, *The Emperor's Adviser: Saionji Kinmochi and Pre-War Japanese Politics*, Croom Helm, 1987.

26. **M. Barnhart**, *Japan and the World since 1866*, Arnold, 1995, ch. 3; Hunter, *Modern Japan*, p. 216. **R.F. Wall**, *Japan's Century: An Interpretation of Japanese History since the Eighteen-Fifties*, Historical Association, 1971, p. 31; Steven, 'Hybrid Constitutionalism', p. 115; Akita, *Foundations of Constitutional Government*, p. 85.

27. Akita, *Foundations of Constitutional Government*, pp. 73, 133.

28. **C. Gluck**, *Japan's Modern Myths: Ideology in the Late Meiji Period*, Princeton University Press, 1985; Reischauer, *Japanese Today*, p. 266.

29. *Japan Weekly Chronicle*, 17 April 1919, 12 February 1925; **G.M. Berger**, 'Politics and Mobilisation in Japan, 1931–1945', in Duus (ed.), *Cambridge History of Japan*, pp. 97–9; Tames, *Traveller's History*, p. 148.
30. Waswo, *Modern Japanese Society*, p. 23.
31. **T.C. Smith**, *Political Change and Industrial Development in Japan: Government Enterprise, 1868–1880*, Stanford University Press, 1965; **D.B. Smith**, *Japan since 1945: The Rise of an Economic Superpower*, Macmillan, 1995, p. 3.
32. See, for example, **T.A. Bisson**, 'Increase of Zaibatsu Predominance in Wartime Japan', *Pacific Affairs*, xviii, 1945. On foreign advisers, see, **H.L. Jones**, *Live Machines: Hired Foreigners and Meiji Japan*, P. Norburg Publications, 1980.
33. Macpherson, *Economic Development*, pp. 36–7; Smith, *Japan*, pp. 4–7; Hunter, *Modern Japan*, p. 119; Allen, *Short Economic History*, pp. 39–40, 178; **E.S. Crawcour**, 'Industrialisation and Technological Change, 1885–1920', in Duus (ed.), *Cambridge History of Japan*, pp. 392–9.
34. **D. Eleanor Westney**, *Imitation and Innovation: The Transfer of Western Organizational Patterns to Meiji Japan*, Harvard University Press, 1987, p. 95. See also **D. Eleanor Westney**, 'The Military', in Jansen and Rozman (eds), *Japan in Transition*, pp. 168–94; Gluck, *Japan's Modern Myths*; Hackett, *Yamagata Aritomo*.
35. Hunter, *Modern Japan*, pp. 110, 269–73; Thomas, *Modern Japan*, p. 99.
36. **B.K. Marshall**, *Learning to be Modern: Japanese Political Discourse on Education*, Westview Press, 1994, p. 60.
37. Marshall, *Learning to be Modern*, p. 62.
38. Norman, *Japan's Emergence*, p. 208.
39. **R.B. Edgerton**, *Warriors of the Rising Sun*, Norton, 1997, p. 223; Tames, *Traveller's History*, p. 117.
40. **H.D. Harootunian**, 'Introduction: A Sense of an Ending and the Problem of Taishô', in **B.S. Silberman** and **H.D. Harootunian** (eds), *Japan in Crisis: Essays on Taishô Democracy*, Princeton University Press, 1974, pp. 9–10.
41. **S. Katô**, 'Taishô Democracy as the Pre-Stage for Japanese Militarism', in Silberman and Harootunian, *Japan in Crisis*, pp. 217–18; **R.M. Spaulding**, 'Japan's Search for Cultural Identity', *Comparative Studies in Society and History*, 14, 1972, p. 514.
42. **S. Minichiello**, *Retreat from Reform: Patterns of Political Behaviour in Interwar Japan*, University of Hawaii Press, 1984, pp. 15–16. For general discussions on the politics of the Taishô era, see **F.O. Miller**, *Minobe Tatsukichi – Interpreter of Constitutionalism in Japan*, University of California Press, 1965; **T. Najita**, *Hara Kei in the Politics of Compromise: 1905–1915*, Harvard University Press, 1967; **P. Duus**, *Party Rivalry and Political Change in Taishô Japan*, Harvard University Press, 1968; **P. Duus**, 'Yoshino Sakuzô: The Christian as Political Critic', *Journal of Japanese Studies*, 4, 1978, pp. 301–26.
43. Minichiello, *Retreat from Reform*, p. 19; Duus, *Party Rivalry*, pp. 146, 176.
44. Despite the existence of a women's suffrage movement which established informal ties with certain members of Katô's party, the Kenseikai, women were not given the vote until 1946. *Japan Weekly Chronicle*, 17 April 1919, 15 July 1920; **J. Dower**, *Japan in War and Peace: Essays on History, Race and Culture*, HarperCollins, 1995, pp. 110–11.
45. *TA*, 29 December 1912; 16 January 1913; *OM*, 12 December 1912; 7 February 1913. See also: *JS*, 15 December 1912; *TA*, 9, 13 January, 18 February 1913. On the political crisis which brought about the movement, see *CS*, 10 December 1912; *OM*, 22 December 1912; A second 'Movement to Protect Constitutional Government'

was initiated by the Kenseikai in 1922 in response to the exclusion of the political parties from cabinet participation and an apparent return to the oligarchic monopolisation of government. Although it largely failed to mobilise the public, it did see a return to party cabinets in 1924. On the second 'Movement to Protect Constitutional Government', see Duus, *Party Rivalry*.

46. *TM*, 1 January 1910.

47. Eccleston, *State and Society*, p. 13; Duus, Introduction, p. 13; **K.B. Pyle**, *The Making of Modern Japan*, Heath, 1978, pp. 121–32, Minichiello, *Retreat from Reform*, p. 63.

48. **T. Mitani**, 'The Establishment of Party Cabinets, 1898–1932', in Duus (ed.), *Cambridge History of Japan*, pp. 55–6; Berger, 'Politics', in Duus (ed.), *Cambridge History of Japan*, p. 97; Banno, *Japanese Constitutional System*.

49. Wall, *Japan's Century*, p. 31; Thomas, *Modern Japan*, pp. 152–4; Najita, *Hara Kei*, pp. 22, 181–2.

50. Duus, *Rivalry*, p. 189.

51. Najita, *Hara Kei*, p. 61; *TM*, 1 February 1915.

52. Eccleston, *State and Society*, pp. 13–14.

53. Baelz, *Awakening Japan*, pp. 82–3; **M. Lewis**, *Rioters and Citizens: Mass Protest in Imperial Japan*, University of California Press, 1990, p. xvii; **J. Orchard**, 'Government Suppression of the Labour Movement', in **J. Livingstone**, **J. Moore** and **F. Oldfather** (eds), *The Japan Reader*, vol. I, *Imperial Japan 1800–1945*, Penguin, 1976; Hunter, *Modern Japan*, pp. 243, 249; Thomas, *Modern Japan*, pp. 154–5. On the Great Treason Incident and one of its leading figures, see **F.G. Notehelfer**, *Kôtoku Shûsui: Portrait of a Japanese Radical*, Cambridge University Press, 1971. See also **T. Arima**, *The Failure of Freedom: A Portrait of Modern Japanese Intellectuals*, Harvard University Press, 1969.

54. *Japan Weekly Chronicle*, 1 May 1930; Hunter, *Modern Japan*, pp. 253–4; Thomas, *Modern Japan*, p. 157.

55. Wall, *Japan's Century*, p. 31; **E. Behr**, *Hirohito: Behind the Myth*, Penguin, 1990, pp. 74–5; Minichiello, *Retreat from Reform*, pp. 31–2.

56. Kase, *Eclipse*, pp. 22–3; Barrington Moore, *Social Origins*; Thomas, *Modern Japan*, pp. 179–8l.

57. *Japan Weekly Chronicle*, 20 February 1930, 3 August 1933, 25 July 1935; Behr, *Hirohito*, pp. 75–6; Wall, *Japan's Century*, p. 33; Eccleston, *State and Society*, p. 140.

58. On Tanaka, see **W.F. Moroton**, *Tanaka Giichi and Japan's China Policy*, Dawson, 1980; **N. Bamba**, *Japanese Diplomacy in a Dilemma*, University of British Columbia Press, 1992.

59. Pyle, *Making*, p. 97; Akita, *Foundations of Constitutional Government*, p. 159. Studies of the political history of the 1930s include **G.M. Berger**, *Parties out of Power in Japan: 1931–1941*, Princeton University Press, 1977; Minichiello, *Retreat from Reform*.

60. *Japan Weekly Chronicle*, 20 February 1930; Berger, 'Politics', pp. 102–5.

61. Najita, *Hara Kei*, pp. 96–7.

62. *Japan Chronicle*, 8 May 1919; Waswo, *Modern Japanese Society*, pp. 83–4; Eccleston, *State and Society*, p. 14; Behr, *Hirohito*, pp. 105, 109–10; **R. Storry**, *The Double Patriots: A Study of Japanese Nationalism*, Greenwood Press, 1957, p. 138. On the military in the 1930s, see **J.B. Crowley**, *Japan's Quest for Autonomy: National Security and Foreign Policy*, Princeton University Press, 1966; **M. Harries and S. Harries**, *Soldiers of the Sun: The Rise and Fall of the Imperial Japanese Army*, William Heinemann, 1991. Factionalism in the military is dealt with in the following: **M. Maruyama**,

Thought and Behaviour in Modern Japanese Politics, expanded edition, **I. Morris** (ed.), Oxford University Press, 1969, first published in 1963; **G. Wilson**, *Radical Nationalist: Kita Ikki, 1883–1937*, Harvard University Press, 1969; **B-A. Shillony**, *Revolt in Japan: The Young Officers and the February 26, 1936 Incident*, Princeton University Press, 1973; Storry, *Double Patriots*.

63. **H. Byas**, *Government by Assassination*, Allen & Unwin, 1943.

64. Waswo, *Modern Japanese Society*, pp. 79–82; Behr, *Hirohito*, pp. 138–9, 166–7.

65. Thomas, *Modern Japan*, p. 174; Waswo, *Modern Japanese Society*, p. 87; Berger, 'Politics', pp. 119–25.

66. Berger, 'Politics', pp. 128–36.

67. Duus, Introduction, p. 36; Berger, 'Politics and Mobilisation', pp. 141–6; Shillony, *Politics and Culture*, pp. 2–3, 28. See also **J. Crump**, 'Anarchist Opposition to Japanese Militarism, 1926–1937', *Japan Forum*, 4, 1992; **E.H. Kinmonth**, 'The Impact of Military Procurements on the Old Middle Classes in Japan, 1931–1941', *Japan Forum*, 4, 1992.

68. Cited in **J.B. Crowley**, 'Intellectuals as Visionaries of the New Asian Order', in **J.W. Morley** (ed.), *Dilemmas of Growth in Pre-War Japan*, Princeton University Press, 1974, pp. 282–3.

69. Berger, 'Politics', pp. 102, 148–9; **A. Iriye**, *Japan and the Wider World: From the Mid-Nineteenth Century to the Present*, Longman, 1997, p. 168.

70. **R.H. Minear**, *Victors' Justice: The Tokyo War Crimes Trial*, Charles Tuttle, 1972; **B.V.A. Roling** and **A. Cassese**, *The Tokyo Trial and Beyond: Reflections of a Peacemonger*, Polity, 1993; **S. Dockrill**, 'Hirohito, the Emperor's Army and Pearl Harbor', *Review of International Studies*, 18, 1992; Waswo, *Modern Japanese Society*, pp. 29, 87; Dower, *Japan*, p. 105.

71. Thomas, *Modern Japan*, p. 229.

72. **C. Browne**, *Tōjō: The Last Banzai*, Da Capo Press, 1998, pp. 157–60; Thomas, *Modern Japan*, pp. 225–43; Harvey, *The Undefeated*, pp. 26–7.

73. **G. Daws**, *Prisoners of the Japanese: POWs of World War II in the Pacific – The Powerful Untold Story*, Robson Books, 1995, pp. 302–20; Thomas, *Modern Japan*, pp. 243–6; Dower, *Japan*, pp. 40–1.

74. Dower, *Japan*, pp. 280–1.

75. Barrington Moore, *Social Origins,* p. 301. One of the most important works on the question of Japanese fascism is Maruyama, *Thought and Behaviour*. **P.M. Brooker** systematically compares German, Italian and Japanese fascism, or 'fraternalism' in *Faces of Fraternalism: Nazi Germany, Fascist Italy, and Imperial Japan*, Clarendon Press, 1991. See also **G.M. Wilson**, 'A New Look at the Problem of "Japanese Fascism"', in *Comparative Studies in Sociology and History: An International Quarterly*, 10, 1967–68, pp. 401–12; **W.M. Fletcher III**, *The Search for a New Order: Intellectuals and Fascism in Prewar Japan*, University of North Carolina Press, 1982.

76. *Japan Chronicle*, 3 August 1933; *Japan Times Weekly*, 2 February 1939; Wall, *Japan's Century*, p. 16; Waswo, *Modern Japanese Society*, pp. 76–7; Barrington Moore, *Social Origins*, p. 304; **R. Griffin**, *The Nature of Fascism*, Routledge, 1991, p. 153.

International relations and imperial expansion

It is even more difficult to examine Japan's international relations and imperial expansion with an open mind than it is her politics, political systems and political culture. Indeed, it is not too much of an exaggeration to suggest that the debate over Japan's domestic politics pales almost into insignificance when compared to the furore which has been generated by the way in which Japan behaved towards her neighbours in Asia and her enemies in Europe and the United States of America. How was it, we ask, that Japan grew, in three-quarters of a century, from an isolated, feudal backwater into a world power whose empire encompassed over 600 million people and stretched from China in the north to the Dutch East Indies in the south, from Burma in the west to the middle of the Pacific in the east (see Figure 3). Why was it, we wonder, that in acquiring her empire, she behaved in a way which became a byword for contempt, cruelty and inhumanity? Is it possible, with the passing of the years, to look back upon Japan's international relations and imperial expansion with something approaching impartiality and objectivity?[1]

It is well known, of course, that the Japanese themselves have found it exceptionally difficult to come to terms with their imperial past. The struggle continued well into the 1990s, for example, over how school textbooks should deal with Japan's policy towards Taiwan, Korea, China and other Asian countries, with the Imperial Army's use of 'comfort women' and with its involvement in the bestialities of Unit 731's biological experimentation. The failure to confront the past meant, critics have claimed, that war criminals went unpunished, that those on the right were able to regain power and that re-militarisation was made a good deal more likely. Those who are not Japanese usually react to Japan's imperial past with a mixture of indignation and incomprehension. One retired major-general wrote to *The Times* on the reaction of the Far East prisoners of war towards the visit of Emperor Akihito, the son of Hirohito, to Britain in 1998,

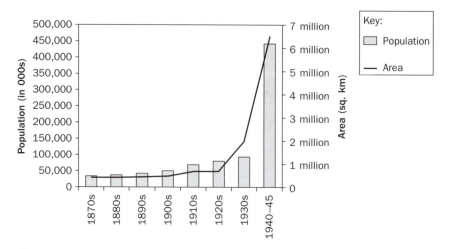

Figure 3: Population and area of the Japanese Empire, 1870s–1945

Note: Figures for 1940 to 1945 are estimates since the population and area of occupied China are not officially recorded.

Source: Compiled from *Nihon teikoku tokei nenkan*; figures for 1940 to 1945 from P. Duus, R.H. Myers and M.R. Peattie (eds), *The Japanese Wartime Empire, 1931–1945*, Princeton University Press, 1996, p. xiii.

> [It] is not the 'scars of war', as the emperor's speech expressed it, which the PoWs bear, but the scars of Japan's failure to obey the laws of war as expressed in the Hague and Geneva Conventions and which her government promised to observe.

Many were far more vitriolic in their criticism, the newspapers condemning the emperor's 'deep sorrow' as nothing more than 'fairy stories' and 'outrageous trickery'. Nor is indignation limited to those from the West who suffered personally at the hands of the Japanese. When the premier of China received the Emperor on a state visit later in 1998, he politely, if pointedly, noted that it was up to the Japanese government to 'contain the denial and distortion of history'. An editorial in *The Times* concluded that, 'The inescapable impression created is that Japan is incapable of outright apology to China, because the Japanese still feel no real guilt about atrocities committed against the Chinese by its Imperial Army.'[2]

Indeed, the inability to address past actions has meant that Japan's post-war efforts to reshape her image as a peaceful nation committed to future international welfare has continually been cast into doubt. As one observer comments, 'while business ties develop, and amity is proclaimed to be spreading, old facts emerging as recent revelations increase their magnetic attraction and pull us into a re-examination of what happened then – and again incite us into debates of how and why'. The *Daily Mail* put it more bluntly, 'Why, if Japan's manufacturers appear precisely to grasp our needs as consumers of cars, cannot their politicians have a better understanding of the more profound feelings of the heart?'[3]

Accordingly, this chapter, like the last, has two broad and very difficult aims: to describe, and attempt to explain, the course of Japan's international relations and imperial expansion between 1868 and 1945. It is important, it is believed, to provide once again a clear exposition of Japan's development. It will be shown, for instance, that the late nineteenth and early twentieth-century policy of enriching the country and strengthening the military was accompanied by war with China and Russia, and that the shift in the late 1920s towards militarism and authoritarianism became associated with expansion into China, and later war with America and the allied powers.

It will be stressed once again that there was nothing preordained about these developments. It will be shown that, whether one starts from the assumption that Japan's imperialism was an aberration or from the assumption that the Japanese were inherently aggressive and expansionist, it is essential to take account of the particular historical circumstances in which policy was made and wars were fought. Indeed, it has been suggested that Japan provides a valuable laboratory for studying international relations and imperial expansion, and in particular the complex relationship between human resources, economic demands, technological change and the policy-making process.

When this laboratory is used, it can be seen that the distinction between formal and informal methods of control (and thus between formal and informal imperialism) is fundamental to the understanding of Japan's international relations. As Robinson and Gallagher suggested many years ago in a pioneering re-examination of British imperialism, studying the formal empire alone 'is rather like judging the size and character of icebergs solely from the parts above the waterline'. Britain, they argued, pursued her interests by diplomacy as well as by belligerency, by ingratiation as well as by annexation. British policy, they believed, 'followed the principle of extending control informally if possible and formally if necessary'.[4]

Armed with this distinction between formal and informal imperialism, it can be seen that there were five broad stages in the evolution of Japanese international relations. There was what may be called the search for security between 1868 and 1890; the establishment of formal empire between 1890 and 1914; the expansion of informal imperialism between 1914 and 1931; the growth of nationalism and militarism between 1931 and 1940; and the inauguration, finally, of what was known as the

Greater East Asia Co-Prosperity Sphere between 1940 and 1945. It can be seen too that, although these stages in Japan's international relations were intimately related, each of them had its own antecedents, its own dynamics, its own strategies and its own consequences.

The search for security

The search for security was part and parcel of the policy of enriching the country and strengthening the military. It was a search that took different forms at different times. Sometimes it was cautious and sometimes aggressive; political pressure and diplomatic manoeuvring were used, but so too were economic sanctions and military might. It was a search which, whatever forms it took, was underpinned in a most profound way by Japan's geographical position. Viewing the world from a small island off the east coast of Asia, Japanese policy-makers were always deeply concerned about what was happening in neighbouring Korea, in nearby islands like Taiwan and Sakhalin, and in major mainland powers like China and Russia whose eastern provinces abutted onto the East China Sea and the Sea of Japan. As scholars like Hoare have argued, 'Japan was reluctantly forced into the nineteenth-century world of power politics by the triple pressures of the British advance in China, the Russian push into north-east Asia and the United States' realisation that it was a Pacific power'.[5]

It was seen in the previous chapter that the fundamental aim of the generation that came to power in 1868 was to build a united, prosperous and powerful nation state. They did what they could to promote economic development by encouraging the use of foreign expertise, creating close ties with the *zaibatsu*, and strengthening the country's financial, transport and communications infrastructure. They also did what they could to enlarge the army and navy, provide them with the equipment they needed, and disseminate military virtues among the population at large. By the early 1880s, the peacetime army numbered over 70,000, a force which at times of war grew to more than a quarter of a million.[6]

The search for security, which was central to the policy of enriching the country and strengthening the military, was also the driving force behind Japan's international relations. The leaders of Meiji Japan knew very well that it had been the *shōgun*'s inability to deal with the American incursion of 1853 and the acceptance of the 'unequal' treaties of 1858 which provided the catalyst that undermined the Tokugawa regime and led to the Restoration of 1868. They did not intend to make the same mistakes, and realised that if Japan's international position was to be strengthened, domestic reform needed to be accompanied by significant foreign policy initiatives.[7]

Respect, recognition and influence

Japan worked hard to secure international respect and recognition. This meant, if nothing else, the renegotiation, or better still the termination, of the 'unequal' treaties of the 1850s. For as one early twentieth-century Japanese commentator pointed out, 'Japan asserted that a great national wrong had been done her by the Powers, whereby she had been robbed of her birthright, namely Judicial and Tariff Autonomy'. What made the feeling of injustice particularly intense was a profound sense of the racial and religious discrimination that they faced. Itô explained that:

> I find ... that the Europeans would harm and deceive us, [and] there is precious little sentiment among them for doing anything to profit or benefit us. . . . The European nations, combining together, are trying to outstrip isolated Japan. This feeling, in fine, stems from none other than racial and religious differences. . . . If they are going to stress that our level of civilization is not up to their standards, what about their recognizing as civilized and independent states Bulgaria, Serbia, Montenegro, and Rumania? These states are peopled by those who do not differ from wild monkeys. . . . The reason that the Europeans show respect and affection for these uncivilized mountain barbarians and do not recognize the progress of those of us in the East is that there is no fellow feeling between us as between correligionists.[8]

So sensitive were the Japanese to the 'humiliation' they suffered at the hands of the Europeans and Americans that by the late 1880s opposition leaders and their supporters included alongside their demands for 'freedom of the press' and 'land-tax reduction', 'the re-assertion [of full control] over diplomacy'. In 1889 Foreign Minister Ôkuma secured the most favourable terms to date for treaty revision, but faced the opposition of privy councillors, imperial advisers and nationalistic sections of the general public because he envisaged the use of foreign judges in the Japanese Supreme Court. Despite numerous attempts by the Japanese government to have the treaties revised, the struggle dragged on until the turn of the century, the foreign powers defending their legal and fiscal privileges on the grounds that the Japanese legal and constitutional system remained inferior to their own. Britain argued, for instance, that it did not wish to jeopardise its good relations with Japan by entrusting the interests of British subjects to the Japanese government 'too soon' in its development. It was not until 1894 that a treaty was signed ending foreign consular jurisdiction, an event which at once enabled the Japanese to reflect on and celebrate their recent achievements while confidently looking to the possibilities of the future as a 'civilised nation' equal with those of the West. The *Jiji Shimpô* commented that the treaty provisions

> are something we . . . have no hesitation in boldly endorsing. . . . The current success is completely with the trend of the times. . . . Recently, Japanese national strength has developed remarkably. Accordingly, foreigners, recognising this, have uncategorically changed their policy towards us . . . the result of this policy is nothing less than the likes of treaty revision. . . . Although there may be feelings of dissatisfaction [*vis-à-vis* the minutiae of the treaty revisions] in the hearts of the masses, the promulgation of this code is for the Japanese; it has nothing to do with foreigners.[9]

The leaders of Meiji Japan were more successful, more quickly, in their search for defensible frontiers and clearly defined national boundaries. The new regime dealt expeditiously with three sets of islands where disputes might bring it into conflict with its neighbours China, Korea and Taiwan, or with world powers such as Britain, Russia and the United States. In the early 1870s, she brought Okinawa and the Ryûkyû islands, to the south-west of Kyûshû, under the jurisdiction and protection of the Japanese state. A few years later, she tackled the problem of the sparsely inhabited islands to the north of Hokkaidô by ceding the large island of Sakhalin to the Russians and retaining for herself the chain of small islands known as the Kurils. Finally in 1876, she managed to incorporate the Bonin islands, 560 miles south-east of Tokyo, into the administrative jurisdiction of the nation's capital.[10]

The search for respect, recognition and territorial integrity developed within a few years into a movement for influence, domination and territorial aggrandisement. The new regime began to look towards the mainland – a process which was to culminate, as we now know, in Japan's domination and colonisation of vast tracts of the Asian continent. Domestic policy and foreign policy were intimately entwined. The 'modernisation' undertaken by the Meiji oligarchs meant, claims Iriye, that 'in the 1880s, when the European powers stepped up their tempo of imperialist domination, the Japanese state, with a centralized bureaucracy and aroused public opinion, was in a far better position to understand and respond to these developments than were the other countries of Asia, the Middle East, or Africa'.[11]

Korea was nearby, important and vulnerable. The fact that it was a client state of China's Qing dynasty did not deter the Meiji government from launching a concerted effort to increase its economic, political and strategic influence over its nearest neighbour. Trade between the two countries was increasing, in 1881 Japan sent an advisory group to begin work on modernising the Korean army and three years later a short-lived coup established a pro-Japanese government that was dedicated to the 'independence' of Korea from China. However, the oligarchs were reluctant at this stage to risk open conflict with the Chinese, and in 1885 the two countries signed a convention whereby they both withdrew their troops from Korea and agreed that neither would replace them without giving the other prior notice.[12]

The establishment of formal empire

The late 1880s and early 1890s seemed to confirm Japan in the view that something more needed to be done. The European powers' growing interest in Asia could scarcely be overlooked, and this coincided with – and encouraged – Japan's development of a more aggressive foreign policy. However, exceptional care needs to be taken when discussing the factors that lay behind late nineteenth-century imperial expansion. It is one thing to distinguish the major stages in Japan's – or any other country's – move towards colonisation and imperialism. It is another thing altogether to disentangle the complex interaction between cause and effect, between attitudes and behaviour, between economic imperatives, ideological presuppositions and international pressures and opportunities.[13]

It is possible, however, to isolate a number of key factors which, towards the end of the nineteenth century, encouraged the Japanese along the path of imperial expansion. The most immediate, most obvious and most important considerations were strategic and military. It was suggested above that the quest for respect, recognition and territorial integrity shifted imperceptibly into a drive for influence, domination and territorial acquisition. It has been claimed in fact that, 'Japan's colonial territories (with the possible exception of Taiwan) were, in each instance, obtained as the result of a deliberate decision by responsible authorities in the central government to use force in securing a territory that would contribute to Japan's immediate strategic interests'. The comments on Russian influence in China made in 1912 by General Tanaka, who later became prime minister, suggest vividly the vulnerability that Japan's foreign policy-makers felt.

> Russia has made great strides toward increasing its military installations in the postwar period. . . . It is almost as powerful as Japan in actual numbers. . . . In

the matter of railroads, too, the double tracking of Siberian lines will be finished in two years. By 1916, the Amur lines will be complete. As a result, Russia's carrying power will have doubled. . . . Add to this the conditions within China from last year [October Revolution of 1911]. . . . China is an area that vitally concerns our security. Should China be subdivided into spheres of influence, how will Japan move forward? For Japan, China must remain independent. In sum, Japan's position in East Asia has become truly dangerous.[14]

As is evident from this extract, these concerns invariably had an economic dimension. It is not necessary to subscribe to a Marxist interpretation of capitalist development to recognise the role that economic considerations frequently played – and play – in shaping the course of foreign policy. Indeed, it is an irony of Japanese history that a country which industrialised in order to set itself free from the threat of Western incursions found that industrialisation generated its own pressure for overseas expansion. An industrialising economy needed secure access to raw materials and consumer markets and an outlet, many felt, for its burgeoning population. Indeed, recent research suggests that the political and business leaders of late Meiji Japan tended to share a common belief in the economic importance and potential of the Asian continent.[15]

However, strategic, military and economic factors alone do not explain the move to, or the timing of, Japanese imperial development. Domestic politics and the desire for international prestige also played a part. An expansive foreign policy could be used to distract attention from day-to-day discontents at home, and the acquisition of an empire provided, it was recognised, one of the key indicators of great power status. Indeed, Japanese leaders were able to claim, without undue hypocrisy, that in establishing their overseas empire they were merely following the example that had been set them by the Western powers.[16]

Nor should the balance of international relations be overlooked. Japan was weaker than the Western powers, but stronger than her Asian neighbours. This meant not only that Japan acquired her imperial possessions later than the Western powers, but that when she did so the empire she established was substantially different from theirs. It is well known, of course, that between 1870 and 1914, the years of the so-called 'Age of Imperialism', the British, French, Germans and Americans expanded their empires by annexing independent, thinly populated countries in distant parts of the world with which they had very little in common.[17]

It is less widely understood, perhaps, that the Japanese empire took a very different form. The Japanese established their empire by asserting control over the neighbouring, often well populated, colonies of the

Western powers with which they had a good deal in common. 'If comparisons are to be made,' suggests Duus, 'then perhaps Japanese expansion on the Asian mainland should be compared with the British in Ireland, the Germans in central Europe, the Russians in the Balkans and Central Asia.' The result was that the Japanese empire was a good deal more homogeneous than those of the Western powers.[18]

Moreover, it became increasingly evident that the Japanese empire, replete with concentric security rings surrounding the 'core area' of the Japanese mainland, was conceived of in highly military terms. As Peattie explains, 'even though Japan was an island nation and her colonial possessions lay literally overseas, the thrust, and ultimately the purpose, of its empire was both region and continent directed . . . no colonial empire of modern times was as clearly shaped by strategic considerations'.[19]

War with China and Russia

During the 1890s, this combination of strategic, military, economic and political pressures culminated in the Sino-Japanese War and the beginning of Japan's formal empire. The catalyst once again was Korea. The Itô government grew increasingly concerned about the weakness of Korea because instability in the peninsula made it difficult to use the kingdom as a bulwark against a possible Russian incursion from the north-west. Indeed, even the most cursory glance at a map of East Asia will show why the Japanese regarded Korea as a dagger pointed at the heart of the homeland. Those directing Japanese foreign policy could not contemplate allowing Korea to become the colony or protectorate of any other power.[20]

When the Korean government requested Chinese assistance to put down a domestic rebellion in 1894, Japan too sent in her troops, fighting ensued and China suffered a series of humiliating reverses, including the loss of Port Arthur. By the beginning of 1895, Japan had driven the Chinese out of Korea, and had begun to advance towards Beijing. In fact, Chinese resistance was so weak that prime minister Yamagata reflected later that, 'Japanese officers did not encounter any serious problems worthy of careful consideration'. When the war ended in the spring of 1895, it was clear that the Japanese had won a stunning success, radically upsetting the balance of power. In the ensuing Treaty of Shimonoseki, the Chinese granted Japan most-favoured nation status in China, agreed to pay a substantial indemnity to offset the costs of the campaign, and ceded to the Japanese four treaty ports, the Liaodong (Liaotung) Peninsula (to the north-west of Korea) and a number of islands including, most importantly, the Chinese province of Taiwan to the south-west of Okinawa.[21]

It was a great victory, greeted with enthusiasm by virtually all shades of domestic opinion. Fukuzawa, Japan's foremost liberal and advocate of Westernisation, declared that, 'it is true that war occurred between the two countries of Japan and China. Yet, if one seeks its [true] origins, it is really a battle for the progress of "civilization and enlightenment", a battle against the obstruction of such progress . . . [a battle in which] the Japanese do not regard the Chinese as enemies.' To be sure, the vast majority of the public were far more hawkish, feeling that 'the right to speak on [behalf of] Korea is Japan's alone!' In either case, victory, as Gluck succinctly puts it, 'enhanced national confidence and pride of empire at the expense of an age-old cultural respect for China'.[22]

But then came a shock. Alarmed by the terms of the treaty, Russia, Germany and France banded together in the so-called 'Triple Intervention' to force Japan to give up the Liaodong Peninsula in return for a more substantial indemnity. It was a development that was received in Japan with a mixture of resentment and resignation. On the one hand, the indignation of the people was captured in a popular song of the day.

> England in the West,
> Russia in the North.
> Don't be caught off guard,
> Countrymen!
> The treaties that bind on the surface
> Do not plumb the depths of the heart.
> International law though there may be,
> When the time comes,
> We must be prepared –
> For with brute force,
> The strong devour the weak.[23]

On the other hand, the war, the treaty and the 'Triple Intervention' confirmed the contradictory position in which Japan found herself: strong enough to begin to impose herself on her neighbours, but not yet strong enough to resist pressure from the West. It was, says Beasley, 'a savage reminder that half a century's work had still not put Japan in a position to ignore or reject the 'advice' of the great powers. The resignation which resulted was captured in an *Osaka Asahi* editorial on the imperial rescript that announced the terms of peace.

It didn't come from His Majesty's heart. As the multitudes read [it] reverentially over and over, and respecting the depths of his heart, there were only blood and tears. At one time, they celebrated victory, waving flags, lighting lanterns. Now, as the subjects of the Empire read [it] with the most solemn respect, the reason for their tears is their loyalty. Ignoring their choked-up emotions when they finished reading [it], these, the subjects of the Empire, with grave patience and diligence wait for another day.

In short, the lesson that both government and people drew from the events of 1895 was, not surprisingly, that they would need to redouble their efforts if they were to approach, let alone achieve, their objective of economic and military autonomy. Indeed, the most popular slogan of the day read 'persevere, overcome, and avenge'.[24]

True to this sentiment, the government took a number of new initiatives. It invested more heavily still in the armed forces. In the year following the war, for example, military expenditure was increased more than six times, so that it accounted for more than half of the entire Japanese budget. Six new divisions were added to the army, and a major shipbuilding programme was started in order to add four battleships, sixteen cruisers, 23 destroyers and more than 600 smaller warships to the existing fleet.[25]

The authorities also contributed to the debate over the long-term strategy to be adopted with regard to the Asian mainland. Some believed that, 'Our programmes in Manchuria should be peacefully and internationally promoted as much as possible and should aim at eradicating difficulties in our path rather than reaping huge profits.' Others advocated a much more aggressive stance:

> we should be prepared to use force in China, should an opportunity present itself either because China becomes incapable of maintaining domestic order or because it encounters some complications in dealing with a foreign power. This will be an excellent opportunity for us to extend our national interests and rights so as to enable our nation to emerge as the hegemon of the Far East.[26]

It was decided eventually to pursue the policy of 'northern advance', a course of action which was generally understood to mean expansion through the Korean peninsula into Manchuria, and on into China proper. Successive governments involved themselves militarily and diplomatically in developments on the Asian mainland. During the 'Boxer Rebellion' of 1900, prime minister Yamagata took the lead in organising and manning the international force of European, American and Japanese troops which rescued the foreign nationals besieged in Beijing's diplomatic compound. Two years later, prime minister Katsura concluded the Anglo-Japanese Alliance, by which each country undertook to remain neutral if the other found itself at war with a third power – and to assist the other if it found itself at war with two or more other powers. The

Alliance, concludes Nish, was of paramount significance both in terms of international relations and of domestic affairs.

> For the Japanese, the treaty was their only significant link with the outside world, the only thing which saved Japan from isolation in a world which was afflicted by suspicions based on fear of the Yellow Peril. It also played an indirect part in solving Japan's domestic problems. Under the shadow of the Alliance, Japan was able to devote her energies to attaining the high industrial and commercial objectives which she had set herself. . . . For Japan, therefore, it was in a real sense an important highway.

Barnhart adds that the alliance conferred on Japan a place of privilege of which she could justifiably feel pride. 'Japan had obtained recognition – in treaty form, no less – of its own great power status in an alliance-between-equals with one of the greatest nations of Europe.'[27]

The Alliance encouraged the Japanese to adopt a firmer line with Tsarist Russia, which had refused to withdraw its troops from Manchuria following the end of the Boxer Rebellion. The refusal threatened the Japanese position in Korea – the soon-to-be colony which the oligarchs agreed should never be given up 'no matter what difficulties are encountered'. With public opinion firmly behind an aggressive stance and a hawkish press calling for the 'protection of the nation's interest and honour' against a disingenuous Russia, Japan entered into the Russo-Japanese War of 1904–5. It was a conflict in which the navy did spectacularly well. It launched an unannounced, and highly successful assault on the Russians' Pacific fleet while it lay at anchor in Port Arthur, and went on to destroy the Russians' Baltic fleet after it had sailed all the way from northern Europe, round the Cape of Good Hope, to the Sea of Japan. The army did less well. The land war dragged on through the bitter Manchurian winter, the Russians struggling with enormously long lines of communication, the Japanese with dreadful losses and increasingly serious economic difficulties. It was not surprising therefore that the two sides accepted the mediation of President Theodore Roosevelt of the United States of America, and by the Treaty of Portsmouth Russia accepted Japanese primacy in Korea and relinquished its economic interests in the south of Sakhalin and the south of Manchuria (including the Liaodong Peninsula).[28]

It was another resounding victory, showing once again the advances that Japan had made since the Meiji Restoration, and demonstrating, for the first time in modern history, that it was possible for an Asian country to defeat one of the world's great powers. Nonetheless, the failure to secure still better terms – and especially better financial compensation

– in the Treaty of Portsmouth led to a great deal of domestic criticism, two days of unprecedented rioting in Tokyo, and the resignation of prime minister Katsura:

> There was hardly an end in sight to the burning of 'police boxes' [neighbour-hood police detachments]; from Hibiya to . . . Kyôbashi, Nihonbashi, and by around twelve, already spreading to Kanda, there was no end. . . . At around two this morning, it reached the central station of Fukagawa, and [one] saw the conflagration at thirteen sites around the city. Such anarchic perversity under the imperial institution, oh, whose sin is it!
>
> [The masses] carrying drawn swords in hand in broad daylight and intruding into the prime minister's residence, it is a shock; setting it ablaze, it is even more shocking. To the extent of drawing police sabres and striking down the people, to the extent of confronting good citizens with soldiers' swords un-sheathed, it's just like the Russian capital all over again. The [treaty] which transformed our triumphant imperial city (and made it into) a second Russian capital, oh, to lead to this, it is nothing less than sin. When the people's hearts are enraged like a fire, smoke and flames burn an emblazoned sky . . . looking at this mass disorder – isn't it sad?[29]

Such responses confirmed once again the contradictory position in which Japan found herself. 'Victory in her first war with one of the European powers', it is explained, 'had the paradoxical effect not of reassuring Japan that she was now a major player able to compete effect-ively with the others as at least an equal but, instead, of convincing her of her continuing vulnerability and the need to strengthen further her military capability.'[30]

Nonetheless, Japan was now both a regional power and 'a major player'. The establishment of the formal empire had been begun by acquiring Taiwan in 1895, appropriating southern Sakhalin in 1905 and establishing a protectorate over Korea in 1905, followed by its annexation five years later. How then did Japan exercise her newly won power? Did the fact that Taiwan and Korea were close neighbours mean that the Japanese dealt more sensitively than Western imperialists with the susceptibilities of their colonial subjects? Or did the Japanese already display signs of the contempt and cruelty with which their country's imperialism was to become associated so indelibly in the years to come?

In answering this question, it is necessary to forget a good deal of what one has learned about Japan's behaviour towards her enemies and her colonial subjects. It cannot be emphasised too strongly that in these early years of empire, the Japanese gained the reputation of behaving with chivalry and generosity. It was found during the 'Boxer Rebellion', for instance, that Japanese troops were less likely than those from Austria,

Britain, France, Germany, Russia or the United States of America to rape, murder and brutalise the Chinese with whom they came into contact. It was reported during the Russo-Japanese War that the Japanese adhered scrupulously to the international rules of war. According to one British observer, 'The Japanese consideration for their prisoners is almost unparalleled in the history of warfare.' In the words of an American army surgeon who inspected Japanese prisoner-of-war camps, their 'treatment of prisoners had established a new standard of humanity for the nations of the future'.[31]

It needs to be emphasised too that it is more difficult than one might imagine to generalise about the ways in which Japan administered her colonial territories. To be sure, Japanese colonialism was portrayed as – and believed by many Japanese to be – a mission of benevolence.

> No matter how low the level of culture, how backward and inefficient – if a people can be given the proper environment [for advancement] and the appropriate education according to their special characteristics as a people, enlightenment is possible. That has got to be the basis of colonization policy.

Yet, despite such rhetoric, the homogeneity of imperial policy must not be allowed to conceal the heterogeneity of imperial administration. For, in spite of the determination of Japan's policy-makers to develop (and later transform) the agrarian economies of Taiwan and Korea to the economic advantage of the metropolitan power, the colonial administrations imposed upon the two countries went about their task in strikingly different ways.[32]

In Taiwan, the behaviour of Japan's colonial administrators was, if not chivalrous and generous, then at least competent and constructive. Within a few years of her occupation, the island was being run by a bureaucracy which, though never popular, fostered economic prosperity and provided efficient transport and communications, a coherent educational system, better social services than were available on the mainland – and what has been described as an 'omnipresent and seemingly omnipotent police force'. The result, claims Peattie, was that 'a backward, economically fragmented, and debt-ridden territory' was transformed into 'a modern economically self-sufficient colonial possession'.[33]

Korea was run anything but benevolently. The Japanese felt themselves superior to the Koreans, and used the cultural background which they shared to justify, rather than challenge, their right to exercise imperial control over their nearest neighbour. The treaty of annexation signed in 1910 was designed, it declared, to promote 'the common wealth of the two nations' and to guarantee 'permanent peace' in Asia. It was a declaration which – like those accompanying the Greater East Asia Co-Prosperity Sphere later in the century – was honoured in the breach rather than in the execution. The Land Investigation Scheme (of 1912–18), for example, amounted to little more than a device by which the Japanese were able to dispossess Korean peasants.

According to Chang, Japanese landlords, most of whom were absentees, comprised less than five per cent of the total farming population yet owned sixty per cent of the arable land and took from their Korean tenants half the crops grown as rent. In fact, such figures only serve to mask much harsher circumstances. As part of the Rice Increase Plan, rice grown in Korea was exported to Japan to feed its growing population. The result was that between 1915/19 and 1930/34, Korean food consumption fell by nearly one-fifth. Indeed, the plight of the Koreans reached such distressing proportions that even the Japanese Governor General of Korea felt compelled to admit in 1935 that, 'About eighty per cent of the agricultural population are "impoverished farmer" tenants'.

> Since they have been suffering from the exploitation resulting from the disorganised traditional administration over a long period of time, they are retarded, demoralized. They lost their hope and aspiration, absorbed into vice, and have no intention of improving their lots. . . . In the time of 'spring poverty' the majority of farmers are short of food supply and thus seek for the root of grass or the peel of tree to fill up their mouths. Although the number of households short of food fluctuates depending upon the result of the harvest, they roughly account for forty-eight per cent of the total farm households, or about 1.2 million households.[34]

As in Taiwan, the colonial government undertook the wholesale transformation of the country's economic, educational and social structures. But, unlike in Taiwan, the imperial policy of economic exploitation was accompanied by a ruthless determination to crush all opposition, and smother any vestiges of indigenous national identity.

> Under the draconian administration of Governor General Terauchi, Korea now entered that dark epoch of developmental shock known to its chroniclers as the 'period of military rule,' a term that in English hardly conveys the crushing impact of the Japanese army and police on every aspect of Korean life.

It was a regime which, despite being constantly adapted, never succeeded in reconciling the Koreans to the demands of imperial rule. It was claimed as early as 1905, for example, that, 'It would be very hard to find a Korean child who does not drink in, almost with his mother's milk, a feeling of dislike against the Japanese'. It was reported in 1919 that, 'divided as the Koreans are in many ways, they are absolutely one in their hatred of the Japanese for the way in which the latter have treated them during the last ten years'.[35]

The expansion of informal imperialism

It is always tempting to divide the past into discrete chronological periods, ascribing to them characteristics which distinguish them from those that came before and after. Although it is a temptation which should certainly be resisted more often than it is, there can be little doubt that the First World War constituted a major turning point in international relations, as in so many other aspects of late nineteenth and twentieth-century world history.

It has been seen that in the years leading up to the First World War, Japan found herself in a curiously contradictory position: stronger than she had been, but not as strong as she wished to be; powerful enough to challenge Russia and dominate her immediate neighbours, but not yet powerful enough to impose herself upon world powers such as Britain, France, Germany and the United States of America. It may seem curious too, at least to modern eyes, that Japan's early twentieth-century imperialism received so friendly a welcome. Visitors from Britain and America commented, for instance, on the 'amazing progress' made by Taiwan, and lauded the 'courage, devotion, and insight' displayed by the colonial administration in Korea. Nor was it unknown, even in countries like China and Korea, for those who were opposed to imperialism to look to Japan as an example of what Asians might hope to achieve. Commenting on the exile of Chinese nationalist Sun Wen (Sun Yat-sen) in Japan, Reginald Johnston, the British tutor of the last emperor of China, Pu Yi (P'u Yi), noted that many Japanese 'were the sincere and generous friends of the cause of reform in China'.[36]

For all the complications that arise from dividing the past into discrete periods, the First World War provides a useful vantage point from which to review Japan's international relations and imperial expansion. The war, we can now see, marked both an end and a beginning. Japan took advantage of the hostilities to declare war on Germany according to the terms of the 1902 Anglo-Japanese Alliance (by which, it will be recalled, Japan and Britain had agreed to assist the other if they found themselves at war with two or more adversaries). As the second Ôkuma cabinet declared, 'Japan must take the chance of a millennium' to 'establish its rights and interests in Asia'. She sent military expeditions to German islands in the north Pacific and to German-leased territory in eastern China, which was still in turmoil following the overthrow of the Qing dynasty in 1911. Military gains were supported by diplomatic efforts, the Japanese delegation to the Paris Peace Conference which brought the war to a close retaining the territory which had been won by armed force. By the beginning of the 1920s, the first phase of Japan's formal expansion was substantially complete.[37]

The establishment of Japan's formal empire was accompanied by a growing emphasis upon informal methods of control. It has been suggested already that this distinction between formal and informal methods of control (and thus between formal and informal imperialism) is fundamental to the understanding of modern imperial development. For example, British policy, Robinson and Gallagher believed, 'followed the principle of extending control informally if possible and formally if necessary'.[38]

Japanese policy was somewhat different. It followed the principle, some argue, of extending informal control as the preparation for, and precursor of, formal control. Of course, Japan had long used such devices of informal control as protectorates, spheres of influence and favourable treaty provisions in order to further her foreign policy aspirations. It has been seen, for example, that at the end of the Sino-Japanese War, Japan won most-favoured nation status in China and that, ten years later, at the end of the Russo-Japanese War, she was able to establish a protectorate over Korea and extend her economic interests in south Sakhalin and the south of Manchuria. Manchuria, in particular, seemed to offer rich possibilities, and prime minister Katsura was determined to exploit the concessions that had been won at the negotiating table. He and his successors renamed the province the Guandong (Kwantung) Leased Territory, acquired the South Manchurian Railway (and excluded the Chinese from investing in it), obtained significant trading concessions, obstructed other countries' merchants and, it was suspected, manipulated the customs system to their own advantage.[39]

The First World War provided Japan with new opportunities for informal, as well as formal, exploitation – indeed, as the navy's Katô argued, 'the Yamato race is destined to emerge as the saviour of East Asia'. With the belligerents preoccupied in Europe, Japan was able to extend her influence in China which, as noted above, had been severely weakened by the fall of the Qing dynasty. In January 1915, the Ôkuma government presented the new republic with a controversial list of 'Twenty-One Demands'. The Chinese found little support when they tried to resist the demands and, despite divisions within the Japanese leadership, they were compelled to agree to the restriction of their economic, financial and political autonomy at the expense of Japan. The 'Demands' not only signalled the weakness of China and the burgeoning power of Japan, but also confirmed vividly the importance of paying attention to informal means of control when considering international relations and imperial expansion.[40]

The circumstances that developed following the First World War encouraged Japan to place greater emphasis still upon informal methods of control. Attitudes towards imperialism were changing across the world. It is easy, of course, to exaggerate the scale and significance of such developments. If one should be careful about dividing the past into discrete periods, one must be exceptionally suspicious when confronted with talk about Zeitgeist, the spirit of the age, or the spirit of the times. Nonetheless, there were new, and powerful intellectual forces at work in the wake of the First World War. 'Wilsonian internationalism trumpeted the right of national self-determination; Leninist anti-imperialism called for the oppressed peoples of the world to light the spark of world revolution; and indigenous nationalism throughout the non-Western world challenged colonial regimes.'[41]

The growth of anti-imperialism abroad coincided with growing pressure at home for overseas expansion. Such a claim may come as something of a surprise, for it was seen in the previous chapter that the First World War saw the emergence of what became known as the era of 'Taishô Democracy'. It is true that prominent liberals such as Ishibashi opposed expansion in China, warning of 'grave consequences' following such 'foolish acts' as the Twenty-One Demands. Yet the widening of the franchise, the consolidation of party government, and the modest liberalisation of domestic policy did little to alter Japan's underlying economic circumstances or silence those favouring expansion. Japan, like Germany, saw herself as a resource-poor 'late-developer'. Her rising population, growing industrialisation and entrenched militarisation made her increasingly dependent upon overseas sources of supply, and overseas markets for her products. Japan imported soybeans from Manchuria, and oil from the United States and the Dutch East Indies; she exported semi-manufactured raw silk to the United States and sold manufactured goods, chiefly cotton, to her neighbours in East Asia.[42]

These developments presented Japan's post-war governments with a disconcerting dilemma. But they also suggested a possible solution. If the growth of anti-imperialist feeling made it difficult to consider further military initiatives, it also made it tempting to contemplate the possibility of turning again to informal methods of exerting influence over independent or nominally independent neighbours. Party cabinets of the mid- to late 1920s discovered that they had considerable room to manoeuvre within the new regional security arrangements established at the Washington Conference of 1921–22. They made concerted efforts, both diplomatically and economically, to extend their influence over China. Governments during and after the War put pressure on the great powers to recognise the Sino-Japanese Treaty of 1915, took an independent position at the Beijing Tariff Conference of 1925, and did their best to undermine efforts to secure Chinese unification. Japan also worked hard, and with increasing success, to integrate China into her widening sphere of economic influence. She invested in China, imported Chinese primary products and used China as a market for her manufactured goods. The result was that by the end of the 1920s, China provided thirteen per cent of Japanese imports and purchased twenty per cent and more of Japanese exports.[43]

The use of informal methods of control was neither peculiar to this period nor anything like as arresting as the expansion of formal empire which occurred before and after it. However, between the First World War and the late 1920s, Japanese policy-makers made increasing use of informal methods of exerting influence over their Asian neighbours. Both Manchuria and Mongolia, it was suggested, might be brought within Japan's 'sphere of influence'. The emphasis upon informal, rather than formal, methods forced governments during the period of 'Taishô Democracy' to confront once again the recurring paradox of Japan's international relations, that growing power was accompanied by a growing sense of vulnerability and inequality *vis-à-vis* the West. Indeed, the replacement of the Anglo-Japanese Alliance with the 'Open Door' framework of the American-sponsored Nine-Power Pact of 1922 was interpreted by many – including many liberals – as a Western ploy to dislodge growing Japanese influence in China.[44]

Nor was this all. The rejection by the Powers of Japanese proposals for the inclusion of a racial equality clause in the Versailles settlement heightened 'the grievance of the Japanese towards the unequal treatments to which the coloured races were subjected by the Western peoples'. Then too the discriminatory immigration laws passed by the US government in 1924 tended to make the vision of 'Asia for Asiatics' all the more appealing.

For the time being, then, the emphasis upon informal, rather than formal, methods seemed to provide Japan's leaders with a way of reconciling the competing intellectual, diplomatic and economic demands of the 1920s. Within less than a decade, however, advocates of informal methods would find themselves open to criticisms of weakness through their 'co-operation' with a racist West. The foundations for the more aggressive foreign policy which was to be pursued during the 1930s and the early 1940s had been laid.[45]

The growth of nationalism and militarism

It is exceptionally difficult to approach Japan's international relations and imperial expansion from the 1930s onwards with anything like an open mind. Many in Japan are reluctant even to discuss this period of their nation's past, few of Japan's neighbours will ever forget what was done in her name and much of the rest of the world remains bewildered by what it regards as Japanese contempt, cruelty and inhumanity. How then should the balance be struck? How is one to explain the course of Japanese foreign policy during the 1930s and early 1940s?

It is always tempting to look deep into the past for the origins of developments which can be seen, with hindsight, to be important or controversial. It is a temptation which is sometimes best avoided, but not when seeking to understand the growth of Japanese militarism and the emergence of the Greater East Asia Co-Prosperity Sphere. It has been seen that the expansion of formal and informal empire during the late nineteenth and early twentieth centuries was followed during the 1920s by a renewed emphasis upon informal methods of influence and control. The two forms of imperialism came together during the 1930s, as Japanese policy-makers attempted to reconcile the competing pressures with which they found themselves confronted. Economic realities jostled with diplomatic demands, national self-interest with a growing assertion of Asian solidarity.[46]

Economic, demographic and political pressures

Economic considerations remained very powerful. Japan, like Germany, believed that it was essential to have guaranteed access to the raw materials and markets necessary for industrial success and military vitality. And it was formal political control, it seemed to many, that still promised the best way of securing such access on a permanent and unhindered basis. When Japanese policy-makers looked abroad in the 1930s, they saw Russia weakened by famine and forcible collectivisation, and China divided by the struggle between Jiang Jieshi (Chiang Kai-shek) and the Communists. The key to Japan's policy in China, explained the

Japan Times Weekly in 1939, was 'the fact that she wants to gain access to the raw materials there available, to secure a ready market for her goods, and to ensure that the resources of that country are attuned to her economic and strategic needs' in the event of war against Russia.[47]

Japan, like Germany, believed that she needed *Lebensraum*. Japan was already the most densely populated country in the world: it was calculated that, with a population of 60 million inhabiting 60.2 million square kilometres in 1925, for example, there were 993 people per square kilometre. Only Holland and Britain were anywhere near as crowded, with 802 and 800 people per square kilometre. (Germany, by contrast, enjoyed the relatively low density of 305.) In fact, the situation appeared more serious still to the country's military planners, with government demographers calculating that a population of at least 100 million would be needed to ensure a margin of safety when dealing with China, Russia and the United States. 'In politicians' and generals' speeches, at this time, Japan was constantly referred to as a small potted tree struggling to extend its roots – and dying in the process.'[48]

Such economic and demographic nationalism was reinforced by the worldwide economic depression of the late 1920s, another catastrophe which reinforced the Japanese people in their sense of vulnerability. The Great Depression hit particularly hard in the countryside. The collapse of the American market for raw silk combined with a sharp decline in rice prices (caused by rising imports and record-breaking domestic production) to undermine the incomes of the country's millions of peasant farmers. It has been estimated, for instance, that between 1925 and 1930, farmers' real incomes, which were modest at the best of times, declined by as much as one third. In the Tôhoku region of Japan (the north-west), famine struck, leading to a host of social ills such as infanticide and the selling of children into prostitution. According to one school of thought, the extreme hardship experienced in this region was of major significance in the rise of militarism.

> We can still remember . . . the plight of the *Tôhoku* peasants. Peasant poverty was the direct cause of the Fascist movement becoming revolutionary and of the right-wing terrorism which broke out after 1931. It had a direct influence on the conversion of young army officers to revolution; as many of them came from medium and small landowner families. And as the peasantry, the *Tôhoku* peasantry especially, were regarded as the core of the army the explanation of their behaviour is clear enough.[49]

While this interpretation is highly contentious, it does demonstrate the influence of the economic crisis of the early 1930s. Indeed, the lesson which many drew from the Depression was that they should reconsider both Japan's domestic policies and her position in the international community. They needed to look again at her adoption of Western-style capitalism, her dependence upon an unpredictable international economy, and her unequal relationships with the leading Western powers. Japan, along with Germany and Italy, believed that the international, Anglo-American world order was grotesquely unfair to late-developing nations like themselves. It was a system, many in Asia came to think, which worked unsparingly to the advantage of the white, Western colonial powers and to the disadvantage of non-Western, non-white countries such as Japan. It was tempting to believe that the colonial powers, satiated with imperial conquests, 'had tricked Japan into giving up its expansion before it had acquired an adequate base to maintain its economic and military power'. Rôyama, a leading Japanese liberal, complained in 1941 that, although 'Japan was faithful to the letter and spirit' of the American-designed Washington Treaties of 1922 and the Open Door system in China they had established, the Americans and British supported by their League of Nations maintained a policy of 'checking the advance of Japan . . . as a protection to their own Far Eastern interests'. This was blatantly hypocritical since, 'In other parts of the world . . . special situations *do* exist, and they *are* recognized', despite the fact that Japanese claims to special interests in China were continually condemned by the West.[50]

Although the crises of the 1920s, and especially of the early 1930s, acted as catalysts in the emergence of a militarist, parochial and, indeed, racial nationalism, it needs to be stressed that the transformation was by no means instantaneous. In fact, as we have seen in the previous chapter, resentment towards Western discrimination and belief in Japanese racial inferiority had a very long history. Indeed, the Meiji Restoration and many of the reforms implemented in its wake were structured in large part as a response to the Western incursion in Japan. And, although nationalism in the Meiji and the Shôwa periods were very different, reflecting the particular historical circumstances in which they emerged, they were related in that the West figured so strongly in them. So it is that Crowley describes the antagonism and hostilities of the 1930s as, in part, a 'racial conflict' between Japan and the West.[51]

Moreover, it needs to be stressed that nationalism in the 1930s was not antithetical to that of the previous twenty years. Japanese liberalism could, and often did, accommodate racist nationalism. During the First World War, for example, one middle-ranking 'liberal' politician was virulent in his criticisms of, and calls to 'destroy white despotism'.

England and the US talk of the horrors of war and advocate a League of Nations based on the ideal of peace among different peoples. Yet, they will not give at all on commercial imperialism and aggressive capitalist politics. . . . The instances of their self-centredness are innumerable. They are for limiting armaments on the one hand, but, on the other, for maintaining their territories, rights, and colonies as they originally were. One does not need to be a great politician or statesman to guess how the future world peace to be secured by this League of Nations will go. There is no way to counter economic power and resources except with economic power and resources.[52]

The growing power of such sentiments received political recognition in 1927 when, as was seen in the previous chapter, a retired general, Tanaka, replaced a civilian politician, Wakatsuki, as prime minister. Tanaka favoured a more 'positive' approach – and a much more aggressive rhetoric – towards Asia than his party-leader predecessors. 'The common formula used', it was reported, 'is that Japan's interests are sealed for ever by the blood and treasure which were expended on the battlefield.'[53]

Tanaka appointed anti-Chinese politicians to his cabinet, placed two of his friends at the head of the South Manchuria Railway, and convened 'The Eastern Conference' of military and government leaders to discuss the policy that should be adopted towards the mainland. In his public pronouncements, Tanaka stressed his intention of defending Manchuria as strongly as he could. In private, he went a good deal further, discussing the possibility of merging the administration of Korea (which was part of Japan's formal empire) with that of Manchuria (which was not). It was an idea which, if carried out, would amount, of course, to the annexation of Manchuria and its incorporation into Japan's formal empire. It was a suggestion that foreshadowed, we can now see, what was to happen in 1931.[54]

However, as hotly contested as the defence of Manchuria was the size of the navy. Arguments about the scale and strength of the imperial navy had been rumbling on since the beginning of the decade, and came to the fore in 1930 when Tanaka's successor, party politician Hamaguchi, signed the London Naval Treaty. The aim of the countries involved in the negotiations was to avoid an arms race by agreeing to limit the size of their naval forces. The Treaty introduced what is generally referred to as the celebrated 10-10-7 formula; that is, for every ten tons of American and British naval vessels, the Japanese imperial fleet would be permitted to contain seven. It was a better deal than the Japanese negotiators had anticipated, but it provoked a great deal of domestic discontent. The navy's general staff was critical of the terms agreed, and those with nationalist views declined to accept the premise that the Western powers had any right at all to curtail the size of the Japanese navy. Equally as significant was the accusation that non-military leaders – the prime minister and the navy minister – had wrongly usurped the navy general staff's 'right of supreme command'. In fact, feelings were running so high that before the end of the year, prime minister Hamaguchi had been shot by a young right-winger who was dissatisfied with the terms of the Treaty.[55]

The annexation of Manchuria

It did not take long for Manchuria to move back to the top of the political agenda. Hamaguchi died from his injuries in the summer of 1931, and was succeeded by the less forceful Wakatsuki whose government was to preside over the seizure of Manchuria. The essentials of what became known as the Manchurian Incident were described in the previous chapter. It will be recalled that a group of army officers, with the tacit support of their superiors, staged an incident near the Manchurian city of Mukden, and used it as a pretext for overrunning the whole of the province and setting up the puppet state of Manchukuo. Afraid of provoking a *coup d'état* if it attempted to discipline those responsible, the Wakatsuki government soon acquiesced in what had been done, and then attempted to justify it to the rest of the world.[56]

The details of what happened are instructive. In September 1931, officers of Japan's Guandong (Kwantung) Army blew up a section of the South Manchuria Railway near Mukden which they were supposed to be guarding. They blamed the explosion on local Chinese troops, and then used the 'guilt' of the troops as a pretext for launching an attack upon them. 'The Manchurian Incident was Planned like This', explained one of those who was involved.

As part of his responsibility for patrolling the railroad, First Lieutenant Kawamoto of the Shimamoto battalion, Kawashima company, set out for Liutiaohu with several of his men. While keeping an eye on the [Chinese troops' barracks], Kawamoto put in place and set alight a small type of explosive used by the cavalry at a spot about an hundred metres to the south which he had chosen. It was just after ten [pm] when a deafening explosion severed the rails and sent railway ties flying . . .

At the same time as the blast, a report reached battalion headquarters and the office of the secret military service. The head of the Kawashima company who was at the barracks of the civil service four kilometres north [of the explosion], immediately ordered soldiers to commence an attack on the Chinese camp situated to the south . . .

> Besides the fact that the majority of [Chinese] had been sleeping knowing
> nothing of the situation, they were without weapons since the officer holding
> the key to the weapons storeroom was away. As the Chinese ran around bewil-
> dered, the Japanese soldiers rushed in . . . A large portion of the Chinese side
> fled at the deafening sound of the 28 cm guns of the artillery attack, and . . . the
> entire city of Mukden fell into [our] hands . . .

The following seizure of Manchuria became an 'unavoidable measure
. . . an extraordinary step to expediently deal with the situation.'[57]

It was a cynical but effective ploy. The officers instigating the conflict calculated correctly that it would be difficult for the authorities in
Japan to abandon their troops once fighting had begun. The cabinet sent
reinforcements, the Guandong Army claimed the 'right of supreme
command', the province was annexed, and in 1932 it was renamed
Manchukuo under the 'independent' rule of Pu Yi, the last descendant of
China's deposed Qing dynasty.[58]

Pu Yi was a figurehead and Manchukuo a puppet state, a colony in all
but name. This 'new frontier' was run by Japanese administrators, Japanese immigration was encouraged, political activity was prohibited, the
military police were given free rein and, as in Taiwan and Korea, the
economy was run for the benefit of the metropolitan power. From his
palace in Changchun, Pu Yi presided over a system administered by
Chinese officials each of whom had a Japanese 'adviser' to assist them in
reaching desirable decisions. Education was reorganised so that the schools
for the Chinese provided vocational training combined with warnings
about the dangers of Marxism, republicanism and democracy. As one of
the leaders of the Guandong Army explained with refreshing candour,
it was only 'by bringing about Japanese–Manchurian co-operation and
Japanese–Chinese friendship that the Japanese people can become rulers
of Asia and be prepared to wage the final and decisive war against the
white races'.[59]

The seizure of Manchuria – and its transmogrification into Manchukuo
– marked a new stage in Japan's imperial development and conduct of
international relations. While Manchuria and much of the territory that
was taken over in the years immediately following the Manchurian
Incident were often handed to the authorities in Tokyo as *faits accomplis*
following renegade actions of individuals and/or sections of the army,
they were incorporated formally into the empire. Thus, the events of
1931–32 signalled a reversion to the policy of formal expansion, a policy
which was to culminate in war first with China, and then, disastrously,
with America and the allied powers.[60]

The Manchurian Incident also signalled Japan's rejection of the Anglo-American world order. It was an order that, for Japan, was symbolised by the Washington Conference of 1921–22, which had sought to organise security arrangements in East Asia, and by the League of Nations, which had been established in the aftermath of the First World War to promote new, equitable and peaceful international relations. It was a system that Japan now began to repudiate almost completely. In 1932, she formally recognised Manchukuo as an 'independent' state, and early in the following year resigned from the League of Nations when it accepted Lord Lytton's highly critical report on her behaviour during and after the Manchurian Incident. The League, the Japanese claimed, 'has been wont to be aggressive and bombastic when it deals with an Asiatic nation'. Foreign minister Uchida announced what he called his 'scorched earth diplomacy'. He would not yield one step, he declared, in achieving the recognition of Manchuria 'even if our country is reduced to ashes'. The rhetoric was prophetic; Japan was well on the way towards making herself an international pariah.[61]

War with China

Japan's progress along this path was speeded by the policy she adopted towards the rest of China. The Manchurian Incident led – almost inevitably it seems – to further expansion, further clashes with Chinese troops, war with China and eventually war in the Pacific. What Japan wanted, claimed the president of the South Manchuria Railway, was peace, an end to racial conflict, a secure supply of raw materials, an outlet for her surplus population and a defensive alliance against the threat posed by communist Russia. The supply of raw materials was crucial, explained Viscount Inoue on a visit to London in 1937.

> Not only do we possess no oil supplies but this is true of very many other materials without which today a nation is helpless in wartime. To secure assured supply of raw materials has become a problem of greatly increased importance. The very life of Japan as a first-class power is dependent on this question.[62]

In 1936, Japan had joined Nazi Germany, and a year later Fascist Italy, in an 'Anti-Comintern Pact'. 'Japan's diplomacy', explained the director of the *Japan Times*, 'is based on her non-compromise with Communist Russia and her friendship with Germany and Italy.' The *Japan Times Weekly* elaborated the point.

> No sensible man can really be indifferent to the danger of a Communist China, and most of all Japan could not tolerate such a neighbour; for apart from

political unrest accompanying the establishment of a Sovietized China, Japan's interests on the Asiatic mainland would be seriously threatened.[63]

What Japan wanted, it seemed to the rest of the world, was domination over China. The Manchurian Incident of 1931 was followed – one is tempted to say replicated – in 1937 by the Marco Polo Bridge Incident. It is true that in this case it is not clear who provoked the crisis. But once the fighting between Japanese and Chinese patrols had started in the suburbs of Beijing, it escalated rapidly, and brought Japan into conflict with the two other powers in the country, the Chinese communists and the nationalist government of Jiang Jieshi. By September, Japan's newly created North China Army contained 200,000 men, and by the end of the year it had captured Beijing, Shanghai and the walled city of Nanjin (Nanking), 200 miles up the Yangtze river from Shanghai. The occupation of Nanjin was followed by the six weeks of looting, rape and murder known as the 'Nanjin Massacre', an atrocity which has become associated indelibly with Japanese savagery, butchery and inhumanity.[64]

During the course of a six-week period, the victorious Japanese troops raped at least 20,000 Chinese women, murdered, it seems, at least ten times as many men, women and children, and looted whatever they could. The barbarities almost defy description. According to one Japanese soldier, he and his colleagues enjoyed killing a pregnant Chinese woman: 'We stuck bayonets in her huge belly, skewered her like a piece of meat.' According to another, 'I beheaded people, starved them to death, burned them, and buried them alive, over 200 in all.' According to yet another, 'rape was against military regulations, so we had to destroy the evidence. While the women were fucked, they were considered human, but when we killed them, they were just pigs.' Some of the evidence from Chinese witnesses is chilling in its simplicity,

> The Japanese military used various methods of murder: cutting victims' heads off, chopping at and smashing the head, ripping the stomach to pieces, digging out the heart, burying Chinese people alive, dismembering arms and legs, cutting up the genital organs, pushing objects into the genital organs and anuses of women, burning people to death, throwing them into deep water and drowning them to death, and mowing them down with machine-gun fire.[65]

The West was horrified. Worse still for Japan, morality and realpolitik coalesced when the Western powers considered how they should respond to Japan's behaviour in eastern Asia. The horrors of Nanjin, the war with China and the pact with Germany and Italy all strengthened the view that something had to be done to halt the spread of Japanese hegemony across the Asian mainland. For two years, Russia and the Western powers considered a number of measures – short of war – that might be used to punish Japan and to assist the Chinese.[66]

The inauguration of the Greater East Asia Co-Prosperity Sphere

Western fears were reinforced by the ideas being floated in Japan for a 'New Order in East Asia' and for a 'Greater East Asia Co-Prosperity Sphere'. Prime minister Konoe encouraged a group of intellectuals to develop a set of ideas consistent with the country's expansionist ambitions. Western imperialism and Japanese imperialism were different, they concluded. Western imperialism was hierarchical, Japanese imperialism was patriarchal; Western imperialism was exploitative, Japanese imperialism was mutually advantageous; Western imperialism sought to subjugate the non-Western world, Japanese imperialism had as its aim the freeing of Asian nations from Western domination.[67]

In November 1938, the Konoe government announced the establishment of a 'New Order in East Asia', the prime minister himself explaining on national radio that, 'What Japan desires is not to destroy China, but to help her progress; not to conquer China, but to co-operate with her'. Just under two years later, the government announced the inauguration of the 'Greater East Asia Co-Prosperity Sphere'. The two initiatives were at once backward-looking and forward-looking.

> Although both of these visionary conceptions of Japan's historic role in world politics were a rationalization for a policy of expansion already under way, they did reflect a widespread belief that the imperialist order established by the European powers in the nineteenth century had come to an end and that the world system would be reorganized into economically self-contained and politically autonomous supranational regional blocs.[68]

The pan-Asian, anti-imperialist rhetoric became relentless. Japan embodied 'the inexorable will of Asia, within her spiritual heritage', explained the *Nippon Times* in 1943. It followed therefore that Japan was 'fighting not for herself only but for the sake of all East Asia peoples also'. It was the imperial powers which were to blame for any conflict: 'The War of Greater East Asia is traceable, in the ultimate, to the Anglo-American idea of racial discrimination.'[69]

However, the rhetoric made clear too that the New Order and Co-Prosperity did not mean that Japan and her neighbours should be regarded as equals. A professor from Tokyo Imperial University suggested in 1939 that it was helpful to 'think of China as a young brother, though a recalcitrant one'. An imperial army document of 1942 divided Asia into 'master races', 'friendly races' and 'guest races'; and a study prepared by the civilian bureaucracy in 1942–43 explained that the Greater East Asia Co-Prosperity Sphere would help to maintain the Japanese 'eternally' as the 'leading race' on the Asian continent.[70]

In 1940, Japan concluded a Tripartite Pact with Germany and Italy, the European powers agreeing to 'recognise and respect the Leadership of Japan in establishing a New Order in East Asia'. By the end of the following year, Japan was at war with the United States of America. It was a conflict with lengthy antecedents. The authorities in the West were becoming increasingly concerned about the direction of Japanese foreign policy. They were receiving serious warnings from their diplomats in Tokyo: the British ambassador reported, for example, that Japan had 'embarked on a policy of aggression no less calculated and methodical than was Hitler's course in Europe after the occupation of the Rhineland'. Relations deteriorated rapidly. In 1939, America repealed her longstanding Treaty of Commerce and Navigation with Japan, and two years later America, followed by Britain and Holland, imposed a virtual ban on oil shipments to Japan. This left her with two choices, explains Edgerton: 'withdraw from China and negotiate with the West from a position of weakness, or seize a major source of oil before her existing two-year reserve was exhausted'. The first option was psychologically and politically unacceptable, the second psychologically, politically – and economically – attractive because it seemed little more than the logical outcome of her existing foreign policy.[71]

The tensions between Japan and the United States culminated, of course, in Japan's surprise attack on Pearl Harbor in December 1941. In the short term, the attack was an outstanding military success. In fact, it was a massacre rather than a battle, the Japanese destroying most of the Americans' Pacific Fleet as it lay at anchor at Hawaii. Germany declared war on America, and the imperial troops launched immediate attacks on Guam and Wake Island, setting in train six months of expansion abroad and euphoria at home. It was seen in the previous chapter that, by the spring of 1942, the Americans had been driven from the Philippines, the Dutch from the Dutch East Indies and the British from Malaya, Burma, Hong Kong and Singapore. The speed, sophistication and success of the onslaught was utterly unexpected in the West. When the governor of Malaya was told that the Japanese had landed, he remarked complacently, 'I trust you'll chase the little men off'. When Winston Churchill reflected on the fall of Singapore, he admitted that, 'The violence, fury, skill and might of Japan far exceeded anything we had been led to expect.'[72]

'This is a war for the emancipation of East Asia', explained one Tokyo paper. 'Western Imperialism in the East Has Become Dirt in the Dustbin of Memory.' In October 1942, a Great East Asia ministry was established in the Japanese capital, and towards the end of the following year it organised the highly publicised Assembly of the Greater East Asia Nations. Attended by representatives from Manchukuo, China, Burma, Siam and the Philippines, and an 'associate' from the 'Free India' Movement, the delegates heard a good deal – and not just from their hosts – about the solidarity of 'a thousand million Asiatics' under Japanese leadership. Such language struck a chord, and it would be a mistake to suppose that – in 1943 at least – the rhetoric of Asian solidarity was simply a device which was foisted onto subordinate nations by the new imperial power.[73]

In the longer term, the attack on Pearl Harbor and the seizure of so much of Asia proved a military and diplomatic disaster. The United States brought its economic and technological force to bear on the struggle, and from the summer of 1942 the allied troops were able to halt, and then reverse, the Japanese series of victories. Defeat followed defeat as the imperial troops sought to defend their gains in a series of bitterly fought, but unsuccessful, island battles: Guadalcanal (August 1942), Attu (May 1943), the Gilbert Islands (November 1943), Truk (February 1944) and Saipan (July 1944).[74]

Then in the spring of 1945, the Japanese mainland came under attack. In April, the allies landed on Okinawa, and in the battle which ensued some 90,000 soldiers and 94,000 civilians perished as men, women and children joined the imperial troops in a desperate struggle to protect the homeland. (In fact, many of the victims died not from enemy attack, but because they killed themselves rather than face the prospect of surrender). From March onwards, the allies launched a series of air raids on the central Japanese cities of Kobe, Osaka, Nagoya and Tokyo. On 10 March, for example, the Americans sent 279 B-29 bombers to attack Tokyo. The Japanese air force was unable to offer effective resistance, with the result that 80,000 people were killed and a million or so made homeless. The devastation reminded Emperor Hirohito of the battlefields of the First World War. His capital, he observed bleakly, 'has become "scorched earth" '.[75]

The New Order and the Greater East Asia Co-Prosperity Sphere proved no more resilient. For however attractive the rhetoric of Pan-Asian solidarity and however appealing the 'independence' granted to countries

such as Burma, Indonesia and the Philippines, the edifice so hastily –
some would say, haphazardly – constructed in Tokyo was unable to
survive the racism, arrogance and cruelty of Asia's new rulers. Dower
explains the situation clearly and with as much detachment as is probably possible.

> As a symbol of Asian audacity, defiance, and – fleetingly – strength *vis-à-vis*
> the West, the Japanese commanded admiration throughout Asia. As the self-
> designated leaders of the Greater East Asia Co-Prosperity Sphere, however, they
> proved to be as overweening as the Westerners had been before them.

Indeed, in many cases the new rulers of Asia proved even more harsh
and insensitive than their predecessors. They dominated local politics,
'taking over local economies, imposing broad programs of "Japanisation",
slapping non-Japanese in public, torturing and executing dissidents, exploiting native labour so severely that between 1942 and 1945 the death
toll among such workers numbered in the hundreds of thousands'.[76]

How was it then that the New Order and Co-Prosperity lasted as
long as they did? Why did the Japanese not surrender sooner? By the
spring of 1945, Italy had surrendered, Germany was all but defeated, the
imperial navy had been destroyed, and the allies were able to attack
the Japanese mainland more or less at will. Determined to protect the
emperor system and the 'fundamental principle' of the Japanese state,
the authorities embarked upon a series of desperate measures, mobilising
all youths and men between the ages of 15 and 60, and all women
between the ages of 17 and 40.[77]

The armed forces could not win the war, but they could delay the end
of it. Indeed, they had good reason to do so, for they believed – and with
good reason – that surrender would mean the end of the imperial army,
navy and air force in anything like their existing form. As a staff officer
at the Imperial General Headquarters explained, it was the struggle which
mattered. 'We merely prepared for the final operations with the philosophy that we must fight in order to glorify our national and military
traditions, that it was an engagement which transcended victory or defeat.' Such was the atmosphere in which the government decided not to
accept the allies' ultimatum, the Potsdam Declaration of 26 July, which
called for Japan's unconditional surrender.[78]

It was a calamitous decision. Less than two weeks later, the allies
dropped the world's first atomic bomb on Hiroshima; three days later
they dropped the second on Nagasaki. Between 200,000 and 300,000
people were killed, injured and left to die in the most dreadful agony.

Predictably perhaps, the army reported that the military had 'counter-measures' in hand, and that the high command did not believe that the war was lost. They were overruled, however, and finally on 15 August, Emperor Hirohito made his celebrated, and unprecedented, broadcast to the Japanese people.

> I cannot bear any longer to see my innocent subjects tormented under the cruelties of war. There are certainly conditions that can hardly be accepted: disarmament of the Imperial Forces by foreign hands for one. But we have to bear it now. I think of the spirit of those who have died for the nation's cause and I reflect on My incapacity to respond to their loyalty. My heart aches as I think of those who have faithfully fulfilled their duties and who now have to bear the disgrace. But this is the time when we must bear the unbearable to restore peace to the nation and to the world.[79]

Exploitation or co-prosperity?

Is it possible to regard Japan's international relations and imperial expansion between 1868 and 1945 with anything other than scorn and contempt? Is it possible to find anything positive to say about the way in which the Japanese treated the countries and individuals with which they came into contact as they became a world power and swept across the Asian continent?

It is obvious, of course, how Japan acquired her evil reputation. The political leaders of late nineteenth and early twentieth-century Japan led her into a series of aggressive wars: against China, Russia, China again, the United States of America, the allied powers and finally much of south-east Asia. They established a chain of oppressive colonial regimes: in Korea, Manchuria, other parts of China and much of south-east Asia. They declined to ratify the Geneva Convention on the treatment of prisoners of war. They condoned the excesses of the armed forces, it seems, whenever and wherever they occurred: the Manchurian Incident, the Nanjin Massacre and innumerable, less well known events throughout the Pacific War. The armed forces themselves behaved with a mixture of cunning, barbarity and apparent fanaticism. They provoked the Manchurian Incident, and possibly the Marco Polo Bridge Incident. They forced thousands upon thousands of Korean and Chinese women into sexual slavery; they abused, exploited and murdered prisoners of war; they conducted experiments on live subjects, they launched themselves to certain death in *kamikaze* raids, and they refused, some of them, even to surrender when the war was over. Japanese imperialism became – and has remained – a byword throughout the world for cruelty, inhumanity and exploitation.[80]

However, it is easy to let one's outrage run away with one's judgement. It is tempting to generalise too broadly about Japan's international relations and imperial expansion, suggesting, for example, that there was no change in policy between the beginning and end of the period, and that there was no difference in the ways that different parts of the empire were acquired and administered. It is a temptation that needs to be resisted. There is no reason to attribute a spurious homogeneity to Japan's international relations and imperial expansion to be able to mount a telling attack on her record in dealing with the rest of the world. There is no need either to use the supposed homogeneity of Japan's international relations and imperial expansion to support the view that it derived from something deep and unchanging in Japanese society and culture.[81]

The heterogeneity of Japan's international relations and imperial expansion can be seen in several ways. It will be recalled from earlier in the chapter that when Japan embarked upon her policy of territorial aggrandisement, her troops were viewed as a model of restraint rather than barbarity and her colonial administration in Taiwan (and even Korea) was regarded – at least in the West – as a model of enlightenment rather than exploitation. It should be recognised too that during the 'Taishô Democracy' of the 1920s, there were some attempts to further a more liberal policy – if that is the proper way to describe the new emphasis that was placed upon the 'assimilation' of the colonial population. In Taiwan, in particular, efforts were made to encourage equal employment opportunities, to stimulate the diffusion of the Japanese language and to bring about intermarriage between Japanese and Koreans.[82]

It should not be forgotten either that, later in the century, the Japanese claimed that it was Western troops, rather than their own, who were notorious for their barbarity; and that it was Western imperialism, not Co-Prosperity, which should be identified with degradation and exploitation. During the late 1930s and early 1940s, papers like the *Nippon Times* and *Japan Times Weekly* carried numerous reports contrasting the barbarity of the Americans with the chivalry of the Japanese. 'The inborn cruelty of the American people', it was argued, 'is clearly manifest in the character of crimes perpetrated by them' against coloured people. The Japanese built hospitals for their prisoners of war, it was explained. 'Unlike the brutal massacre of helpless Japanese soldiers and the wanton attacks on hospital ships by the enemy, kind considerate treatment is accorded to the war prisoners interred in Japan.'[83]

This, of course, was selective reporting with a vengeance. But neither were Western troops or Western imperialists by any means as fastidious as those in the West have been led to believe. In fact, it has been seen already in this chapter that even the victims of Japanese imperialism sometimes regarded it as an example of what the East might achieve.

Japan's military expansion after 1941 toppled colonial regimes in the Dutch East Indies, Malaya, the Philippines, and eventually French Indochina. The Japanese occupying forces had difficulty in finding collaborators who saw the Japanese, initially at least, as liberators, and Japan's encouragement of anticolonialist nationalism in Southeast Asia paved the way for the wave of antiimperialist revolutions, civil wars, and liberation movements, successful and unsuccessful, that swept the region after 1945.[84]

It is important to stress, once again, how difficult it is to avoid the 'presentism' and ethnocentrism which colour so many Western judgements about late nineteenth and early twentieth-century Japanese history. There is no denying, of course, that Japan's international relations and imperial expansion inflicted misery both upon her own people and upon untold millions in Asia and the rest of the world. There is no denying either that many of the policies adopted by Japan were similar to those which had been pursued by other imperial powers. The comparison may help to explain, but it does nothing to excuse, the course which was adopted by Japan's political and military leaders. It is a record with which many in Japan still have to come to terms.

Notes

1. **D.B. Smith**, *Japan since 1945: The Rise of an Economic Superpower*, Macmillan, 1995, pp. 164–5; **P. Duus**, Introduction, in **P. Duus** (ed.), *The Cambridge History of Japan*, vol. 6, *The Twentieth Century*, Cambridge University Press, 1988, pp. 6–11; **A. Iriye**, *Japan and the Wider World: From the Mid-Nineteenth Century to the Present*, Longman, 1997, p. 63.
2. *The Times*, 28 May, 30 May, 27 November 1998.
3. *South China Morning Post*, 29 August 1997. See also 'Behind the Textbook Controversy', *Japan Echo*, 24 March 1997; *The Times*, 29 May 1998.
4. In retrospect, it appears as though Japanese international relations were directed exclusively towards imperialistic aggrandisement. Nevertheless, a closer examination of the period reveals that various foreign policy strategies were debated and pursued, often in tandem. The most important of these included the pursuit of an alliance with the predominant Western nation of a given era, and benevolent co-operation with Asia (Pan-Asianism). For an analysis of foreign policy throughout the period, see **M. Mayo** (ed.), *The Emergence of Imperial Japan: Self-Defense or Calculated Aggression*, Heath, 1970; **I.H. Nish**, *Japanese Foreign Policy, 1869–1942. Kasumigaseki to Miyakezaka*, Routledge & Kegan Paul, 1977; **W.G. Beasley**, *Japanese Imperialism 1894–1945*, Oxford University Press, 1987. For the distinction between formal and informal imperialism, see **R. Robinson** and **J. Gallagher**, 'The Imperialism of Free Trade', *Economic History Review*, vi, 1954, esp. pp. 1–13.
5. **J.E. Hoare**, 'Japan's Road to War', *Asian Affairs*, 18, 1997, p. 57.

6. Beasley, *Japanese Imperialism*, pp. 136–7; **J. Dower**, *Japan in War and Peace: Essays on History, Race and Culture*, HarperCollins, 1993, p. 315; **R.G. Edgerton**, *Warriors of the Rising Sun*, Norton, 1997; **M.A. Barnhart**, *Japan and the World since 1868*, Arnold, 1995.

7. Iriye, *Japan*, p. 5; Barnhart, *Japan and the World*, pp. 1–16. A classic Marxist interpretation of 'enriching the country and strengthening the military' is found in the works of **E.H. Norman**: *Japan's Emergence as a Modern State: Political and Economic Problems of the Meiji Period*, Institute of Pacific Relations, 1940; *Origins of the Modern Japanese State: Selected Writings of E.H. Norman*, **J. Dower** (ed.), Pantheon Books, 1975.

8. Japan regained full control over her tariff policy in 1911. **R.F. Wall**, *Japan's Century: An Interpretation of Japanese History since the Eighteen-Fifties*, Historical Association, 1971, pp. 19–22; **G. Akita**, *Foundations of Constitutional Government in Modern Japan, 1868–1900*, Harvard University Press, 1967, p. 13. Details on the 'unequal treaties' and attempts to revise them can be found in **F.D. Jones**, *Extraterritoriality in Japan and the Diplomatic Relations Resulting in its Abolition, 1853–1899*, Yale University Press, 1931.

9. *JS*, 28 August 1894; Barnhart, *Japan and the World*, pp. 1–16; **J. Hunter**, *The Emergence of Modern Japan: An Introductory History since 1853*, Longman, 1989, pp. 10, 42; **A. Iriye**, 'Japan's Drive to Great-Power Status', in **M.B. Jansen** (ed.), *The Emergence of Meiji Japan*, Cambridge University Press, 1995.

10. **L. Blusse**, 'Japanese Historiography and European Sources', in **P.C. Emmer** and **H.L. Wesseling** (eds), *Reappraisals in Overseas History*, Leiden University Press, 1979, p. 195; Iriye, 'Japan's Drive', pp. 286–9; Wall, *Japan's Century*, pp. 22–3. Studies of the Ryûkyû, Bonin and Kuril Islands include **J.J. Stephen**, *Sakhalin: A History*, Clarendon Press, 1971; **J.J. Stephen**, *The Kuril Islands, Russo-Japanese Frontier in the Pacific*, Clarendon Press, 1974; **S. McCune**, *The Ryûkyû Islands*, David & Charles, 1975.

11. Iriye, 'Japan's Drive', p. 296.

12. Iriye, 'Japan's Drive', pp. 302–3. On the development of Japanese imperialism in Korea, see **C.I.E. Kim** and **H.K. Kim**, *Korea and the Politics of Imperialism: 1876–1910*, University of California Press, 1968; **H. Conroy**, *The Japanese Seizure of Korea, 1868–1910: A Study of Realism and Idealism in International Relations*, University of Pennsylvania, 1974; **M. Deuchler**, *Confucian Gentlemen and Barbarian Envoys: The Opening of Korea*, University of Washington Press, 1977; **G.T. Ladd**, *In Korea with Marquis Itô*, Charles Scribner's Sons, 1908; **M.J. Rhee**, *The Doomed Empire: Japan in Colonial Korea*, Ashgate, 1997.

13. A concise overview of Japanese colonialism is found in **M.R. Peattie**, 'The Japanese Colonial Empire, 1895–1945', in Duus (ed.), *Cambridge History of Japan*, pp. 217–70.

14. Peattie, 'Colonial Empire', p. 218; **T. Najita**, *Hara Kei and the Politics of Compromise, 1905–1915*, Harvard University Press, 1967, p. 91.

15. **C. Howe**, *The Origins of Japanese Trade Supremacy: Development and Technology in Asia from 1540 to the Pacific War*, Hurst, 1996; Peattie, 'Colonial Empire', pp. 222–3. Cf. **S. Akita**, '"Gentlemanly Capitalism", Intra-Asian Trade and Japanese Industrialisation at the Turn of the Last Century', *Japan Forum*, 8, 1996.

16. Hunter, *Modern Japan*, p. 42.

17. Iriye, *Japan*, p. 13.

18. **P. Duus**, review of Beasley, *Japanese Imperialism*, in *Journal of Japanese Studies*, 14, 1988, p. 453.

19. Peattie, 'Colonial Empire', pp. 217–18.

20. Iriye, *Japan*, pp. 4, 11.

21. E. **Baelz**, *Awakening Japan: The Diary of a German Doctor: Edwin Baelz*, Indiana University Press, 1974, p. 343; C. **Browne**, *Tôjô: The Last Banzai*, Da Capo Press, 1998, pp. 16–17; Barnhart, *Japan and the World*, p. 16; P. **Duus**, *The Abacus and the Sword: The Japanese Penetration of Korea, 1895–1910*, University of California Press, 1995; Iriye, *Japan*, p. 151.

22. Y. **Fukuzawa**, 'Nisshin no sensô wa bunya no sensô nari' in **Rekishigaku kenkyûkai** (eds), *Nihonshi shiryô*, vol. 4. *Kindai*, Iwanami Shoten, 1998, pp. 221–2; *JS*, 29 July 1894. See also *JS*, 24 July 1894.

23. Edgerton, *Warriors*, pp. 48–50; Iriye, *Japan*, p. 33; C. **Gluck**, *Japan's Modern Myths, Ideology in the Late Meiji Period*, Princeton University Press, 1985, p. 131. For further reading on the Sino-Japanese War and the 'Triple Intervention', see S. **Takeuchi**, *War and Diplomacy in the Japanese Empire*, Allen & Unwin, *c.* 1935; M.B. **Jansen**, *Japan and China: From War to Peace: 1894–1972*, Rand McNally, 1975; M. **Kajima**, *Diplomacy of Japan: 1894–1922*, vol. 1, *Sino-Japanese War and the Triple Intervention*, The Kajima Institute of International Peace, 1976; S. **Lone**, *Japan's First Modern War: Army and Society in the Conflict with China, 1894–95*, St Martin's Press, 1994.

24. *OA*, 14 May 1895; *NP*, 15, 27 May 1895; Beasley, *Japanese Imperialism*, p. 164. See also *JS*, 22, 26, 28 May, 1 June 1895; *KS*, 1 June 1895.

25. Edgerton, *Warriors*, p. 49.

26. Iriye, *Japan*, p. 32.

27. I.H. **Nish**, *The Anglo-Japanese Alliance: The Diplomacy of Two Island Empires, 1894–1907*, The Athlone Press, 1966, pp. 373, 377; T. **Kawahara**, *Hirohito and His Times: A Japanese Perspective*, Kôdansha International, 1990, p. 10; Beasley, *Japanese Imperialism*, pp. 64–7; Barnhart, *Japan and the World*, pp. 30–5; Peattie, 'Colonial Empire', pp. 271–4. See M. **Kajima**, *Diplomacy of Japan: 1894–1922*, vol. 2, *Anglo-Japanese Alliance and Russo-Japanese War*, The Kajima Institute of International Peace, 1978, 1980.

28. Iriye, *Japan*, p. 16; Baelz, *Awakening Japan*, p. 317; Kawahara, *Hirohito*, p. 12; *JS*, 24 January 1904. On the Russo-Japanese War, see S. **Okamoto**, *The Japanese Oligarchy and the Russo-Japanese War*, Columbia University Press, 1970; I.H. **Nish**, *The Origins of the Russo-Japanese War*, Longman, 1985.

29. Hunter, *Modern Japan*, p. 26; S. **Okamoto**, 'The Emperor and the Crowd: The Historical Significance of the Hibiya Riot', in T. **Najita** and J.V. **Koschmann** (eds), *Conflict in Modern Japanese Society: The Neglected Tradition*, Princeton University Press, 1982, pp. 258–75; *NP*, 6 September 1905.

30. Peattie, 'Colonial Empire', pp. 174–5; J.N. **Westwood**, *Russia Against Japan, 1904–1905: A New Look at the Russo-Japanese War*, Macmillan, 1986.

31. Baelz, *Awakening Japan*, p. 256; Edgerton, *Warriors*, pp. 17–18. See also: D. **Borg** and S. **Okamoto** (eds), *Pearl Harbor as History: Japanese–American Relations, 1931–1941*, Columbia University Press, 1973.

32. Taiwan and Korea were, of course, at very different stages of development. S. **Minichiello**, *Retreat from Reform: Patterns of Political Behaviour in Interwar Japan*, University of Hawaii Press, 1984, p. 80; Peattie, 'Colonial Empire', pp. 253–7. A general study of the Japanese Empire is R.H. **Myers** and M.R. **Peattie** (eds), *The Japanese Colonial Empire, 1895–1945*, Princeton University Press, 1984.

33. Peattie, 'Colonial Empire', pp. 229–30, 251–7. See also: G.H. **Kerr**, *Formosa – Licensed Revolution and the Home Rule Movement, 1895–1945*, University of Hawaii Press, 1974; C.-M. **Ka**, *Japanese Colonialism in Taiwan: Land Tenure, Development, and Dependency: 1895–1945*, Westview Press, 1995.

34. **Y.-S. Chang**, 'Planned Economic Transformation and Population Change', in **C.I.E. Kim** and **D.E. Mortimore** (eds), *Korea's Response to Japan: The Colonial Period 1910–1945*, pp. 58–9; **K.Y.K. Kim**, 'The Impact of Japanese Colonial Development on the Korean Economy', in Kim and Mortimore (eds), *Korea's Response*, p. 91.

35. *Japan Chronicle*, 17 April 1919; Peattie, 'Colonial Empire', pp. 230–1; **J.E. Thomas**, *Modern Japan: A Social History since 1868*, Longman, 1996, pp. 134–5; Beasley, *Japanese Imperialism*, pp. 148–9. The Japanese empire in Korea is discussed in Kim and Mortimore (eds), *Korea's Response to Japan*; **A.C. Nahm** (ed.), *Korea Under Japanese Colonial Rule: Studies of Policy and Techniques of Japanese Colonialism*, Proceedings of the Conference on Korea, 12–14 November 1970, Center for Korean Studies, Western Michigan University, 1973.

36. Duus, Introduction, p. 7; Peattie, 'Colonial Empire', pp. 232–3; **R.F. Johnston**, *Twilight in the Forbidden City*, with an Introduction by **P. Atwell**, Oxford University Press, 1985, p. 116.

37. Duus, Introduction, p. 9; Peattie, 'Colonial Empire', p. 228; **E.O. Reischauer**, *The Japanese Today: Change and Continuity*, Belknap Press, 1988, p. 349; **I. Hata**, 'Continental Expansion', in Duus (ed.), *Cambridge History of Japan*, p. 279. See **R.P. Dua**, *Anglo-Japanese Relations During the First World War*, S. Chand, 1972; **H.T. Patrick**, 'The Economic Muddle of the 1920s', in **J.W. Morley** (ed.), *Dilemmas of Growth in Prewar Japan*, Princeton University Press, 1971, pp. 211–66; **B.S. Silberman** and **H.D. Harootunian** (eds), *Japan in Crisis: Essays on Taishô Democracy*, Princeton University Press, 1974.

38. Robinson and Gallagher, 'Imperialism of Free Trade', esp. pp. 1, 13.

39. Beasley, *Japanese Imperialism*, pp. 94–5; Barnhart, *Japan and the World*, p. 43; Thomas, *Modern Japan*, p. 166.

40. Iriye, *Japan*, pp. 45–6; Beasley, *Japanese Imperialism*, pp. 108–15; Barnhart, *Japan and the World*, pp. 52–3; Hata, 'Continental Expansion', pp. 280–1. In fact, the 'Twenty-One Demands' revealed growing divisions within the nation's political elites. Yamagata, the predominant *genrô*, strongly objected to the demands and, as a result, the Dôshikai (later, the Kenseikai), was forced into the political wilderness while its leader, Katô, became *persona non grata*. **P. Duus**, *Party Rivalry and Political Change in Taishô Japan*, Harvard University Press, 1968, p. 95.

41. Duus, Introduction, pp. 8–9.

42. Reischauer, *Japanese Today*, p. 349; Wall, *Japan's Century*, p. 34; **S. Okamoto**, 'Ishibashi Tanzan and the Twenty-One Demands', in **A. Iriye** (ed.), *The Chinese and the Japanese*, Princeton University Press, 1980, p. 185; **G.C. Allen**, *A Short Economic History of Modern Japan 1867–1937*, Allen & Unwin, 1946, pp. 104–5; Hata, 'Continental Expansion', p. 283; **A. Iriye**, *The Origins of the Second World War in Asia and the Pacific*, Longman, 1987, p. 56.

43. *Japan Weekly Chronicle*, 29 July 1920; Iriye, *Japan*, pp. 53, 63–4; Iriye, *The Origins of the Second World War*, p. 2; Duus, Introduction, pp. 9–10; Beasley, *Japanese Imperialism*, pp. 115, 122–3. See also **P.M. Coble**, *Chinese Politics and Japanese Imperialism, 1931–1937*, Harvard University Press, 1991.

44. *Japan Weekly Chronicle*, 22 January 1925. See **N. Bamba**, *Japanese Diplomacy in a Dilemma: A New Light on Japan's China Policy, 1924–1929*, University of British Columbia Press, 1972.

45. Peattie, 'Colonial Empire', p. 229; **M. Rôyama**, *Foreign Policy of Japan: 1934–1939*, Greenwood Press, 1975 (originally printed by the Japanese Council, Institute of Pacific Relations, 1941), pp. 28–31; *NN*, 15 April 1924. A contemporary analysis of

the Immigration Exclusion Act is found in **R. D. McKenzie**, *Oriental Exclusion: The Effect of American Immigration Laws, Regulations, and Judicial Decisions upon the Chinese and Japanese on the Pacific Coast*, University of Chicago Press, 1928.

46. *Japan Times Weekly*, 1 January 1939; **E. Behr**, *Hirohito: Behind the Myth*, Penguin, 1990, p. 106. Cf. *Japan Weekly Chronicle*, 22 July 1920.

47. **J. Dower**, *War Without Mercy: Race and Power in the Pacific War*, Faber & Faber, 1986, p. 278; Behr, *Hirohito*, p. 106; **T. Kase**, *Eclipse of the Rising Sun*, Cape, 1951, pp. 24–5.

48. **W.R. Crocker**, *The Japanese Population Problem: The Coming Crisis*, Allen & Unwin, 1931, p. 51.

49. Allen, *Economic History*, p. 98; Barnhart, *Japan and the World*, p. 91; **R. Dore** and **R. Sinha** (eds), *Japan and World Depression: Then and Now. Essays in Memory of E.F. Penrose*, St Martin's Press, 1987; **R. Storry**, *The Double Patriots: A Study of Japanese Nationalism*, Greenwood Press, 1957, p. 99; **M. Hane**, *Peasants, Rebels and Outcastes: The Underside of Modern Japan*, Pantheon Books, 1982, p. 3.

50. Reischauer, *Japanese Today*, p. 350; **J.B. Crowley**, 'Intellectuals as Visionaries of the New Asian Order', in **J.W. Morley** (ed.), *Dilemmas of Growth in Pre-War Japan*, Princeton University Press, 1974, pp. 319–73, Rôyama, *Foreign Policy*, pp. 82, 133–4, 158, 166.

51. Rôyama, *Foreign Policy*, p. 28; **J.B. Crowley**, 'A New Asian Order: Some Notes on Prewar Japanese Nationalism', in Silberman and Harootunian (eds), *Japan in Crisis*, p. 270.

52. Minichiello, *Retreat from Reform*, pp. 32–3, 42.

53. *Japan Chronicle*, 10 March 1927. So-called 'Tanaka Diplomacy' is frequently and misleadingly contrasted with the informal, co-operative and internationalist tenets of 'Shidehara Diplomacy', named after one of Japan's ablest foreign ministers (1924–27, 1929–31). Although Tanaka was more hawkish in his pronouncements and plans, his diplomatic efforts did not represent a significant break with the world order in the way that post-1933 diplomacy did. See **A. Iriye**, *After Imperialism: The Search for a New Order in the Far East, 1921–1931*, Harvard University Press, 1965; **S. Takemoto**, *Failure of Liberalism in Japan: Shidehara Kijûrô's Encounter with Anti-Liberals*, University Press of America, 1978; **W.F. Morton**, *Tanaka Giichi and Japan's China Policy*, Dawon, 1980.

54. Hata, 'Continental Expansion', pp. 286–90; Hunter, *Modern Japan*, p. 54; Barnhart, *Japan and the World*, pp. 83–4.

55. Kase, *Eclipse*, p. 24; Behr, *Hirohito*, pp. 107–8; Barnhart, *Japan and the World*, pp. 87–90; *OM*, 29 March 1930, 16 April 1930, 25 April 1930, 24 May 1930; *TA*, 30 April 1930, 22 July 1930, 18 September 1930, 28 September 1930. See **T.F. Mayer Oakes** (trans.), *Fragile Victory: Saionji-Harada Memoirs*, Wayne State University Press, 1968. Minobe Tatsukichi's three-part discussion on the 'right of supreme command' is found in *TA*, 2, 3, 5 May 1930.

56. Kase, *Eclipse*, p. 17; Barnhart, *Japan and the World*, p. 93; Iriye, *Origins*, pp. 14, 22–3.

57. *JS*, 20 September 1931. The extract cited is from 'The Manchurian Incident was Planned like This'. It is a reconstruction of events based on statements made by Hanatani Tadashi, a key player in the planning and execution of the incident. The article first appeared in 1956. **T. Hanatani**, '*Manshû jihen wa kô shite keikaku sareta*', in **Rekishigaku kenkyûkai** (ed.), *Nihonshi shiryô*, vol. 5. *Gendai*, Iwanami Shoten, 1998, pp. 14–15. See also: *TA*, 20 September 1931. See **T. Yoshihashi**, *Conspiracy at Mukden: The Rise of the Japanese Military*, Yale University Press, 1963; **S. Ogata**,

Defiance in Manchuria: The Making of Japanese Foreign Policy, 1931–1932, University of California Press, 1964; **M. Peattie**, *Ishiwara Kanji and Japan's Confrontation with the West*, Princeton University Press, 1975; **G. McCormack**, *Chang Tso-Lin in Northeast China, 1911–1928: China, Japan, and the Manchuria Idea*, Stanford University Press, 1978; **J.W. Morley** (ed.), *Japan Erupts: The London Naval Conference and the Manchurian Incident, 1928–1932*, Columbia University Press, 1984; **P. Duus, R.H. Myers** and **M.R. Peattie** (eds), *The Japanese Informal Empire in China, 1895–1937*, Princeton University Press, 1989; **I.H. Nish**, *Japan's Struggle with Internationalism: Japan, China and the League of Nations, 1931–1933*, Kegan Paul, 1993; **L. Young**, *Japan's Total Empire: Manchuria and the Culture of Wartime Imperialism*, University of California Press, 1999.

58. Barnhart, *Japan and the World*, pp. 93–4; Hata, 'Continental Expansion', p. 297.
59. *Japan Chronicle*, 20 July 1933; *Japan Weekly Chronicle*, 4 July 1935; Hunter, *Modern Japan*, pp. 56–7; Beasley, *Japanese Imperialism*, pp. 194–7. See **K.C. Sun**, *The Economic Development of Manchuria in the First Half of the Twentieth Century*, Harvard University Press, 1969.
60. Iriye, *Japan*, p. 64. See **J.B. Crowley**, *Japan's Quest for Autonomy: National Security and Foreign Policy, 1930–1938*, Princeton University Press, 1966; **S. Okamoto**, *Pearl Harbor as History: Japanese–American Relations, 1931–1941*, Conference on Japanese–American Relations, 1931–1941, **D. Borg and S. Okamoto** (eds), Columbia University Press, 1973; **W.J. Morley** (ed.), *The Fateful Choice: Japan's Advance into South-East Asia, 1931–1941*, Columbia University Press, 1980; **W.J. Morley** (ed.), *The China Quagmire: Japan's Expansion on the Asian Continent, 1933–1941*, Columbia University Press, 1983.
61. *Japan Times Weekly*, 13 October 1938; Iriye, *Origins*, pp. 2, 4, 11, 18–20, 71; Barnhart, *Japan and the World*, pp. 101–2; Hata, 'Continental Expansion', p. 298.
62. Browne, *Tôjô*, p. 74; Iriye, *Origins*, pp. 41–3, 67.
63. *Japan Times Weekly*, 15 December, 22 December 1938; 9 March 1939.
64. Iriye, *Origins*, pp. 41–3, 67; Hata, 'Continental Expansion', pp. 303–6. On Japanese war atrocities, see **H.J. Timperley**, *Japanese Terror in China*, Modern Age Books, 1938; **D. Boling**, *Mass Rape, Enforced Prostitution and the Japanese Imperial Army: Japan Eschews International Legal Responsibility*, University of Maryland School of Law, 1993; **G. Hicks**, *The Comfort Women: Japan's Brutal Regime of Enforced Prostitution in the Second World War*, Norton, 1995; **Xu Zhigeng**, *Lest We Forget: Nanjing Massacre, 1937*, **Zhang Tingquan and Lin Wusun** (eds), Panda Books, 1995; **K. Honda**, *The Nanjing Massacre*, F. Gibney (ed.) and K. Sandness (trans.), M.E. Sharpe, *c.* 1999. A recent work about the Nanjin Massacre that has been well received by Western scholars but has caused considerable controversy among specialist Japanese historians is **I. Chang**, *The Rape of Nanking: The Forgotten Holocaust of World War II*, Penguin, 1997.
65. **T. Iritani**, *Group Psychology of the Japanese in Wartime*, Kegan Paul International, 1991, pp. 197–8; Beasley, *Japanese Imperialism*, p. 203; Edgerton, *Warriors*, pp. 14, 244–50.
66. Iriye, *Origins*, pp. 41, 88.
67. **H. Cortazzi**, review of Iriye, *Origins*, in *Asian Affairs*, xviii, October 1997, p. 362; Beasley, *Japanese Imperialism*, p. 204; **J. Dower**, *War Without Mercy: Race and Power in the Pacific War*, Faber & Faber, 1986, p. 278; Browne, *Tôjô*, p. 167. Studies of the New Order in East Asia and the Greater East-Asian Co-Prosperity Sphere include **J.C. Lebra** (ed.), *Japan's Greater East Asia Co-Prosperity Sphere in World War II:*

Selected Readings and Documents, Oxford University Press, 1975; F. Jones, *Japan's New Order in East Asia: Its Rise and Fall, 1937–1945*, AMS Press, 1978; P. Duus, R.H. Myers and M.R. Peattie (eds), *The Japanese Wartime Empire, 1931–1945*, Princeton University Press, 1996. A detailed analysis of the political origins of the New Order Movement is found in G.M. Berger, *Parties out of Power in Japan: 1931–1941*, Princeton University Press, 1977.

68. *Japan Times Weekly*, 10 November 1938; Duus, Introduction, p. 10.

69. *Nippon Times*, 30 May, 19 June, 5 September 1943; Wall, *Japan's Century*, p. 38; Behr, *Hirohito*, p. 224; Iriye, *Japan*, p. 91.

70. *Japan Times Weekly*, 2 February 1939; Dower, *War Without Mercy*, p. 8.

71. Behr, *Hirohito*, pp. 180, 223; Edgerton, *Warriors*, p. 311; Peattie, 'Colonial Empire', pp. 310–13; Iriye, *Japan*, pp. 79–80, 160. For the Tripartite Pact, see F.W. Ikle, *German–Japanese Relations, 1936–1940*, Bookman Associates, 1956; J.M. Meskill, *Hitler and Japan: The Hollow Alliance*, Atherton Press, 1966.

72. L. Warner and J. Sandilands, *Women Beyond the Wire*, Arrow, 1997, p. 27; Barnhart, *Japan and the World*, pp. 141–2; Behr, *Hirohito*, p. 114; Edgerton, *Warriors*, pp. 260–1; A.D. Coox, 'The Pacific War', in Duus (ed.), *Cambridge History of Japan*, pp. 344, 348; Kawahara, *Hirohito*, pp. 114–15.

73. *Nippon Times*, 30 May, 1 August, 11 September 1943; Dower, *War Without Mercy*, pp. 6–7; Wall, *Japan's Century*, p. 39; Behr, *Hirohito*, p. 323.

74. Kawahara, *Hirohito*, pp. 116–17; Coox, 'Pacific War', pp. 350–7; Iriye, *Japan*, pp. 88–90.

75. Kawahara, *Hirohito*, pp. 118–20; I. Buruma, *Wages of Guilt: Memories of War in Germany and Japan*, Vintage, 1995, p. 225. Authoritative works on the Pacific War include R. Butow, *Tôjô and the Coming of the War*, Stanford University Press, 1961; D. Lu, *From the Marco Polo Bridge to Pearl Harbor*, Public Affairs Press, 1961; T. Havens, *Valley of Darkness: The Japanese People and World War Two*, Norton, 1978; S. Ienaga, *Japan's Last War: World War II and the Japanese, 1931–1945*, Blackwell, 1979; J.W. Morley, *The Fateful Choice: Japan's Advance into South-East Asia, 1931–1941*, Columbia University Press, 1980; M. Barnhart and H. Wray, *Japan Prepares for Total War: The Search for Economic Security, 1919–1941*, Cornell University Press, 1987; Iriye, *Origins*; H. Conroy (ed.), *Pearl Harbor Re-examined: Prologue to the Pacific War*, University of Hawaii Press, 1990.

76. Dower, *War Without Mercy*, p. 7. Numerous works exist on the history of collaboration and the anti-Japanese resistance including N. Smith and T.B. Clark, *Into Siam, Underground Kingdom*, Bobbs-Merrill, 1946; U.S. Baclagon, *The Philippine Resistance Movement Against Japan, 10 December, 1941–14 June, 1945*, Munoz Press, 1966; F.H. Conroy, 'Thoughts on Collaboration', in *Peace and Change*, 1, 1972, pp. 43–6; E. Rice, *BAAG: Hong Kong Resistance, 1942–1945*, Oxford University Press, 1981; F. Aurillo Sr, 'The Leyte Guerilla Movement', in *Leyte–Samur Studies*, 17, 1983. M.E. Miles deals with the Sino-American Cooperative Organisation and its role in the anti-Japanese resistance guerrilla effort in *A Different Kind of War*, Doubleday, 1967.

77. Coox, 'Pacific War', pp. 368–71.

78. Barnhart, *Japan and the World*, p. 146; Coox, 'Pacific War', pp. 372–3. See R. Butow, *Japan's Decision to Surrender*, Stanford University Press, 1954; H. Feis, *The Atomic Bomb and the End of World War II*, Princeton University Press, 1966; J. Dower, *Empire and Aftermath: Yoshida Shigeru and the Japanese Experience, 1878–1954*, Harvard University Press, 1988.

79. Coox, 'Pacific War', pp. 373–6; Thomas, *Modern Japan*, p. 246. On the decision to drop the atomic bomb, see **X. Freedman** and **S. Dockrill**, 'Hiroshima', in **S. Dockrill** (ed.), *From Pearl Harbor to Hiroshima: The Second World War in Asia and the Pacific, 1941–45*, Macmillan, 1994; **R. Takagi**, *Hiroshima: Why America Dropped the Atomic Bomb*, Little, Brown, 1995.

80. **K. Howard** (ed.), *True Stories of the Korean Comfort Women*, Cassell, 1995; **V. Chiv**, 'China's House of Shame', *South China Morning Post*, 6 June 1998; Dower, *War Without Mercy*, pp. 284–7; Peattie, 'Colonial Empire', pp. 232–7. **G. Daws**, *Prisoners of the Japanese: POWs of World War II in the Pacific – The Powerful Untold Story*, Robson Books, 1995. For the biological experiments of Unit 731, see Behr, *Hirohito*, pp. 202–9; **S.H. Harris**, *Factories of Death: Japanese Biological Warfare, 1932–1945 and the American Cover-up*, Routledge, 1994; **J. Powell**, 'Japan's Biological Weapons: 1930–1945', *Bulletin of the Atomic Scientists*, 37, 1981; **P. Williams** and **D. Wallace**, *Unit 731 – The Japanese Army's Secret of Secrets*, Hodder & Stoughton, 1989.

81. For the continuities, see Peattie, 'Colonial Empire', pp. 238–40.

82. It should not be forgotten that 'this benign view from abroad was in large part shaped by the fact that, outwardly at least, Japanese colonialism at this stage closely resembled that of the European nations themselves'. Peattie, 'Colonial Empire', pp. 233, 240–2, 248; **N. MacKenzie** (ed.), *The Letters of Sidney and Beatrice Webb*, vol. II, Cambridge University Press, 1978, pp. 374–5.

83. *Nippon Times*, 30 May 1943. Also *Japan Times Weekly*, 19 January 1939; Dower, *Japan*, ch. 8.

84. Duus, Introduction, p. 11.

4

Economic growth, industrial relations, consumption and saving

There has been a profound ambivalence in Western attitudes towards Japan. Whereas Japanese political practices, international relations and imperial expansion are castigated as precedents to be avoided, her economic performance, industrial relations and patterns of consumption and saving were, until the mid-1990s, revered as models to be studied, and if possible emulated. Indeed, some of the praise heaped on late twentieth-century Japan reached quite extraordinary levels of hyperbole. 'The Japanese economy', it was said, 'might well be considered one of the wonders of the world.' The Japanese company, it was said, 'becomes in a real sense the property of the people who make it up', and of course, 'Everybody knows that the Japanese are prodigious savers.' In fact, it was claimed in the mid-1970s that, 'Japan may well be showing the rest of the world not only how to survive the twentieth century but how to prepare for the twenty-first'.[1]

Although the praise lavished upon Japan's so-called 'economic miracle' was directed overwhelmingly at the years following the Second World War, it is commonly believed that the 'miracle' had its roots deep in the country's history. Between the middle of the nineteenth century and the middle of the twentieth century, it is explained, Japan transformed herself from a feudal backwater into one of the world's leading industrial nations, achieving enviable rates of economic growth, remarkably harmonious industrial relations and unparalleled levels of personal saving.[2]

But how tenable are such views? Did the Japanese really find the answer to so many of the problems confronting the world's modern industrial economies? Can it be true that Japan's economic growth was uniquely rapid, her industrial relations uniquely harmonious, her people's propensity for saving, rather than consumption, uniquely powerful and persistent? If it is true, how did it all come about? What was it in Japanese psychology or Japanese society which enabled her to do so much better than her Asian neighbours, and so much better too than her competitors in the rest of the world?

It is the purpose of this chapter to submit such issues to the serious and sustained scrutiny which they undoubtedly deserve. Its aim, more specifically, is to describe, and attempt to explain, the course of Japan's economic growth, industrial relations, and consumption and saving between 1868 and 1945. It will be argued that the claims which are made about these aspects of Japan's economic history reveal, at best, only part of the story. It will be stressed that Japan's economic development was more uneven than is often supposed: short-term fluctuations and the 'dual' nature of the economy meant that growth, harmony and foresight were characteristic only of certain periods of time, and certain sectors of the economy. It will be suggested, in other words, that insofar as growth, harmony and foresight constituted a Japanese tradition, it was an 'invented tradition', a product of the particular economic and social circumstances prevailing in the years during, and following the First World War.[3]

Economic growth

The economic performance of late nineteenth and early twentieth-century Japan has never attracted the same media attention as the 'economic miracle' of the post-war years. Nonetheless, the achievements of the years between 1868 and 1945 are widely recognised by specialists in Japanese economic and social history. Japan was a late developer, it is explained, but she managed not only to catch up with the Western powers but also to overtake a large number of them. Indeed, it has been suggested that this 'ascent into the ranks of the industrial elite . . . was the true economic "miracle" of modern Japanese history'. It 'not only defied the apparent logic of Japan's situation at the time but also created much of the basis for Japan's rise to "economic superpower" status in the decades following its defeat in the Second World War'.[4]

These economic achievements should be neither discounted nor exaggerated. Accordingly, it is the purpose of this, the first section of the chapter, to consider Japan's economic performance between 1868 and 1945, showing how important it is to pay attention to all parts of the period and all sectors of the economy if one is to avoid over-estimating the speed, scale and significance of the changes which occurred.

The true economic 'miracle'?

Japan's reputation for economic dynamism was fully deserved. Her economic performance between 1868 and 1945 – or at least between 1868 and 1938 – was, by any measure, exceptionally impressive. The Japanese

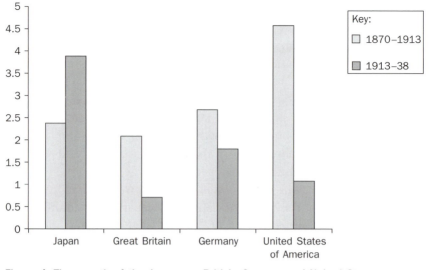

Figure 4: The growth of the Japanese, British, German and United States economies, 1870–1938 (% real growth pa)

Source: T. Nakamura, *Economic Growth in Prewar Japan*, Yale University Press, 1983, p. 2.

economy was growing, growing fast, and from the First World War onwards growing faster than those of her major competitors. There are a number of indicators that can be used to measure economic perform-ance but the most serviceable is real gross national product, the value, in real terms, of all the goods and services produced by the economy.[5]

Figure 4 uses the estimates which have been made of real gross na-tional product to reveal the rapid, and accelerating, growth of the Jap-anese economy between 1870 and 1938. It shows that the economy as a whole grew by an average of almost 2.5 per cent a year between 1870 and 1913, and by nearly 4 per cent a year between 1913 and 1938. These are impressive figures, and even those critical of the ways in which such growth was accomplished have little choice but to acknowledge the very substantial achievement which it represented.[6]

Japan's performance appears more impressive still when viewed from an international perspective. Figure 4 allows us to take this broader view by presenting Japanese growth rates alongside those of Germany, Great Britain and the United States of America. It shows that between 1870 and 1913, Japan's economy grew at a rate similar to those of Germany and Great Britain, albeit a great deal more slowly than that of the United States. Thereafter, however, Japan began to outstrip the Western powers. Between 1913 and 1938, the Japanese economy grew more than twice as fast as that of Germany, three-and-a-half times as fast as that of the United States, and five-and-a-half times as fast as that of Great Britain. In fact, it has been calculated that during the 1930s, Japan's economy was growing at practically 5 per cent a year – and this at a time when much of the rest of the world was struggling to recover from the ravages of the Great Depression. It was difficult not to be impressed. The Japanese, it seemed to some, had begun to find the secret of long-term, accelerating and perhaps sustainable economic growth.

> The progress of Japanese industry forms one of the romances of modern enter-prise. At the beginning of the Meiji era, in 1868, there was in the country but one infant factory in the modern sense. . . . During the more than half a cen-tury since then the progress of native enterprises has been nothing short of phenomenal. . . .
> The story of Japan's abnormal trade development, and her appearance as a rival of more advanced nations in the great trade-fields, is no less interesting and remarkable.[7]

This, of course, is to exaggerate. Indeed, the very grandiloquence of such claims can lead, paradoxically, to a misunderstanding of the Japa-nese people's enormous economic achievements during the late nine-teenth and early twentieth centuries. Japan's economic performance between 1868 and 1945 did not constitute a miracle, but it was suffi-ciently robust to surprise, impress and in some cases alarm her compet-itors. 'One of the great questions which agitate the European economists is that of knowing if Japan is going to become a dangerous competitor from the industrial point of view', it was reported in 1910. 'Personally I do not believe that we need be afraid, at least, for a very long time of the industrial yellow peril.'[8]

Short-term fluctuations and the dual economy

Even this more modest assessment of Japan's performance can lead to a misrepresentation of the speed, scale and success of the country's eco-nomic development. For what has not been made clear in the previous discussion is that Japan's economic growth was neither uniform nor universal. It is essential to recognise that generalisations based upon long-term trends and/or the economy as a whole need to be treated with the greatest possible caution. It is essential to understand, once again, that generalisations based on the supposed homogeneity of Japanese behaviour – and explanations based on the supposed homogeneity of Japanese character and culture – simply cannot be sustained.

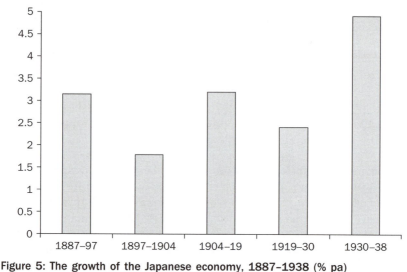

Figure 5: The growth of the Japanese economy, 1887–1938 (% pa)

Source: W.J. Macpherson, *The Economic Development of Japan 1868–1941*, Macmillan, 1987, p. 16.

It has been seen already that the economy tended to grow more quickly after 1913 than it did before. Figure 5 allows us to examine this tendency in more detail. It shows that the long-term acceleration which occurred between 1870 and 1938 must not be allowed to conceal the short-term fluctuations which took place throughout the whole of the period. It is difficult, of course, to know how best to subdivide the period under discussion. However, it can be seen that the economy grew rapidly between 1887 and 1897, grew more slowly between 1897 and 1904, grew rapidly again between 1904 and 1919, grew somewhat more slowly between 1919 and 1930, and grew most rapidly of all between 1930 and 1938. These short-term fluctuations confirm the perils of generalising too readily on the basis of long-term trends, and the mistake therefore of believing that Japan had somehow discovered the secret of perpetual growth.[9]

It must be stressed too that generalisations based upon the development of the economy as a whole can be seriously misleading. The Japanese economy was no more homogeneous than those of other industrialising nations. It developed what is commonly – if rather crudely – described as a dual structure, with a large-scale, capital-intensive, technologically advanced, 'modern' sector operating alongside a small-scale, labour-intensive, 'traditional' sector.[10]

Figures 6 and 7 reveal something of the changes which were taking place. They show that in the early years of the period, the primary industries of farming, forestry and fishing accounted for over 60 per cent

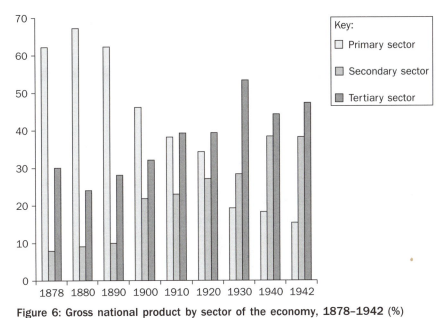

Figure 6: Gross national product by sector of the economy, 1878–1942 (%)

Source: *Hundred-Year Statistics of the Japanese Economy*, Statistics Department, Bank of Japan, 1966, p. 32.

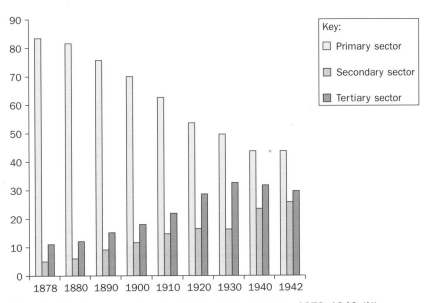

Figure 7: Working population by sector of the economy, 1878–1942 (%)

Source: *Hundred-Year Statistics of the Japanese Economy*, Statistics Department, Bank of Japan, 1966, pp. 56–7.

of gross national product (and for over 80 per cent of the country's workers), while secondary and tertiary industries such as mining, manufacturing, transport, finance, services and administration together comprised less than 40 per cent of gross national product (and barely 16 per cent of recorded employment). Figures 6 and 7 show too how dramatically the situation had changed by the end of the period. In 1942, for example, the primary sector of the economy accounted for just 15 per cent of gross national product (though it still employed more than 40 per cent of the country's workers), while the secondary and tertiary sectors now accounted for 85 per cent of gross national product (and 57 per cent of recorded employment).

Growth was certainly fastest in the modern sector of the economy. And if any organisation epitomised the modern sector of the economy it was the zaibatsu. It has been seen already that the Meiji oligarchs fostered close ties with some of the country's leading entrepreneurs, and that this facilitated the emergence of the four great conglomerates which, clustering first around transport, finance and energy production, were to prove so crucial to the country's economic development. What has not been made clear, however, is the range of their interests or the extent of their influence. By the 1920s, the zaibatsu had assumed a significant role, to a lesser extent, in manufacturing industries like steel-making and shipbuilding and also, in service industries such as commerce and finance. Indeed, by 1945 the four largest zaibatsu, Mitsui, Mitsubishi, Sumitomo and Yasuda, controlled 25 per cent of the country's entire economic activity.[11]

Nonetheless, it is easy to exaggerate the part played by the zaibatsu in Japan's economic development. Although they assumed a leading role in the modern sector of the economy, there was also significant growth among independent undertakings engaged in industries such as textiles, iron and steel-making, and motor manufacturing. Indeed, it has been shown recently that even in the mid-1930s, only ten of the 60 largest mining and manufacturing firms in the country were zaibatsu-related.[12]

Textiles was the first of the light industries to modernise: within four years of its establishment in 1884, the Osaka Spinning Company had increased its paid-up capital five times over and was able to pay dividends of 30 per cent. Iron and steel-making were the first of the heavy industries to follow a similar path: co-operating closely with the state, firms like Fuji Steel and Kobe Steel achieved considerable success during the early years of the new century before coming under the control, eventually, of the major zaibatsu. The motor industry too depended heavily upon state support. In its early years, the industry mostly assembled

components from Ford and General Motors, but the Automobile Manufacturing Industry Law of 1936 licensed Toyota and Nissan (one of the new
zaibatsu) to undertake the entire production process, the state providing
half their capital and favouring them with tax and trade concessions.[13]

However, even the modern, industrial sector of the economy was less
modern and less industrial than one might suppose. Growth depended
not just upon the success of the small number of large, highly capitalised
concerns which were to become bywords for managerial excellence and
technological innovation. Growth depended too upon the activities of
any number of small, modestly capitalised, technologically unsophistic-
ated undertakings whose activities remained virtually unknown except
to those with whom they came into immediate contact. It was found
that as late as 1930, for instance, 53 per cent of all workers employed in
manufacturing industry still worked in establishments which contained
fewer than five people. As the *Japan Chronicle* had observed a few years
previously, 'it has become one of the most exasperating facts in Japan
that, as soon as one leaves the beaten track of mass production, one has
to pay very high prices for very little service'.[14]

Growth was always slower in the traditional sector of the economy.
Retailing, for example, changed a great deal more gradually than mining
or manufacturing. A census taken by the Cabinet Bureau of Statistics in
1939 revealed that even in cities like Tokyo, Yokohama, Osaka, Kyoto,
Kobe and Nagoya there were an 'insignificant' number of department
stores, and that those which did exist were vastly outnumbered by the
'great number' of stores selling food and drink. In fact, Tatsuki claimed
as recently as 1995 that, 'The Japanese distributive system was established in the mid eighteenth-century under the Tokugawa Shôgunate,
and has remained relatively unchanged ever since.'[15]

Farming too was slow to change. Growth rates in agriculture averaged
only a half of those in services and barely a fifth of those achieved in
manufacturing and construction. It is not difficult to see why. The rural
population remained very large, and economies of scale difficult to
secure: as late as 1940, over 33 per cent of farms were smaller than 0.5
hectares (1.25 acres), and a further 57 per cent were between 0.5 and 2
hectares (5 acres). In fact, the nature and pace of rural change continues
to be highly disputed. Some historians have interpreted the years from
the 1880s to 1945, not as a period of progress and modernisation however slow, but as one of stagnation and dislocation. The problems caused
by the introduction of a fixed-rate land tax in 1873 they believe were
aggravated by the draconian deflationary policies of the early 1880s. The

result, it is claimed, was that hundreds of thousands were forced into tenancy and/or bankruptcy. Economic hardship created, in turn, a host of social problems: the dislocation of traditional family structures, the break-up of two million households through out-migration, infanticide, the selling of children into prostitution and violent riots on a large scale. One farmer in the north-west commented in 1905 that,

> There were many people whose means of livelihood was gone, and who, even if they had not eaten for two or three days, felt it debasing to ask others for food; they managed to stay alive by eating unspeakably strange things. Among the poor people in Kawasaki-mura, Motoshakin, Shibata-gun, some left the village telling their neighbours that they were going on a pilgrimage to the Grand Shrine of Ise, but actually went to other villages, where no one knew them, to beg for food there. But in their own villages, they never complained of their hard life.

Meanwhile, a popular song of 1904 laments the plight of a young girl who had been sold into prostitution.

> I parted from my beloved man
> For the sake of my parents
> I was sold to another province,
> Whether north, south, east, or west, I do not know.
> I have these painful duties to perform
> But it's for my parents and it can't be helped.
> Though I don't begrudge my duty
> I may be hurt having private parts
> Examined by cold-hearted doctors
> A treasure box that I wouldn't even show my parents
> I hate to have examined . . .[16]

Although anecdotal evidence concerning the stagnation and misery of rural Japan is not hard to find, great caution is necessary. For just as the modern sector of the economy was less modern than one might imagine, so too the traditional sector was less traditional than one would probably suppose. The countryside was far from unchanging: semi-feudal landlords became more commercial; and simple, but significant, improvements in seed selection and pest control were adopted, first around Osaka and Tokyo and then further afield. The result, Moore goes so far as to claim, was that between the Meiji Restoration and the end of the First World War, Japanese agriculture made what can legitimately be regarded as a successful adaptation to the economic requirements of a modern industrial society.[17]

The fixed-rate nature of the land tax acted as an incentive to increase productivity; and the increase in tenancy can be interpreted less as the result of financial distress than as a rational economic strategy to increase production. So although it is true that there was an 80 per cent increase in tenanted arable land between 1868 and 1912, it needs to be recognised that much of it was contracted out to local farmers, allowing them to expand their production and therefore their profits. In short, the claim that the 'Meiji leaders industrialised and modernised their nation at the expense of the peasantry' seems to be untenable. Smethurst even goes so far as to suggest that, 'the doubling of real income during the Meiji period seems to have raised even the poorest tenant farmer well above, rather than driven him toward or below, the margin of subsistence'.[18]

It is easy of course to exaggerate the success of the late nineteenth and early twentieth-century Japanese economy. Yet whatever caveats are entered about discontinuity, the dual economy and the dangers of generalisation, it remains undeniable that Japan's economic performance proved notably better than those of her major competitors. It is a record which, along with the 'economic miracle' of the post-war years, has attracted a considerable amount of domestic pride and an enormous amount of overseas interest, admiration, surprise and resentment.

Natural advantages, state intervention, entrepreneurial ingenuity and cultural conservatism

How then are we to explain Japan's economic performance? How was it that the Japanese economy grew so fast, and from the First World War onwards so much faster than those of her major competitors? Some commentators mention the natural advantages that Japan enjoyed. It is pointed out, for example, that although the country possessed few raw materials, her position off the east coast of Asia meant that she was well placed geographically to benefit both from trade within the western Pacific and from the contacts which developed more broadly between east Asia and the United States of America.[19]

Still others incline to the view that Japan was better placed historically and culturally than one might imagine to challenge the hegemony of the Western powers. Japan was a late – but not too late – developer. 'Given the relatively recent invention and relative simplicity of many industrial technologies in the nineteenth century', it is explained, 'the gap to be closed by a new aspirant to industrial status may well have been narrower than at any time since.' E.H. Norman concurs. He pointed out as long ago as 1940 that, 'The tempo of Japanese progress ... was increased by the fact that those nations which Japan had singled out as a model or instructor had already proceeded a great distance along the road of technological improvement and economic organization. Japanese industry thus stood to profit from the experience of others.'[20]

It is suggested a great deal more often, and with a great deal more insistence, that Japan's economic success can be traced primarily to the interventionist role played by the Japanese state or to the country's conservative cultural traditions. According to this view, Japanese growth provides a telling illustration of what could be achieved when those in power assumed responsibility for the direction of economic policy. Politicians, bureaucrats and businessmen worked together, it is claimed, to promote the economic growth that the country required to enable it to survive and prosper in a hostile world. 'Japan is first and foremost a bureaucratic state', explains Dower, 'and its version of capitalism is brokered by conservative interests in a manner that retains the market while controlling "excessive" competition and promoting nationalistic goals.'[21]

State intervention was particularly important at the beginning and the end of the period. The Meiji oligarchs inaugurated a form of managed capitalism which has sometimes been dubbed 'laissez-faire in a box'. They began by intervening directly in the industries which they regarded as strategically important, modernising their own arsenals, ironworks and shipyards, and importing advisers and new technology from overseas. Then from the 1880s, they began to turn to less direct methods of influence, making particular efforts to privatise trade and industry, reform the public finances, improve the country's transport and communications infrastructure, and further the interests of the *zaibatsu*.[22]

The governments which came to power after the First World War intervened less actively in the market. Nevertheless, they sought to protect Japanese agriculture and manufacturing by imposing import duties on food and luxury goods, and made efforts to encourage exports by promoting rationalisation and quality control with the Exporters' Association Law and the Major Export Industries Association Law. The late 1920s and 1930s were, according to one commentator, 'a period of indispensable gestation in the evolution and perfection of a genuine Japanese institutional invention, the industrial policy of the developmental state'.[23]

The governments which came to power during the late 1930s had new challenges with which to contend. At war with China in 1937 and embroiled in a life-and-death struggle with America and the allies from the end of 1941, they saw no alternative but to extend their influence and to impose what amounted to a planned economy. They learned what they could about Soviet planning and drew upon their own experience of organising state capitalism in Manchuria. Eventually, it will be recalled, the national government led by Prince Konoe passed the National Mobilisation Law which gave it unprecedented power over the operation of the economy (and the expression of free speech). With control over raw materials, production, labour supply, wages, prices and dividends, state intervention was more pervasive and more powerful than it had ever been before.[24]

If there is a lesson to be learned from Japanese economic growth, some would say, it is that the state had a vital role to play. Indeed, they invert the correlation that is so often made between economic liberalism and economic success. According to this reading of the country's development, Japan's economic achievements should be associated not with unfettered private enterprise but with planning, intervention and regulation.[25]

Such claims have not gone unchallenged. Critics of state activity concede that the Japanese state has been more interventionist than they would wish, but do not accept that this interference with the operation of the market proved beneficial, let alone crucial, in the promotion of economic growth. Japan's economic achievements, they are certain, should be associated not with planning, intervention and regulation but with limited state involvement, modest public expenditure and the maximum possible freedom for individual enterprise.[26]

Recent research into the relationship between government policy and economic growth certainly seems to undermine the claims made for the efficacy of state intervention. Tipton argues, for example, that the bureaucratic elite of nineteenth-century Japan was much less important in stimulating economic growth than has generally been believed. 'Direct government investment was neither extensive nor successful. Government-sponsored institutional change, notably in financial structures, had little if any beneficial impact.' Yonekura agrees. He suggests that the growing international importance of the late nineteenth and twentieth-century iron and steel industry, one of the great success stories of Japanese manufacturing, owed less to government initiatives than to the entrepreneurial flair of industrialists with an eye to changing market conditions.[27]

Nor is this all. Critics of state intervention suggest not simply that it was ineffective in promoting economic growth but that it was all too effective in encouraging industrial–military aggrandisement. It has been calculated, for instance, that military spending increased from just over 2 per cent of gross national product in the early 1890s to 18 per cent in 1940 (with a record 24 per cent in 1905). Because the state's military spending culminated during the 1930s and early 1940s in expansion, war and defeat, it is generally agreed that government involvement in the economy served as a stimulus to Japan's military aggression rather than as a brake upon it.[28]

Tipton concludes his study of Japan's late nineteenth-century political economy by calling into question development strategies based upon government control. 'At best, central government policy hinders the broadly based economic growth upon which long-term social stability depends. At worst, it leads down the road to war and destruction.' Yamamura disagrees. 'Meiji Japan's sustained efforts to build a "strong army" and its decision to wage a war with China in 1895, and another with Russia in 1904, contributed in substantive ways to building the technological foundations for Japan's successful industrialization.' In fact, there is every reason to believe that the association between state intervention, industrialisation and militarism became a good deal more pronounced during the 1930s. It has been claimed, for example, that 'The Manchurian incident played a role in Japan similar to that of the New Deal in the United States. The reflationary effects of increased military expenditure and increased war production revived the Japanese economy from stagnation.'[29]

However, neither natural advantages nor state intervention can explain fully Japan's economic performance between 1868 and 1945. After all, other countries enjoyed far greater natural advantages than Japan, and other governments involved themselves much more closely than Japan's in the direction of economic policy. It is not surprising therefore that commentators of all persuasions have found themselves forced to look elsewhere for explanations of Japan's rapid, and accelerating economic growth.

The answer, more now believe, is to be found in the business acumen of Japanese entrepreneurs, and in particular their willingness to learn from the technological advances of their competitors overseas. Minami claims, for example, that Japan's technological borrowing provides a prime example of the benefits to be derived from 'relative backwardness'. Odagiri and Gotô stress that, 'The Japanese were extraordinarily open and creative in searching out and learning to use modern technologies.'

> The managers of many Japanese business firms were highly entrepreneurial. They aggressively sought out and took aboard foreign techniques, and did the hard work of tailoring these to the Japanese scene. The investments and risks were substantial. And Japanese firms, after taking aboard new technology, made the further continuing investments necessary to stay up with its development worldwide, and increasingly contributed their own invention and innovation to those developments.

What was seen once as slavish copying tends to be regarded now as entrepreneurial adaptability.[30]

The reason for Japan's rapid and accelerating economic growth, many more believe, is to be found in the work ethic, social cohesion and authoritarian attitudes which were encouraged by Japan's conservative cultural traditions. Indeed, it is not too much of an exaggeration to suggest that for some years the discussion of so-called 'Asian values' appeared to be one of the few growth industries in Western countries seeking to replicate the success of the 'tiger economies'. Francis Fukuyama is one of the most influential observers of the differences between West and East. 'According to the precepts of Western liberalism,' he explains, 'lifetime employment should damage economic efficiency by making employees too secure, like professors at universities who stop writing the moment they receive tenure.'

> And yet, in the context of the group consciousness fostered by Japanese culture, the paternalistic loyalty shown by a company to its worker is repaid by a higher level of effort on the part of the worker, who is working not only for himself but for the glory and reputation of the larger organization.[31]

Industrial relations

The mention of group consciousness, paternalistic loyalty and worker effort leads inescapably to a consideration of the possible correlation between industrial relations and economic performance. Did Japanese employers and employees really combine together in the pursuit of common goals? Were Japanese industrial relations really as consensual, harmonious and constructive as we are so often led to believe? If they were, could this be the reason that the Japanese record of economic growth proved so impressive when set alongside those of her major competitors?

The 'three treasures'

Those looking to the East for lessons on how to improve economic efficiency often fastened, until recently, onto what have been called the 'three treasures' of Japanese industrial relations: lifetime employment, seniority-based wages and company unionism. There were any number of eulogies to Japan's work practices and industrial relations. According to a former British ambassador to Japan, 'loyalty has traditionally been a highly prized virtue. If a Japanese is asked what he does he is more likely to reply that he works for such and such a company than to describe himself as a manager or an engineer.' According to a former United

States ambassador, 'managers and workers suffer no loss of identity but rather gain pride through their company. . . . Company songs are sung with enthusiasm and company pins are proudly displayed in buttonholes.'[32]

Yet one should not be persuaded too easily. However important such features of industrial relations may have been in accounting for Japan's post-war economic 'miracle', it does not follow that they explain her economic performance in the years between 1868 and 1945. It follows even less that such practices emanated from something deep and un-changing in Japanese society and psychology. Indeed, it is the purpose of this section of the chapter to show that such characteristics of the Japanese system as lifetime employment, seniority-based wages and com-pany unionism were neither universal nor traditional – nor necessarily effective. The 'three treasures' were 'invented' traditions, a product of the particular combination of circumstances pertaining to a particular time, in a particular part of the economy. Japan's apparently unique system of industrial relations was rooted, it will be argued, not in un-changing national characteristics but in the specific nature of the inter-war labour market.[33]

The inter-war labour market

The Japanese system of industrial relations had its origins not in na-tional character, but in the rational, profit-maximising behaviour of managers in the modern sector of the economy as they attempted to grapple with the social and economic dislocation of the years following the First World War. It is clear beyond all reasonable doubt that lifetime employment, seniority-based wages and company unions were intro-duced for hard-headed, commercial reasons: to attract and retain skilled labour, and to avoid and resolve industrial disputes.

The First World War shifted the balance of power from employers towards employees. The economic boom brought about by the conflict made it difficult for industries like steel-making and shipbuilding to secure the supply of skilled and semi-skilled workers they required, or to deal effectively with a trade-union movement made more confident and aggressive by the buoyant demand for labour. Labour mobility in heavy industry reached levels as high as 70 to 90 per cent a year; the number of trade unions increased two and a half times between 1918 and 1920; and in 1919 there were more than 2,300 industrial disputes. The employers decided that they needed to take action. By the end of the war, explains Gordon, 'Japanese managers offered an impressive array of enticements to security'.

Promotions, wage hikes, bonuses and welfare programmes such as retirement pay all favoured senior workers and theoretically encouraged long-term employment. These benefits had emerged largely as a piecemeal response to the persistence of high turnover, although in a few cases, organized workers had demanded and gained them.[34]

The balance of power soon began to redress itself. The boom ended in 1920, to be followed in rapid succession by the Great Kantô Earthquake of 1923 (which destroyed, *inter alia*, 9,000 factories), a series of depressions and, of course, the Great Depression at the end of the decade. The introduction of factory committees undermined trade unionism in large companies, labour turnover fell to less than 10 per cent a year and, as might be expected, managers grew markedly less enthusiastic about the benefits to be derived from seniority bonuses, regular pay rises and retirement schemes.

Yet this did not mean the end of the 'three treasures'. In the late 1920s, firms like Hitachi began to encourage long-term service by hiring graduates and offering seniority wages. Indeed, there emerged a new awareness of the benefits to be derived from modern technology, and this encouraged a number of employers to make serious efforts to retain the loyalty of their most skilled – and most expensively trained – workers. Firms like the Mitsui Shipbuilding Company and the Kobe Iron and Steel Company were among the first to set up in-house technological training programmes, and during the course of the 1920s such schemes became common in many of the country's larger industrial undertakings.[35]

These and similar devices were revived from the mid-1930s onwards. There was nothing new, of course, about employers wishing to attract and retain skilled labour, and hoping to avoid or resolve industrial disputes. What was new was that with economic recovery, a weakened labour movement and the need to mobilise for war with China, it was the government which took the initiative in pushing employers and employees towards what was to become known as the 'Japanese' system of labour management.

In 1938, the home ministry's police bureau (with the support of the right wing of the labour movement) established the Society for Service to the State through Industry, a sort of state-run company union. Known by its abbreviation *Sanpô*, the new organisation (the Greater Japan Industrial Patriotic Association) stressed the need to replace self-interest and work-place confrontation with a new spirit of industrial service to the nation. With slogans such as 'Enterprise as one family', the leaders of the movement sought to establish a unit in every plant, and so recreate the harmonious, hierarchical relations which they believed existed, or ought to exist, within the Japanese family.

By 1940, *Sanpô's* 3.5 million members included 40 per cent of those employed in manufacturing, and just over 10 per cent of the working population as a whole. It drew upon military organisation and discipline in its attempt to inculcate a common sense of belonging and a shared sense of purpose in the factories where it was active. It encouraged early morning assemblies and helped to diffuse in-house training schemes. It introduced the idea of the 'family-supporting' wage (whereby minimum pay for each age band was supplemented by additional allowances for each dependant), and it popularised the practice of awarding the same annual pay rise to all workers regardless of their length of service.

It is no longer possible to be sure what impact *Sanpô* had upon the development of the Japanese system of industrial relations. Recent research suggests that the new organisation was welcomed by employees – and opposed by employers – because it recognised formally the importance of both labour and capital in the achievement of national economic objectives. 'In a sense', claims Taira, 'it brought about a remarkable social revolution. Because Japan surrendered before the homeland was invaded, Japanese workers made their transition to the postwar period maintaining a high degree of organization and morale in their workplaces.' However, it is important not to overlook more traditional, and much less sanguine, views of *Sanpô* influence on industrial relations. These suggest, not surprisingly, that the organisation deprived working people of their hard-won trade-union rights and so condemned them to impotence at the workplace.[36]

Unemployment, absenteeism and protest

The Japanese system of industrial relations, with its lifetime employment, seniority wage systems and company or state-run unions, was introduced only from the 1920s onwards, and then only among certain groups of workers, in certain large companies which were active in the modern, industrial sector of the economy.

Even where it was in operation, the Japanese system of industrial relations by no means guaranteed loyalty, harmony and goodwill. It will never be easy to judge whether, and to what extent, the 'three treasures' moderated or redirected the tensions that were always likely to arise between employers and employees. However, what can be said is that layoffs occurred, that labour turnover was often high, that absenteeism continued to be common – and that the industrial unrest which took place did so predominantly in those parts of the economy where efforts had been made to establish the so-called Japanese system of industrial relations.

Layoffs occurred more often than the rhetoric of lifetime employment would lead one to suppose. They peaked, as might be expected, during the 1920s and early 1930s. In 1920, for example, the Japan Iron Manufacturing Works laid off five hundred manual workers (and a small number of officials) on the northern island of Hokkaidô. Ten years later, the Woollen Cloth Company of Osaka decided that it had no choice but to dismiss half the 7,000 clerical and manual workers whom it employed. The ideological and material force of such challenges to the concept of lifetime employment should not be underestimated. Hitherto, it was explained, 'the unemployed townsman has gone back to his relations in the country, but this is no longer invariably feasible. Many city dwellers are losing touch with their rural relatives.'[37]

Labour turnover too was often surprisingly high. Even large firms which attempted to discourage labour mobility by hiring graduates and offering seniority wages sometimes pursued their policies inconsistently and ineffectively. It has been found, for instance, that between 1920 and 1939, Hitachi recruited only 10 per cent of its workers at graduation, did not necessarily increase wages in line with seniority, and tended to dismiss its longer-serving, older workers when business was slow. Indeed, when labour was no longer in short supply, many firms replaced schemes whereby wages rose according to length of service with ones whereby earnings were based much more upon individual performance and productivity. The result was that workers continued to move between firms with remarkable frequency: it has been calculated, for example, that between the two world wars the turnover of skilled labour in manufacturing industry averaged as much as 50 per cent and more a year.[38]

Absenteeism too seemed stubbornly intractable. During the Second World War, for instance, absenteeism rates among industrial workers proved particularly problematic for governments whose war efforts depended on the maximisation of production. Averaging 20 per cent even before the American air raids began to disrupt economic activity in the autumn of 1944, they climbed to 50 per cent or so by the time the war ended late the following summer. Of course, it is difficult to know how to interpret such high levels of absenteeism when they occur during the exceptional circumstances of a major international conflict. 'Part of this monumental disruption could be attributed to the physical destruction of factories,' concedes Dore, 'part to illness in the workforce.'

A great portion of such absenteeism, however, came from workers who placed private needs above the demands of the state and abandoned their jobs to forage for food in the countryside or simply to find jobs with higher pay. Whatever the reason, here once again was imposing evidence of hearts not beating as one, workers far more intent on surviving than on fighting on to the bitter end.[39]

Nevertheless, the statistical evidence, while scarce, suggests that absenteeism rates during the war were far from unique. The anecdotal evidence which is available also suggests that Japanese workers between the wars failed to absorb the work ethic. 'Loaf!', advised one of the disgruntled.

> If all there is in life is the sweat of factory labor, we'd be better off as horses and cows. The harder we work, the fatter they get, the thinner we get. We have to enjoy while we can. There's no point in sweating our guts for the profit of capitalists. Don't believe the propaganda that hard work is its own reward.[40]

Strikes and lockouts also remained a great deal more serious than some eulogistic studies of Japanese industrial relations would lead one to suppose. It is true that the incidence of disputes was low by international standards, with fewer than 5 per cent of the industrial workforce taking action annually between 1917 and 1930. It is true too that in some years there were virtually no recorded disputes at all: just eight in the whole of 1902, nine in 1903, six in 1904, eleven in 1909, ten in 1910 and thirteen during the first six months of 1945.[41]

Yet one should not be misled. There are several ways by which one can gauge the success of an industrial relations system, but if one pursues the conventional procedure of recording the incidence of industrial disputes, there emerges a somewhat surprising view of the way in which Japan's employer–employee relationships developed. Figures 8a and 8b show that the number of strikes climbed steadily during the first forty years of the century, with peaks in 1918 and 1919 (when there were up to 490 incidents involving nearly 66,500 workers) and 1931 (when there were 940 incidents involving over 59,260 workers). When the total number of disputes including strikes, lockouts, and slowdowns (for which statistics are available from 1924) are considered, the number of incidents rises to nearly 2,500 in 1931 (involving 155,000 workers). Although the average number of participants were greatest in the years around the First World War and the final year of the Second World War, these figures suggest, on the face of it, that the introduction of new, and supposedly more enlightened management practices coincided with the deterioration, rather than the improvement, of Japan's industrial relations.[42]

Women workers, the unskilled, the casually employed and those working in the traditional sectors of the economy rarely joined trade unions

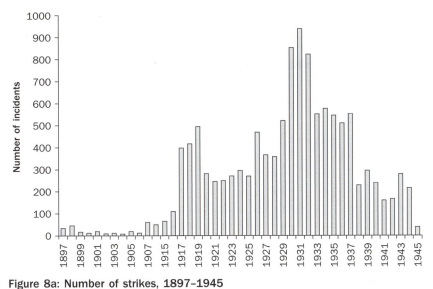

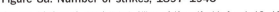

Figure 8a: Number of strikes, 1897–1945

Source: **Rôdô undô shiryô iinkai**, *Nihon rôdô undô shiryô*, vol. 10, 1959, pp. 442–3.

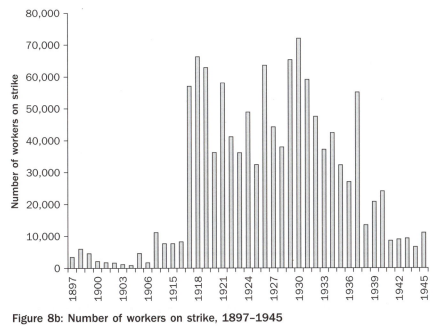

Figure 8b: Number of workers on strike, 1897–1945

Source: **Rôdô undô shiryô iinkai**, *Nihon rôdô undô shiryô*, vol. 10, 1959, pp. 442–3.

and seldom took part in strike action. But in Kôfu protests did occur. In 1886, for example, 100 women employees of a textile factory near Tokyo protested (successfully) when its owners decided to reduce wages and increase the working day by thirty minutes (to fourteen and a half hours). At another factory in Osaka, female workers were particularly active, striking in 1889 for a pay rise and doing so again in 1894.[43]

Tsurumi has shown, too, that although the women working in the textile factories of Meiji Japan found it difficult to sustain strike action, they had other ways of asserting their interests against those of the employers. They stayed away from work, they moved from job to job and they offered each other a range of emotional and psychological support. Tsurumi's research is most important. She establishes that the songs the women sang and the stories they told reveal not only their despair at the conditions in which they found themselves; they reveal too their developing sense of class – and gender – consciousness, and their apparently deep-seated desire to exercise a degree of control over the way in which they lived their lives. One song popular among the women of the Suwa district early in the century told the story of a factory girl, Iwataru Kikusa, who fought off an attack by a man who had murdered several local women.

> Don't scornfully say,
> 'Factory girl, factory girl.'
> Iwataru Kikusa is
> A real factory girl.
>
> Iwataru Kikusa is a shining
> Model of a factory girl.
> Let's wrench the balls
> Of the hateful men!
>
> Mr Overseer, Mr Supervisor,
> You'd better watch out!
> There is the example
> Of Iwataru Kikusa.
>
> Who dares to say that
> Factory girls are weak?
> Factory girls are the
> Only ones who create wealth.

It is not surprising perhaps that the textile factory girls of Meiji Japan began to define themselves as a distinct group with a distinct class and gender identity. What is surprising, concludes Tsurumi, 'is the strength of the positive images of self-worth that emerged' among such a weak and marginalised group.[44]

This discussion of the factory girls' growing class and gender consciousness serves as a useful reminder of the danger of accepting too readily the glowing picture of Japan's industrial relations with which we are so often presented. Japan's industrial relations were good but they were far from perfect, and they were certainly not the product of something deep and unchanging in Japanese society and psychology.

The 'three treasures' – employment for life, seniority wages and company unions – were introduced during the 1920s as a way of providing large companies with a reliable supply of skilled labour at a time when managers found it hard to attract the workers that they required. Yet one should not mistake ambition for achievement, the unusual for the usual. The companies which introduced the 'three treasures' did not necessarily secure the loyalty and commitment of the workers they employed. Indeed, these same companies continued to employ large numbers of temporary workers who were laid off whenever trade was poor – and these same companies were always vastly outnumbered by firms which did not display the slightest inclination to adopt anything approximating to the so-called Japanese system of industrial relations.

This reassessment of employer–employee relationships has important implications for our understanding of the correlation between industrial relations and economic performance. It makes it difficult to sustain the argument that it was Japan's much vaunted system of industrial relations which made possible her impressive rates of economic growth. It means therefore that we must look elsewhere for explanations of Japan's formidable economic record between 1868 and 1945.

Consumption and saving

It has become common in recent years for scholars from many disciplines and many parts of the world to point to the importance of consumer demand. For a country to industrialise, it is emphasised, the population has to learn to respond 'rationally' to the economic incentives which are placed before them. They need to be taught to prefer work to leisure, to value the joys of consumption above the demands of subsistence. According to this analysis, there was – and is – an intimate relationship between consumer attitudes and economic growth. It is the ambitious and respectable worker who drives on economic growth by working hard to earn the money to enable him (or her) to consume the growing range of goods and services that a new industrial economy is able to provide.[45]

It is an interpretation which seems, on the face of it, to sit rather uneasily with popular views of Japanese economic development. For, despite Japan's rapid economic growth, it is often assumed that the Japanese people remained reluctant to consume, suspicious of new products, and wedded to the importance of saving. Indeed, it was seen at the beginning of the chapter that some aspects at least of this abstemious trinity have been championed by those on the right as key elements in Asian economic success.

A reluctance to consume?

It was not that Japanese consumers lacked money to spend or products to purchase. Japanese incomes were reasonably high by international standards, and rose significantly between the Meiji Restoration and the end of the Second World War. It is not easy to provide precise statistics, but those who have studied this aspect of the country's economic history are in no doubt about the level and growth of disposable incomes. The economy was growing, the number of those in work was increasing, and unemployment was much less common than in other industrialised nations. Figure 9 shows that the amount of disposable income available to individual consumers increased substantially between the late nineteenth century and the mid-1930s. Once again, it is difficult to know how best to subdivide the period under discussion. Once again, however, the major shifts can be readily discerned. Income rose quickly between

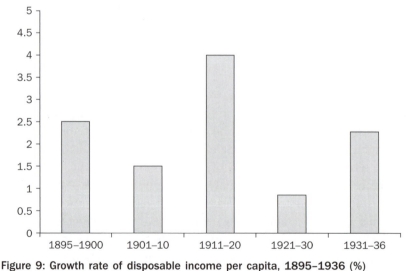

Figure 9: Growth rate of disposable income per capita, 1895-1936 (%)

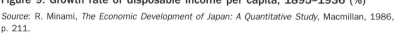

Source: R. Minami, *The Economic Development of Japan: A Quantitative Study*, Macmillan, 1986, p. 211.

1895 and 1900, edged up slowly between 1901 and 1910, rose quickly again between 1911 and 1920, rose slowly (of course) between 1921 and 1930, and quickly again between 1931 and 1936.[46]

The increase in disposable incomes was accompanied by an expansion in the volume and variety of the goods and services on which they could be spent. As in other industrialising countries, the restructuring of the economy, the introduction of mechanisation and the adoption of organisational innovation exercised the most profound effect. As in other countries, indigenous economic change reduced the relative cost of traditional items such as food and drink. The greatest change during the Meiji period was the spread of bread and polished white rice (hitherto confined to the *samurai* classes and religious ceremonies) as the main staples, and the mass production of basic goods such as soy sauce, soybean paste, rice wine and cigarettes. Only in the Taishô and Shôwa periods did foreign foods like beef, beer, Worcestershire sauce and omelettes begin to become more widely known. Prior to this, Hanley notes, 'there is really no evidence of any transition to a diet including new types of Western-influenced foods. . . . Even those Japanese who did occasionally eat imported cuisine at restaurants ate traditional food at home.'[47]

One of the most important consequences of the decreasing cost, the greater availability and wider variety of food was a gradual improvement in the diet of the typical Japanese consumer. Figure 10 shows that daily

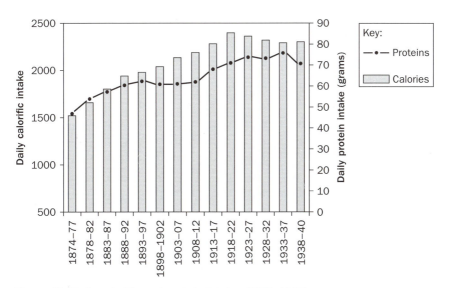

Figure 10: Daily calorific and protein intake, 1874–1940

Source: C. Mosk, 'The Decline of Marital Fertility in Japan', *Population Studies: A Journal of Demography*, XXXIII, 1979, p. 25.

calorific intake rose significantly. In the mid-1870s, the typical Japanese citizen consumed 1,500 calories per day (which, according to Mosk, did not match even the rates for many developing countries in the 1950s and early 1960s). Forty-five years later, daily intake had risen to 2,400 calories and, although this dropped slightly in the following decade, the quality of the Japanese diet continued to improve as protein intake increased. Improvements in diet were reflected in changes to the body. Surveys of the heights of military recruits show that the average man in the mid-1930s was over two centimetres taller than his grandfather half a century earlier and a kilogram heavier than his father at the end of the First World War.[48]

Moreover, an influx of imports made accessible a range of new products, from pianos and patent medicines, to American cars and European wines. The introduction of foreign goods and styles began to change the appearance of Japan, at least in the major cities. Yanagida comments that, by 1860, traditional male hair styles and fashions were becoming rare and, as one popular song in 1871 indicated, were considered somewhat gauche:

> If you tap a shaven and top-knotted head you will hear the sound of retrogression;
> If you tap an unshaven head you will hear the sound of the Restoration;
> If you tap a close-cropped [the current fashion] you will hear the sound of culture and enlightenment.[49]

Nonetheless, change was slow. Food, clothing and housing were affected far less than one might imagine. Straw-mat floors (*tatami*) and papered screens, for example, long remained cheaper and more popular than European-style sitting rooms.[50]

It is not difficult to see how the Japanese earned their reputation for consumer conservatism. Figure 11 shows that the proportion of gross national product devoted to personal consumption declined, rather than increased, as the economy grew and disposable incomes increased. With the growth of government and military spending, consumption's share of gross national product fell by nearly a quarter in a touch over fifty years: from 80 per cent in 1887, to 76 per cent in 1911 and 62 per cent in 1938. Moreover, consumption was low by international standards: the proportion of gross national product devoted to personal consumption was lower, and declined more rapidly, in Japan than in many of the countries with which she competed, and with which she is so often compared.[51]

There are grounds for believing therefore that the Japanese were unwilling, rather than unable, to behave in the way that modern consumers

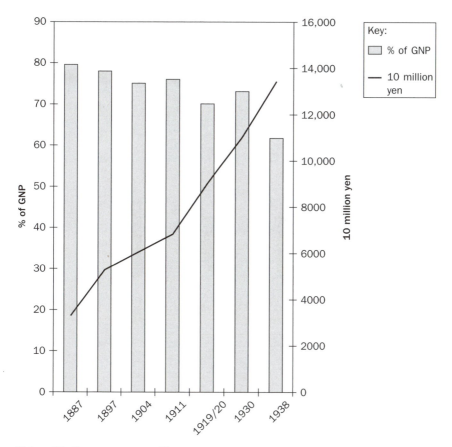

Figure 11: Consumer expenditure

Note: Consumer expenditure as per 10 million yen is based on figures for 1885, 1900, 1915 and 1940.

Source: **S. Nishikawa** and **T. Abe**, 'Sangyôka no jidai', in *Nihon keizaishi*, vol. 4, Iwanami Shoten, 1990, pp. 46–7; **T. Nakamura**, *Economic Growth in Prewar Japan*, Yale University Press, 1983, p. 5.

were supposed to respond to the incentives before them. Indeed, it is not unusual for those looking back from the vantage point of the late twentieth century to contrast the care and caution of those living before the Second World War with what seems like the frivolity and fecklessness of those brought up during the 1960s and 1970s. 'Frugality was held in high regard in traditional Chinese and Japanese societies,' explained Lee in 1991, 'but it has been replaced by consumerism today. Before the war, the Japanese regarded consumer buying as a kind of vice, but after the war it became a virtue.'[52]

Whether or not those living before the war regarded consumer buying as a vice, they appeared well able to resist the blandishments of advertisers

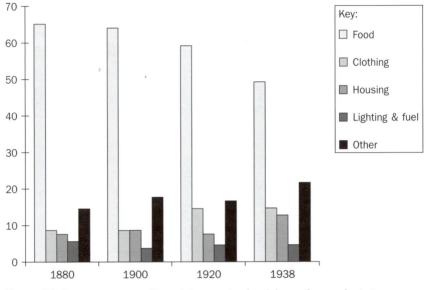

Figure 12: Consumer expenditure (at current prices) by major product groups, 1880–1938 (%)

Source: R. Minami, *The Economic Development of Japan: A Quantitative Study*, Macmillan, 1986, p. 398.

tempted to extol their products as new, exciting or fashionable. The Japanese copied the West, it has been said, in everything but consumption. Figure 12 reveals the extent to which consumer expenditure remained dominated by spending on food. Even in the late 1930s, food spending accounted for 50 per cent of all consumer expenditure, with rice alone providing 60 per cent of the nation's calorific intake. John Morris lived in Tokyo from 1938 to 1942, and was struck by how well those living in the capital were able to cope with wartime shortages of food.

> Nobody likes living on an unchanging diet of fish and rice, but it should be realized that the Japanese have something of a genius for austerity. It is the consequence, perhaps, of an age-long training, and of having in the past been forced by their rulers to live in accordance with sumptuary laws, so that they can be called upon by their government to subsist for long periods on a diet so frugal that no European people would put up with it.

Morris's analysis is obviously not without its limitations, but it does support the mass of other evidence, both qualitative and quantitative, suggesting that consumption habits in Japan were different from those in the West.[53]

It is well known, of course, that economic orthodoxy in the West has shifted in recent years from Keynesianism to monetarism, from the study of demand to the study of supply. It is less well known perhaps that historical concerns have tended to move in the opposite direction, with historians of economic growth now paying particular attention to the role that is – or might be – played by consumer demand. It is a realignment whose value, though recognised by scholars in both West and East, may seem to be undermined by the examination of the Japanese experience.

However, it is important not to be misled. Figure 11 shows that, as one would expect, consumer expenditure was growing in absolute – if not in relative – terms. It increased from 3.3 thousand million yen in 1885, to 5.3 thousand million in 1900, 6.8 thousand million in 1915 and 13.4 thousand million in 1940. Herein then lies the key to understanding the role played by consumption in Japanese economic growth. 'While absolute increases in consumption were a major demand factor in growth, the declining share of personal consumer expenditure released resources for capital formation.'[54]

A propensity to save?

The obverse of a reluctance to consume is, of course, a propensity to save. It will presumably come as no great surprise therefore to discover that the decline (in relative terms) of personal consumption before the Second World War is often associated with the rise (both relatively and absolutely) of individual and family saving. However, what might come as a surprise is to discover that the new patterns of consumer behaviour which emerged during the prosperity of the 1960s and 1970s failed to dislodge traditional attitudes towards saving. The result is that, until very recently, the Japanese have enjoyed a reputation both for high levels of consumption and for high levels of saving.

Those who believe that there are lessons to be learned from the Japanese experience have generally been highly complimentary – and have sometimes waxed almost lyrical – about Japanese thrift and foresight. For example, in the early 1990s, the former British ambassador to Japan, Sir Hugh Cortazzi, listed what he believed to be the reasons for the country's post-war economic success, among which he included the fact that 'Japan's saving rates have traditionally been high'. It is more striking still that even those who wish to challenge the view that the Japanese have saved more than other nationalities recognise the power and persistence of the stereotype. Critics like Emmott claim, for instance, that both Italy and Taiwan boast higher saving rates than Japan, but concede the pervasiveness of the myth 'that the Japanese are the industrial world's most prolific savers and that these peculiar creatures resist all inducements to spend their hard-earned cash'.[55]

These are complicated issues. In attempting to disentangle the relationship between consumption and saving, and between consumption, saving and economic growth, there are three things that need to be done. It is necessary first to assess the level of saving in Japan, then to decide whether the level of saving was related to the level of consumption (or indeed to anything else), and finally to judge whether and to what extent saving (or consumption) contributed towards the country's rapid economic advance.

It is not too difficult to assess the level of saving. Statistical evidence confirms that the Japanese people most certainly lived up to their reputation during the first forty years of the century. Saving rates were high (and higher than in other countries), and tended to grow higher still as time went by. The saving rate, was, by the time comparisons can be made, a great deal higher than those to be found in countries like the United Kingdom or the United States of America. Indeed, the saving rate increased by over 70 per cent during the first forty years of the century: it grew steadily until the late 1920s, dipped slightly during the early 1930s, before climbing rapidly towards the end of the decade.

Armed with these figures, it is possible to address the second of the three questions that need to be asked. Was the level of saving related to the level of consumption? Common sense suggests, of course, that the more people consumed, the less they were likely to save; and that the less they consumed, the more they were likely to save. It is a view which finds powerful support from the evidence which has been presented in this chapter. It has been seen that, as the economy grew and disposable incomes increased, the proportion of gross national income devoted to personal consumption declined, while the proportion of disposable income devoted to individual and family saving increased. It has been seen, as might be expected, that there was an inverse relationship between saving and consumption.

It is a great deal more difficult to know whether the level of saving was related to any of the other factors that those interested in Japanese thrift have suggested. Some seem to believe that the Japanese were inherently and instinctively thrifty. Others accept that the Japanese propensity to save was economically driven, but that it was the consequence, rather than the cause, of the country's economic growth. They suggest that a rise in the saving rate was the natural concomitant of a rise in the growth rate and/or the level of disposable income. Thus Yoshihara concludes from his examination of post-war developments that 'there was a positive relation between growth rate and the saving ratio', with the former 'an independent variable determining' the latter.[56]

Others believe that what seemed like natural frugality or economic determinism was the product of cultural conditioning, of encouragement, of compulsion or even of geography and climate. It is pointed out, for example, that Confucian teaching with 'its ideological queasiness toward money' encouraged saving rather than consumption, that firms like Mitsubishi Shipbuilding ran private savings banks, and that in the aftermath of the war with China the government set a savings target of 30 per cent of gross national product. And, even if these explanations do not convince, it has been suggested that 'the incidence of typhoons and earthquakes may be common enough to encourage the Japanese to place more emphasis on precautionary motives for saving'.[57]

Such geographical determinism may well seem utterly implausible. Nonetheless, it is of value insofar as it raises the possibility of a link, much more broadly, between insecurity and the propensity to save. It is a link with two quite distinctive strands: it is argued on the one hand that insecurity leads to irresponsibility; but it is suggested too that insecurity – be it physical, financial or psychological – tends to make people careful, cautious and responsible. It is the latter argument which has been adopted by those attempting to account for the Japanese people's supposed reluctance 'to spend their hard-earned cash'.

Proponents of this view point to the failings of the country's social security system, suggesting that it left – as it leaves – the Japanese with little or no choice but to save for the future. These, and similar, arguments have been taken up by monetarists and right-wing commentators keen to stress the bracing effects of individual effort and sturdy self-reliance. However, one does not need to subscribe to the monetarist agenda to accept that the more people received – or expected to receive – from social security, the less they were likely to try to save; and that the less they received – or expected to receive – by way of social security benefits, the more they were likely to attempt to save.

There seems little doubt that the inverse relationship between consumption and saving was matched by a similarly inverse relationship between welfare and saving. It is undeniable that the state took little interest in the needs of the poor. So, while it is true that spending on social security increased substantially in real terms between the late nineteenth century and the late 1930s, it never accounted for more than 1.2 per cent of gross national product. As Lockwood pointed out more than forty years ago,

Japan lagged behind most industrial countries in the public provision of social security and consumer services, except elementary education. Apart from the case of agricultural subsidies during the interwar years, the State Treasury was never regarded seriously as an instrument for equalizing the distribution of income.... As a result, the inequalities and insecurities inherent in the economic situation were allowed to develop largely unchecked by political action. Personal security continued to depend mainly on family thrift; in no other way could one provide for the future.[58]

The debate about what it was that made the Japanese save so hard cuts to the core of the attempt to understand Japanese attitudes, assumptions and behaviour. It is a task which, as must be apparent by now, is shot through with difficulty and needs to be approached with considerable caution and humility. It is easy enough to suggest that it was a combination of economic insecurity and inadequate welfare which encouraged the Japanese to save so heavily. But this simply will not do. Other nationalities were economically insecure, other nationalities had to get by with inadequate welfare. But other nationalities did not save like the Japanese.

It is a question which has intrigued scholars and commentators for many years. Fortunately, part of the answer at least is to be found in the work of two North American economists, Williamson and de Bever. Indeed, by yoking together saving, accumulation and economic growth, they touch on the third of the issues that needs to be addressed when attempting to disentangle the relationship between consumption, saving and economic growth. They raise the possibility that Japan's distinctive pattern of economic growth may be accounted for by her low level of consumption and/or by her high level of savings.

According to Williamson and de Bever, the reason for Japan's high saving rate lay in a combination of demography and political economy. Concentrating primarily on the Meiji years, they suggest, *inter alia*, that low rates of population growth meant that families needed to spend only a relatively small proportion of their income on housing; and that government monetary, fiscal and foreign policies combined, on balance, to foster saving and accumulation. 'Did "state militarism" retard accumulation and growth?', they ask. 'In the short run, it most assuredly did since war-related "stop–go" explains most of Japanese long swing experience and investment "spurts".' However, they go on to argue that 'In the longer run, at least during late Meiji, militarism appeared to *foster* accumulation'.[59]

It is as clear an answer as one is likely to get. Insofar as it is possible to trace a relationship between consumption, saving and economic growth, all that can be said with any confidence is that Japan's high levels of individual and family saving contributed, in some measure at least, towards the country's rapid economic growth between 1868 and 1945.

Good luck or good planning?

This is the question that confronts everybody examining the economic history of modern Japan. Whether they are interested in the past for its own sake or in order to learn lessons for the present and the future, they will inevitably need to explain what has been, by any measure, an outstanding economic performance. How was it that between the late 1870s and the late 1930s, Japan, with so few natural advantages, was able to perform so well, and so much better than her neighbours and competitors? Was it really all because of her uniquely harmonious industrial relations, her unnaturally cautious consumers, and her wonderfully farsighted savers?

The truth, as one might suspect, is somewhat more complicated. It has been shown, it is hoped beyond all reasonable doubt, that growth was uneven, and that harmony and foresight were traditions invented and introduced in the particular economic and social circumstances prevailing in the years immediately following the First World War. What remains to be explained – beyond all reasonable doubt – is why it was in Japan that such traditions were invented, nurtured and celebrated.

Notes

1. **J. Woronoff**, *Japan As – Anything But – Number One*, Macmillan, 1990, pp. 12, 16, 82, 268.
2. **D.B. Smith**, *Japan Since 1945: The Rise of an Economic Superpower*, Macmillan, 1995, p. 4; **E. Pauer**, 'The Years Economic Historians Lost: Japan, 1850–1890', *Japan Forum*, 3, 1991.
3. **E.J. Hobsbawm** and **T. Ranger** (eds), *The Invention of Tradition*, Cambridge University Press, 1983.
4. **A. Waswo**, *Modern Japanese Society 1868–1994*, Oxford University Press, 1996, p. 36. Also **G. Stein**, *Made in Japan*, Methuen, 1935; **A. Gerschenkron**, *Economic Backwardness in Historical Perspective*, Harvard University Press, 1962; **K.D. Brown**, *Britain and Japan: A Comparative Economic and Social History since 1900*, Manchester University Press, 1998, ch. 3.
5. **W.J. Macpherson**, *The Economic Development of Japan 1868–1941*, Cambridge University Press, 1995, p. 3.
6. e.g. Stein, *Made in Japan*; **W.H. Chamberlain**, *Japan over Asia*, Duckworth, 1938; Smith, *Japan*, pp. 11–12; **G.C. Allen**, *A Short Economic History of Modern Japan 1867–1937*, Allen & Unwin, 1946, pp. 154–60; **T. Nakamura**, *Economic Growth in Prewar Japan*, Yale University Press, 1983, pp. 1–4.

7. J. Dower, *Japan in War and Peace: Essays on History, Culture and Race*, HarperCollins, 1993, p. 13; **E.S. Crawcour**, 'Industrialization and Technological Change, 1885–1920', in **P. Duus** (ed.), *The Cambridge History of Japan*, vol. 6, *The Twentieth Century*, Cambridge University Press, 1988, p. 388; **J.I. Bryan**, *Japan from Within: An Inquiry into the Political, Industrial, Commercial, Financial, Agricultural, Armamental and Educational Conditions of Modern Japan*, T. Fisher Unwin, 1924, pp. 39, 53.

8. Stein, *Made in Japan*; Chamberlain, *Japan*, chs 8, 12; **J.E. Hunter**, *The Emergence of Modern Japan: An Introductory History since 1853*, Longman, 1989, p. 127; **J. D'Autremer**, *The Japanese Empire and its Economic Conditions*, T. Fisher Unwin, 1910, p. 203.

9. **R. Minami**, *The Economic Development of Japan: A Quantitative Study*, Macmillan, 1986, pp. 47–8; Nakamura, *Economic Growth*, p. 8.

10. The 'traditional' sector is notoriously difficult to define, but 'In the main, it consists of family labour and at times it is based on a small business which is dependent on the engagement of a few.' See **T. Nakamura**, *Meiji Taishôki no Keizai*, Tokyo Daigaku Shuppankai, 1988, p. 177. Also pp. 182–3; **T. Nakamura**, *Nihon Keizai – sono seichô to kôzô*, Tokyo Daigaku Shuppankai, 1986, p. 90. Cf. Crawcour, 'Industrialization', p. 388.

11. The new *zaibatsu* such as Nissan developed rapidly in Korea and Manchuria, attracting a good deal of military and popular support. **T.A. Bisson**, 'Increase of Zaibatsu Predominance in Wartime Japan', *Pacific Affairs*, xviii, 1945; **H. Takeda**, *Zaibatsu no jidai*, Shinyôsha, 1996, pp. 197–8; **B. Eccleston**, *State and Society in Post-War Japan*, Polity, 1989, p. 13; Allen, *Economic History*, pp. 125–8; Smith, *Japan*, pp. 52–3; **E.O. Reischauer**, *The Japanese Today: Change and Continuity*, Belknap Press, 1977, pp. 305–7; Crawcour, 'Industrialization', p. 390.

12. T. Okazaki, 'Keikakukeizai to kigyô', in Tokyo Daigaku Shakaikagaku Kenkyûjo (ed.), *Gendai nihon shakai*, vol. 4, Tokyo Daigaku Shuppankai, 1991, pp. 367–8.

13. Macpherson, *Economic Development*, pp. 18–19; Crawcour, 'Industrialization', pp. 425, 431, 439.

14. *Japan Chronicle*, 20 January 1927; **W.M. Fruin**, *The Japanese Enterprise System: Competitive Strategies and Cooperative Structures*, Clarendon Press, 1992; Nakamura, *Economic Growth*.

15. 'Wholesale and Retail Trade in the Big Six Cities', *Tokyo Gazette*, January 1940, pp. 267–71; **M. Tatsuki**, 'The Rise of the Mass Market and Modern Retailers in Japan', *Business History*, 37, 1995, pp. 70–1.

16. Macpherson, *Economic Development*, p. 48; **M. Hane**, *Peasants, Rebels, and Outcastes: The Underside of Modern Japan*, Pantheon Books, 1982, pp. 21, 44, 177; **D. Irokawa**, *The Culture of the Meiji Period*, **M.B. Jansen** (ed. and trans.), Princeton University Press, 1985, pp. 31, 199, 221, 226–7, 274; **K. Yanagida** (ed.), *Japanese Manners and Customs in the Meiji Era*, **C.S. Terry** (trans.), Ôbunsha, p. 111.

17. Waswo, *Modern Japanese Society*, pp. 40–1, 68; **S.D. Barrington Moore Jnr**, *Social Origins of Dictatorship and Democracy: Lord and Peasant in the Making of the Modern World*, Penguin, 1967, pp. 275, 280; **W.G. Beasley**, *The Rise of Modern Japan: Political, Economic and Social Change since 1850*, Weidenfeld and Nicolson, 1990 (2nd ed., 1995), p. 197.

18. The impact of the land tax upon landlord–tenant relations remains highly contentious. It is claimed, for example, that the tax provided the Meiji government with the financial basis for industrial growth – and that Japan industrialised therefore on the backs of the peasants. **K. Yamamura**, 'The Meiji Land Tax Reform and Its

Effects', in **M.B. Jansen** and **G. Rozman** (eds), *Japan in Transition: From Tokugawa to Meiji*, Princeton University Press, 1986, pp. 49, 393; **R.J. Smethurst**, *Agricultural Development and Tenancy Disputes in Japan, 1870–1940*, Princeton University Press, 1986, pp. 53, 61, 66, 71, 75.

19. For a useful guide, see **E. Abe** and **R. Fitzgerald**, 'Japanese Economic Success: Timing, Culture, and Organizational Capability', *Business History*, 37, 1995.

20. Waswo, *Modern Japanese Society*, p. 39; Gershenkron, *Economic Backwardness*; Minami, *Economic Development*, pp. 8, 38–41; **T. Morris-Suzuki**, *The Technological Transformation of Japan: From the 17th to the 21st Century*, Cambridge University Press, 1996. Cf. Dower, *Japan*, p. 311; **E.H. Norman**, *Japan's Emergence as a Modern State*, Institute of Pacific Relations, 1940, pp. 208–9.

21. Dower, *Japan*, p. 26; Eccleston, *State and Society*, pp. 91–2; **S. Metzger-Court**, 'Towards National Integration: A Comparative Study of Economic Progress in the Prefectures of Wakayama, Okayama and Hiroshima during the Nineteenth Century', in **G. Daniels** (ed.), *Europe Interprets Japan*, Paul Norbury Publications, 1984, p. 19.

22. Minami, *Economic Development*, p. 8.

23. Macpherson, *Economic Development*, pp. 32–3.

24. Brown, *Britain and Japan*, p. 80.

25. Reischauer, *Japanese Today*, pp. 304–5.

26. Eccleston, *State and Society*, pp. 88–90.

27. **F.B. Tipton, Jr** 'Government Policy and Economic Development in Germany and Japan: A Skeptical Reevaluation', *Journal of Economic History*, 41, 1981, p. 139; **S. Yonekura**, *The Japanese Iron and Steel Industry, 1850–1990: Continuity and Discontinuity*, St Martin's Press, 1994.

28. *Japan Weekly Chronicle*, 19 August 1920; Hunter, *Modern Japan*, p. 11; Dower, *Japan*, p. 14; Macpherson, *Economic Development*, p. 26.

29. Tipton, 'Government Policy', p. 150; **K. Yamamura**, 'Success Illgotten? The Role of Meiji Militarism in Japan's Technological Progress', *Journal of Economic History*, 37, 1977, p. 113; **I. Hata**, 'Continental Expansion, 1905–1941', in Duus (ed.), *Cambridge History of Japan*, p. 299. Cf. **T. Nakamura**, 'Depression, Recovery, and War, 1920–1945', in Duus (ed.), *Cambridge History of Japan*, p. 470; **Y. Yasuba**, 'Did Japan Ever Suffer from a Shortage of Natural Resources before World War II?', *Journal of Economic History*, 56, 1996.

30. Minami, *Economic Development*, p. 417; **H. Odagiri** and **A. Gotô**, *Technology and Industrial Development in Japan: Building Capabilities by Learning, Innovation, and Public Policy*, Clarendon Press, 1996, p. x.

31. **F. Fukuyama**, *The End of History and the Last Man*, Hamish Hamilton, 1992, pp. 231–2; **F. Fukuyama**, *Trust: The Social Virtues and the Creation of Prosperity*, Hamish Hamilton, 1995; Abe and Fitzgerald, 'Economic Success'; **J.F. Wilson**, *British Business History, 1720–1994*, Manchester University Press, 1995, p. 82. See also *Japan Weekly Chronicle*, 6 March 1930.

32. Woronoff, *Japan*, p. 12; **H. Cortazzi**, *Modern Japan: A Concise Survey*, Macmillan, 1993, p. 131; Dower, *Japan*, p. 19; **S. Yonekawa**, 'Recent Writing on Japanese Economic and Social History', *Economic History Review*, 38, 1985, p. 116; Fukuyama, *Trust*, pp. 188–90.

33. The following discussion draws heavily upon **T. Matsumura**, 'Employers and Workers in Japan between the Wars', in **P. Mathias** and **J.A. Davis** (eds), *The Nature of Industrialization*, vol. 3, *Enterprise and Labour: From the Eighteenth Century to the Present*, Blackwell, 1996.

34. **A. Gordon**, *The Evolution of Labor Relations in Japan: Heavy Industry, 1853–1955*, Harvard University Press, 1985, p. xx; Dower, *Japan*, p. 115. Cf. **T.C. Smith**, 'The Right to Benevolence: Dignity and Japanese Workers, 1890–1920', *Comparative Studies in Society and History*, 26, 1984.

35. **K. Taira**, 'Economic Development, Labor Markets, and Industrial Relations in Japan, 1905–1955', in Duus (ed.), *Cambridge History of Japan*, pp. 624–36.

36. Taira, 'Economic Development', pp. 610, 644–6; Gordon, *Evolution*, p. 157; *Nippon Times*, 6 September 1943; **S.S. Large**, 'Perspectives on the Failure of the Labour Movement in Pre-War Japan', *Labour History*, 37, 1979.

37. *Japan Weekly Chronicle*, 9 September 1920, 2 January 1930, 13 March 1930. Also 15 July 1920, 1 May 1930.

38. **S. Yonekawa**, 'University Graduates in Japanese Enterprises before the Second World War', *Business History*, 26, 1984; **B.K. Marshall**, review of Gordon, *Evolution*, in *Journal of Japanese Studies*, 13, 1987, pp. 215–16.

39. Dower, *Japan*, pp. 114–16, 119.

40. Gordon, *Evolution*, pp. 241–2.

41. Dower, *Japan*, p. 115.

42. Waswo, *Modern Japanese Society*, pp. 63, 69–71; Dower, *Japan*, p. 114. There were also trade unions in small firms, and they were often dominated by the Communists.

43. Hane, *Peasants*, p. 194.

44. **E.P. Tsurumi**, *Factory Girls: Women in the Thread Mills of Meiji Japan*, Princeton University Press, 1990, pp. 194–8; **J. Hunter**, 'Japanese Women at Work, 1800–1920', *History Today*, May 1993.

45. See, for example, **D. Miller** (ed.), *Acknowledging Consumption: A Review of New Studies*, Routledge, 1995.

46. Macpherson, *Economic Development*, pp. 42–3; Taira, 'Economic Development', p. 634. Also **O. Saitô**, *Chingin to rôdô to seikatsusuijun*, Iwanami Shoten, 1998, p. 47.

47. According to Yanagida, changes in diet were in part attributable to military service. 'Young men who learned the flavour of rice during their military service took a yearning for it back home with them, and the grain came to be transported even to remote parts of the interior.' Yanagida (ed.), *Japanese Manners*, pp. 34–5; **S.B. Hanley**, 'The Material Culture: Stability in Transition', in Jansen and Rozman (eds), *Japan in Transition*, pp. 458–9.

48. The figures for calorific intake are, if anything, underestimates; the figures for average weight are not available for the years before 1918 or after 1937. **C. Mosk**, 'The Decline of Marital Fertility in Japan', *Population Studies: A Journal of Demography*, 33, 1979, p. 25.

49. Yanagida, *Japanese Manners*, p. 28.

50. Hanley, 'Material Culture', pp. 465–7; *Japan Times*, 22, 25 March 1897, 1 March 1910; *Nippon Times*, 13 June, 5, 11 September 1943, 11 June 1944; Minami, *Economic Development*, p. 375.

51. See, for example, **P. Deane** and **W.A. Cole**, *British Economic Growth 1688–1959: Trends and Structure*, Cambridge University Press, 1962, pp. 332–3.

52. **W.O. Lee**, *Social Change and Educational Problems in Japan, Singapore and Hong Kong*, Macmillan, 1991, p. 44.

53. **J. Morris**, *Traveller from Tokyo*, The Book Club, 1945, pp. 112–13; **W.W. Lockwood**, *The Economic Development of Japan: Growth and Structural Change 1868–1938*, Oxford University Press, 1955, pp. 419–22. An interesting study of dietary changes

in Chôshû in the late Tokugawa to early Meiji periods is found in: **S. Nishikawa**, 'Grain Consumption: The Case of Chôshû', in Jansen and Rozman (eds), *Japan in Transition*, pp. 421–46.

54. Reference mislaid.
55. Cortazzi, *Modern Japan*, p. 135; Eccleston, *State and Society*, p. 45; **B. Emmott**, *The Sun also Sets: Why Japan will not be Number One*, Simon & Schuster, 1989, p. 234.
56. **K. Yoshihara**, 'The Growth Rate as a Determinant of the Saving Ratio', *Hitotsubashi Journal of Economics*, 12, 1972, p. 70. Also *Japan Weekly Chronicle*, 9 September 1920; Minami, *Economic Development*, p. 203.
57. **C. Gluck**, *Japan's Modern Myths: Ideology in the Late Meiji Period*, Princeton University Press, 1985, p. 259. e.g. *Japan Chronicle*, 10 April 1919; Eccleston, *State and Society*, pp. 99–100.
58. Lockwood, *Economic Development*, p. 285. Also *Japan Weekly Chronicle*, 15 July 1920; Minami, *Economic Development*, p. 408.
59. **J.G. Williamson** and **L.J. de Bever**, 'Saving, Accumulation and Modern Economic Growth: The Contemporary Relevance of Japanese History', *Journal of Japanese Studies*, 4, 1978, p. 164.

5

Education, religion and the media

Those attempting to understand Japan's political history, international relations and economic development often turn with something like relief to education, religion and the media. These were the means, many believe, by which the state shaped attitudes and behaviour, the means by which those in power were able to persuade the population at large to accept totalitarianism, dictatorship and emperor-worship, to support overseas adventures and imperial expansion, and to work hard, spend cautiously and save assiduously. Education, religion and the media provide, it is suggested, one way at least of understanding attitudes and behaviour which otherwise appear to be almost inexplicable.

Most of these commentators place particular emphasis on the role played by religion and education. 'In Japan, as elsewhere', it has been claimed, 'the ruling class have long viewed both religion and education as vehicles for furthering the purposes of the state . . . religious practice and formal instruction have been manipulated by those in power to enhance their own influence and that of their administration.' Others agree. 'Education', it is said, 'has been the chief tool in shaping national uniformity. In prewar Japan one could know that on a certain day every sixth-grade child throughout the land would be learning the same Chinese characters, the same historical facts, and the same arithmetic rules.' One or two scholars, however, choose to emphasise the importance of the media. Huffman's research is the result, he tells us, of twenty years studying the late nineteenth and early twentieth-century press.

> Without denying the importance of education, political movements, or economic transformation, it contends that no single institution did more to create a modern citizenry than the Meiji newspaper press, a collection of highly diverse, private voices that provided increasing numbers of readers – many millions, in fact, by the end of Meiji – with both a fresh daily picture of the world and a changing sense of their own place in that world.[1]

Huffman's argument immediately brings us up against a problem that confronts – and frequently confounds – those attempting to explain, rather than simply describe, the attitudes and behaviour of the Japanese. This is the age-old difficulty of ascribing cause and effect, of determining the impact, in this case, that education, religion and the media had upon popular attitudes and behaviour. It is tempting to believe that, if teachers, priests or journalists advocated particular attitudes and actions, and if large numbers of people thought and behaved in these ways, then the former must have caused the latter. But this can be both condescending and illogical: it is condescending in that it suggests that people were merely the passive victims of forces beyond their control, and it is illogical insofar as it suggests that they did not have their own reasons for thinking and behaving as they did.

Accordingly, it is the purpose of this chapter to examine these issues in something like the detail they deserve. It will be suggested that, while it is easy enough to show that those involved professionally in education, religion and the media made serious, and increasingly determined, efforts to promote particular ideas and values, it is enormously difficult to decide whether their efforts had anything like the impact that is commonly supposed.

Education

It was shown when discussing politics and political systems that those who came to power in 1868 made it one of their priorities to establish a system of education which would further the aims of the new state. There is the danger, of course, of exaggerating the coherence of educational policy-making (and of underestimating the broader 'educational' function performed by the family, neighbourhood associations, the armed forces, labour discipline and companies' in-house training programmes). However, there is no denying that the system which was put in place from the 1870s onwards was both highly centralised and tightly controlled. Its aims, it has been seen, were to enable Japan to compete with her rivals in the West, to encourage meritocratic competition and to bind the nation together by inculcating in the minds of the population unquestioning obedience to the emperor and those who ruled in his name.[2]

Centralisation and control

The new system operated at three levels, with three different types of institution: elementary schools, middle schools and universities. For the twenty years or so following the Fundamental Code of 1872, those in government concentrated upon putting in place a comprehensive system of elementary education, with all children in the country required to complete four years (and from 1907 six years) at primary school. From the 1890s onwards, those formulating policy directed their attention much more towards secondary and university provision. The system they established was highly selective: those children (the boys at least) whose parents wished – and were able to pay for – them to continue their studies had a number of choices open to them. They could spend five years in a middle school or a lower technical school, three years in a higher school or a higher technical school, and then three or four years at university depending on the subject to be studied. At the apex of the pyramid stood Tokyo Imperial University, below which were the other imperial universities, a small group of private institutions and eventually a much larger number of less well known – and less well regarded – universities and women's colleges.[3]

There was considerable debate about the direction educational policy should take, but those responsible for the new system were very much agreed about what it was intended to achieve: a committed and effective workforce, and a loyal and enthusiastic citizenry. The system, like so many others, was tailored closely to what the country's leaders saw as its economic needs. The first task was the modernisation of the curriculum. By stripping the curriculum of such 'impractical pursuits as the study of obscure Chinese characters . . . [and] reading ancient texts which are difficult to make out', education, according to the 'civilisation and enlightenment' intellectual Fukuzawa, was to become the foundation for national progress through the adoption of Western techniques.

> Japan's civilization, itself barely attained by our ancestors, is no match with that of the West. We must therefore lament our own inadequacies to follow the ways of the West. . . . We have not yet reached the level of the West in the areas of scholarship, business, and law. But modern civilization is chiefly built on the foundation of these three areas of endeavor. Without sufficient progress in these areas, a nation's independence can clearly not be maintained. But in Japan, not one of these spheres has reached maturity.[4]

In accordance with the widely agreed view that education should consist of 'practical learning' which was 'closer to ordinary human needs', the authorities put in place a system designed to create a huge number of elementary school graduates ready to work at routine tasks in industry and the armed forces. It was also designed to produce a modest number of middle school graduates able to serve as managers and technicians, and a tiny number of university graduates destined for leading positions in industry, government and the professions. The reasons for the meritocratic emphasis were made clear by Fukuzawa,

> I find that Japanese civilization will advance only after we sweep away the old spirit that permeates the minds of the people. But it cannot be swept away by either government decree or private admonition. Some persons must take the initiative in doing things in order to show the people where their aims should lie.[5]

In the intellectual climate of the 1870s, progress based on meritocratic elitism was seen by many political leaders as the best way of promoting egalitarian – and even democratic – openness in a society that hitherto had 'suffered under despotic rule'.

> If the people pursue learning, understand the principle of things, and follow the way of modern civilization, then the laws of the government will also become more generous and compassionate . . . if people want to avoid tyrannical government, they must immediately set their mind to the pursuit of learning, to elevate their own talents and virtues to a position of equality with the government.[6]

As the Meiji reforms became more established, the authorities, not surprisingly, became less comfortable with this 'spirit of independence of a people'. From the 1880s, when a reaction set in against the 'civilisation and enlightenment' advocacy of wholesale Westernisation, enormous effort was devoted to ensuring the inculcation of Japanese values acceptable to those in power. An 1879 pronouncement issued from the imperial household in the name of the emperor made it clear that there should be a return to the Confucian ideals of piety, obedience and benevolence. Government control was strengthened, and in 1881 the Ministry of Education issued a Memorandum for Elementary School Teachers which explained that 'Loyalty to the Imperial House, love of country, filial piety towards parents, respect for superiors, faith in friends, charity towards inferiors, and respect for oneself constitute the Great Path of human morality.' The increasing emphasis placed on Confucian-style patriotism in the 1880s found its ultimate expression in the Imperial Rescript on Education that was issued in 1890. On the instructions of the Ministry of Education under Inoue, a copy of the Rescript was placed in every state school alongside pictures of the emperor and empress.

> Know Ye, Our subjects:
> Our Imperial Ancestors have founded Our Empire on a basis broad and everlasting and have deeply and firmly implanted virtue. Our subjects ever united in loyalty and filial piety have from generation to generation illustrated

the beauty thereof. This is the glory of the fundamental character of Our Empire, and herein also lies the source of Our education. Ye, Our subjects, be filial to your parents, affectionate to your brothers and sisters; as husbands and wives be harmonious, as friends be true; bear yourselves in modesty and moderation; extend your benevolence to all; pursue learning and cultivate arts, and thereby develop intellectual faculties and perfect moral powers; furthermore advance public good and promote common interests; always respect the Constitution and observe the laws; should emergency arise, offer yourselves courageously to the State; and thus guard and maintain the prosperity of Our Imperial Throne coeval with heaven and earth. So shall ye not only be Our good and faithful subjects, but render illustrious the best traditions of your forefathers.[7]

Although the principles of the Rescript remained in place until the end of the Second World War, they were subtly interpreted and reinterpreted, in line with changing political, diplomatic and military circumstances. At the turn of the century, there could still be found an officially sanctioned ' "liberal interpretation" of the Rescript and a favourable attitude to many Western political, ethical, and intellectual values'. Proponents of the so-called 'New Education' or 'Free Education' stressed the need for less rigid thinking and established private schools to put their ideas into practice.

Nonetheless, during the Sino-Japanese War, patriotic anecdotes were compiled in order to strengthen nationalistic feeling and, by the close of the Russo-Japanese War, the tenets of the Rescript had been cast as immutable, sacred truths. Indeed, one woman who attended a girls' school in the southern city of Kagoshima in the late 1910s and early 1920s recalled that the document was considered so sacred that it was kept inside a fire-proof shrine outside of the school building, and that, whenever one passed it, one was expected to bow. Although all students were required to memorise and understand the Rescript, it was only read by the principal of the school at formal assemblies commemorating events such as graduation and National Foundation Day.[8]

With the host of external and internal crises in the 1930s, the Rescript was thrust once again to the forefront of educational thinking. In 1933, for instance, the Education Department introduced a plan 'to foster sound popular ideas'. It was agreed at a conference held at the premier's official residence that, 'In the appointment of teachers and professors from the primary school upwards, special regard should be paid to their personality, refraining from choosing such persons as harbour dangerous ideas'. It was emphasised that 'special importance should be attached to the teaching of history, so that the spirit of the foundation of the country and the national idea may be inculcated'.[9]

In response to the many crises of the 1930s, and a vociferous debate over the nature of Japanese constitutionalism in 1935, the Ministry of Education released its *Cardinal Principles of the National Polity* in 1937. This stressed that the way to serve the emperor was to make the 'minds of one hundred million people unite as one'. Two years later prime minister Hiranuma used his first speech to the Diet to press on the country 'the necessity of renovating the educational system so as to enhance the national spirit'. One result of these initiatives was the National Schools' Law of 1941 which demanded that physical improvement, the elevation of national spirit, the cultivation of scientific intelligence and the refinement of moral sentiment should be incorporated into the teaching of all subjects in the elementary school curriculum. Another was the establishment in 1943 of the Student War-Time Mobilization System, regulations which were designed, as their name suggests, to recruit university students to the armed forces.[10]

It is easy to overestimate the competence of the teaching profession, it is difficult to know how such legislation was interpreted and implemented, and it is impossible to be sure exactly what went on in classrooms, laboratories and lecture theatres up and down the country. But what evidence there is suggests that most school teachers did their best to ensure that the wishes of central government were put into practice. Western visitors were invariably struck by the discipline, and later the militarism, of the Japanese system. When Isabella Ford visited rural Japan in the late 1870s, she was both impressed by the importance attached to education and intrigued by the rote learning practised and the unquestioning obedience of the children. She never, she claimed, came across 'a child troublesome or disobedient'. When Erwin Baelz attended a school celebration just after the turn of the century, he too was struck by the way in which discipline and patriotism were 'inculcated into the Japanese from their earliest years'. Indeed, when John Morris taught in Tokyo in the late 1930s and early 1940s, he reported that militarism was even more deeply embedded in the city's schools and universities than the government's legislation would lead one to believe.

> The amount of time devoted to military instruction is supposed to be about five or six hours a week, but 'special' periods of instruction are now often added, usually allotted to one or other of the foreign teachers, or at some time when the students would otherwise be studying what in the senior officer's opinion is some unnecessary subject, literature or philosophy for instance.[11]

The severity of education in the 1930s and early 1940s is corroborated by those who were teachers and pupils. For example, the southern island of Kyûshû was known for its traditions of military prowess and male dominance. In one school at least,

> Students were not permitted to wear shoes and stockings. . . . They were not allowed to wear overcoats either . . .
>
> The teachers, who wore shoes and stockings, explained this would conserve materials and enable students to sympathize with the soldiers who were fighting in China . . .
>
> None the less it was a bitter experience, and they found it hard to concentrate on lessons when their frozen feet were paining them. When it was below freezing . . . the older pupils were posted to record the names of those who ran, and they were called before the teachers and scolded . . .

However, 'this was only part of their training'. Each day, students were led by the physical director in a 'cold water rubbing exercise'. Stripped to their underpants, students rubbed themselves with towels which they had earlier dipped in cold water and which, in winter, were often frozen completely stiff. Students also received biweekly training in mastication, the idea being that 'careful chewing would conserve food and aid digestion'. The following instructions were given over the loudspeaker.

> Are you ready? Put a bit of relish and rice into your mouth. Move it to the left side. Now chew it. One, two, three. . . . Now move it to the right side. Now chew it. One, two, three. . . . Now swallow. Now put some more into your mouth from your lunch box. Put your hands on your knees. Straighten up. Ready?[12]

It is true that education in Kyûshû was particularly severe. Nevertheless, it appears that all around the country, the curriculum was militarised, text books censored and corporal punishment more or less endemic. Discipline was enforced by beating and slapping, and by forcing children to run, stand still, carry some heavy object or sit in an uncomfortable position until they were exhausted.

> For example, on the occasion of worshipping the Imperial Palace or worshipping in the hall of enshrinement, one of the girls bowed and then threw her head aside in order to remove the hair that was covering her eyes. This was something that was strictly forbidden because it was extremely irreverent. But on the spur of the moment, one of the girls broke the rule. It was said that, 'The teacher required the "collective responsibility" of all the pupils. The pupils were forced to make a line, and the teacher walked past the line slapping the face of each pupil with a slipper.'[13]

Attendance, dissatisfaction and self-justification

The establishment of the Meiji system of education, the interest taken in it by the emperor, and the attempts that were made to inculcate imperial

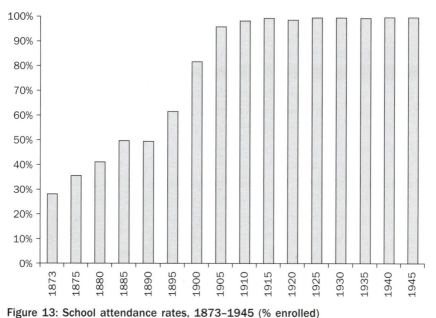

Figure 13: School attendance rates, 1873–1945 (% enrolled)

Source: Ministry of Education, *The Role of Education in the Social and Economic Development of Japan*, Japanese National Commission for UNESCO, 1966, p. 64.

and military values all bear testimony to the drive and determination of those directing policy between 1868 and 1945. Yet care should be taken to exaggerate neither the speed nor the success with which the new system was put into place. The Meiji ideal of 'no family without primary education' took many decades to achieve – see Figure 13. In the mid-1880s fully 50 per cent of children were not yet attending school, and as late as the early 1900s nearly 10 per cent of boys and almost 30 per cent of girls of primary school age still had to be enrolled. For many years, parents had to pay for their children's education, there was a shortage of school buildings, the quality of teachers was poor (with actors, Buddhist and Shinto priests pressed into service) and the idea of securing individual advance by means of education was slow to take root. It was not until the 1920s, fifty years and more after the Fundamental Code, that virtually every child in the country was finally receiving an elementary school education.[14]

Moreover, for many years after the Restoration only a tiny proportion of those attending elementary school went on to middle school or to university. In 1885, for instance, fewer than one elementary school pupil in a hundred studied at middle school, and of this tiny minority fewer than a half went on to university. It was not until the turn of the century, when government priorities had begun to change, that the number of children taking advantage of post-compulsory education started to increase. It is true that the number of university students remained very small indeed, accounting for just 1 per cent of their age group in 1915, and 3 per cent in 1935. But when attendance at middle schools began to increase, it did so dramatically: the proportion of elementary school pupils going on to secondary education leapt from one in a hundred in 1885 to one in six by 1913, and one in five by the end of the Second World War.[15]

The delay in enforcing attendance at elementary school, and the continuing imbalance between the numbers receiving elementary, middle and university education must inevitably throw into question the claims that are made for the efficacy of the Japanese system, and for the impact that it had upon popular attitudes and behaviour. If the case is to be made for education explaining the way in which the Japanese thought and behaved, it must be done on the basis of what was taught from the late nineteenth century onwards, and on the basis primarily of what was taught in the country's elementary schools.

It is a case that can be made, but not without considerable difficulty. It must be conceded that late nineteenth-century intellectuals and press commentators were sometimes highly critical of the education which was provided for the nation's children. When Tokutomi, the founder of the weekly journal *Kokumin no Tomo* (*People's Friend*) visited a third-grade ethics class in 1893, he was shocked by what he found.

> *Teacher*: Why must we be loyal to the Emperor?
> *Pupil*: Because the Emp . . . (He stopped, at a loss; only titters were heard)
> *Teacher*: Because we are indebted to the Emperor. . . . Now why are we indebted to him?
> *Pupils*: (mumbling and looking around at each other)
> *Teacher*: Coming here to school, being safely at home – You owe all these things to the Emperor.
> *Tokutomi*: Children, you always hear about what is good and bad. What kinds of things are good?
> *Pupils*: To practice loyalty and filial piety.
> *Tokutomi*: (silent, appalled at the mechanical response).[16]

A few years later, the *Nippon* and the *Japan Times* led a vigorous campaign against the Department of Education, arguing that its policies had failed to produce the results that the country required. Education, they claimed, lacked a moral dimension with the result, *inter alia*, that there was 'growing subordination among the student body'. The system, they alleged, also involved too much cramming, so that pupils were left physically and emotionally stunted. 'Many intelligent children, giving every promise of a bright future, are in this way converted into physical and intellectual pygmies, with a store of unassorted knowledge, but quite helpless to turn it to good account for purposes of practical life.'[17]

In a few cases, even the patriotic and militaristic values around which so much of the ethics curriculum centred came in for criticism. In 1903, for example, the *Yorozu Chôhô* newspaper carried this report by the leading Christian Uchimura:

> Those who excite the soldiers to attack foreign enemies will in the end become themselves the ones the soldiers attack. The Japanese who made the soldiers attack China have, for the past ten years, come to be the ones who have suffered, devoting most of their wealth to this military training they so revere. . . . Japan will be transformed seemingly into one giant barrack where, instead of rice, the people will eat saltpeter, and instead of wheat, they will gather sabres![18]

This distinction between speaker and audience, between what teachers taught and what pupils learned is crucial, of course, in judging the success of any educational policy and any educational system. It is a distinction that is particularly important – but can prove particularly opaque – when attempting to evaluate the effects of the militarisation of Japanese education which accelerated during the 1930s and early 1940s. There are two major difficulties. It cannot be assumed that those who attended school and university at this time were uncritical of the teaching they received. However, it cannot be assumed either that those who were critical in later years of the teaching they received did not have pressing, albeit non-pedagogic, reasons for expressing dissatisfaction with the way in which they had been educated.

Nevertheless, there is some evidence of dissatisfaction which is untainted by hindsight and self-justification. There were more examples than one would imagine of teachers and pupils challenging the system that was imposed upon them. In 1891, Uchimura resigned from his high school after being accused of bowing his head – rather than bowing – to the Imperial Rescript on Education. In 1927, several elementary teachers were accused of not respecting the emperor because they had held a party while he was ill, and six years later a number of elementary school teachers in Nara prefecture were arrested for what were described as 'offences of thought'. In fact, in 1935, the Japan Cultural Association announced that it would be holding a course of lectures for the 470 elementary school teachers who had been converted from Communism since being arrested for ideological offences.[19]

The students could be just as disruptive. In the early 1920s, middle and high school students, like the girls from the Female Normal School in Shimane prefecture, struck for the dismissal of unpopular teachers (and for the reinstatement of those who were popular). By the end of the decade, protests were more likely to arise over policy issues like the prohibition on studying political theory. Sometimes, of course, a number of concerns coalesced. In 1930, for example, the pupils at one high school went on strike because they wanted their termly exams to be postponed and, when this dispute was settled, they rebelled, it was reported, 'against the military training given to them'. When English lecturer John Morris described pupils' reactions to the militarisation of Tokyo schools between 1938 and 1942, he expressed himself in unequivocal terms: 'I have no hesitation in saying that military training is the most unpopular feature of Japanese school life. Every student I knew loathed it and would seize eagerly upon the slightest opportunity to avoid attendance.' Morris's observations are corroborated by a primary school teacher from Kyûshû.

> The indoctrination in boys' schools was more unremitting than in those for girls, and they were under the direct control of military officers who used harsh measures to repress the slightest deviation. [My] brother reacted more and more against this and was insubordinate at school and unruly at home.[20]

However, even the most forceful assertion of dissatisfaction emanating from ex-pupils is open, almost inevitably, to charges of hindsight and self-justification. It was always tempting for those brought up during this period to blame what was seen after the war as unacceptable adult behaviour onto the evils of their childhood education. Kojima, for instance, attended school during the late 1920s and early 1930s, went on to university, joined the imperial army in 1939 and served in China where he admitted that he was responsible for spreading cholera, murdering women and children, torturing prisoners of war and using them for bayonet practice. 'Yet', as he reflected thirty years later, 'when we were doing these things, we had no sense of guilt or of doing anything wrong. It was for the emperor – or for the country!' The passage in which he attempts to explain his behaviour and lack of guilt is worth quoting at some length.

> We were born and raised in a society of emperorism. A person's absolute responsibility above the army and government was to the emperor. The emperor was a living deity. The emperor's command was supreme and controlled the entire country. We were told how we must serve the emperor, how we should behave toward our parents, how we should behave toward our teachers,

and how we should behave toward our siblings. We were taught that Japan is a sacred country, that the people of Japan are a superior race, that the people of China, Korea, Southeast Asia, and Russia were all inferior races, and the superior races must govern them. And, by doing so, we would bring them happiness. This was the cause to which Japan must devote itself. . . . This was our prewar education.[21]

Makise makes a similar point. 'As loyal subjects of the Emperor, we thought it was prestigious to send our sons and husbands to war. But at the same time and at the bottom of our hearts we did not want them to go. Why, then, did we let our love for our sons and husbands succumb to our sense of loyalty to our country?'

> I entered the primary school immediately after the Sino-Japanese War [1894–95]. In those days, most of the children wished to become soldiers, and I felt sorry to be a girl and not to be able to become a soldier. . . . We unquestioningly accepted what was taught at school. We were not supposed to ask why when the myth of the gods and goddesses was taught as an integral part of our national history. The children who simply believed in what the elders told them were the exemplary pupils. School education nurtured the mind to accept the wars that the government had made ever since the Sino-Japanese War. The high school children today do not know this shameful history of our school education. That is why they do not know why their mothers were blindly driven into the last war. It was the education that produced the ignorant mothers.[22]

Such cases signal the difficulty of judging what went through the minds of these generations of pupils as they took their oaths to the emperor, listened to their teachers, learned their lessons, did their drills, tackled their homework and talked to their friends. It is more difficult still to decide whether what went through their minds was internalised, remembered and acted upon in years to come. It is well nigh impossible to distinguish what was remembered in years to come from all the many other influences that crowded in upon the members of these much reviled generations during their formative years.[23]

Education, behaviour and attitudes

The evidence which is available is simply too consistent – and insistent – for it to be ignored. It suggests that, insofar as it is possible to generalise about the relationship between education, behaviour and attitudes, it is safe to conclude that the system established in Japan following the Restoration did a great deal to stimulate literacy, a great deal to encourage discipline and hard work, and a great deal to foster a sense of national superiority.

The Meiji state built effectively upon pre-Restoration levels of literacy. The increase in the number of children attending elementary school led directly, though not inevitably, to an increase in the proportion of the population that was able to read and write. Reading was easier, of course, than writing, and it has been calculated that, by the turn of the century, 94 per cent of the male population and 82 per cent of the female population were able to read. There is other evidence besides. It was found in 1912, for example, that well over 90 per cent of military recruits in the Osaka region were able to pass the literacy tests they sat, and that practically 70 per cent of a sample of working-class households in Tokyo took a daily newspaper as well as weekly and monthly magazines. By the 1920s, it is commonly accepted, the full impact of mass literacy was being felt across both urban and rural Japan.[24]

However, the spread of literacy, like the attainment of near-universal attendance, was not realised as smoothly as these statistics might suggest. As Figure 14 shows, there were prominent regional variations: in the

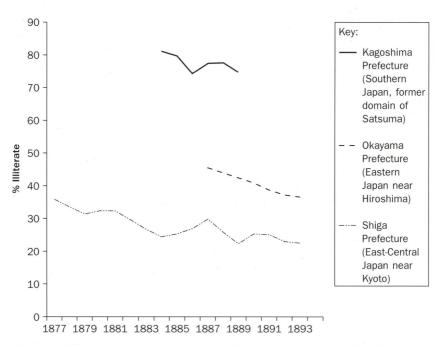

Figure 14: Illiteracy rates in selected areas in the early to mid-Meiji period, 1877–93

Note: Based on the results of tests measuring individuals' ability to write their names.

Source: Ministry of Education, *The Role of Education in the Social and Economic Development of Japan*, Japanese National Commission for UNESCO, 1966, p. 69.

1. Commodore Perry meets the Imperial Commissioners at Yokohama, 8th March 1854. Photo: Peter Newark's Pictures.

2. The Meiji Emperor (1868–1912).
Photo: Peter Newark's Pictures.

3. Russo-Japanese War: Battle of Tsushima, 1905.
Photo: Peter Newark's Military Pictures.

4. Tokyo after the Great Kantō earthquake of 1923.
Photo: Peter Newark's Historical Pictures.

5. The "new" Tokyo 1933, ten years after the Great Kantô earthquake of 1923: view of Ginza. Photo: Peter Newark's Pictures.

6. Women in 1929 making demands for voting power during municipal elections in Tokyo.
Photo: Peter Newark's Pictures.

7. A woman practising calligraphy in traditional surroundings, 1933.
Photo: Peter Newark's Pictures.

8. Women cotton workers at Toyoda, 1937.
Photo: Peter Newark's Pictures.

9. Japanese troops march through the Great Wall of China following the Japanese
occupation of Manchuria.
Photo: Peter Newark's Pictures.

10. The Japanese air attack on Pearl Harbor, Hawaii, 7th December 1941.
Photo: Peter Newark's Military Pictures.

11. Hideki Tôjô, wartime leader and prime minister from 1941 to 1944.
Photo: Peter Newark's Military Pictures.

12. Japanese soldiers show their respect for the Emperor's dead warriors at the Yasukuni Shrine, Tokyo, April 1944. Photo: Peter Newark's Military Pictures.

mid-1880s, for example, illiteracy rates – measured by the inability of those tested even to write their own names – varied from fewer than 30 per cent in Shiga Prefecture to well over 70 per cent in Kagoshima Prefecture. Indeed, when illiteracy rates did eventually drop, they did not necessarily do so in a straightforward linear fashion: an improvement in figures one year was often followed, in the next, by a deterioration in standards.

It is not easy to show therefore that it was the educational system which was responsible for the Japanese people's internationally acclaimed discipline and hard work. Yet education must certainly take some of the responsibility. It was not just that individual teachers and lecturers, the curriculum they followed and textbooks they used, all set enormous store by authority and acquiescence. It was that the system itself epitomised authority and acquiescence; as Mori, one of the architects of the Japanese educational system and Education Minister in the first modern cabinet, explained, education was undertaken 'on behalf of the state, not on behalf of the individual student'.[25]

There is little doubt either that Japan's educational system – like those in many other countries – did a good deal to strengthen popular notions of national identity and national superiority. As Mori explained in 1887, the state had a responsibility to teach children to think in the approved way: 'the aim of education is to cultivate persons who can be of service to the State and nation'. The authorities worked hard to put policy into practice. Ten years later, in the wake of the Sino-Japanese War, schoolchildren no longer studied the glories of Chinese civilisation, learning instead about Japanese military and moral superiority over the 'smelly', 'cowardly' and 'despicable' ' "Chinamen" . . . from "pigtail land" who "ran from battle disguised in women's clothes" '.[26]

Throughout the decade preceding the Russo-Japanese War, the educational system played a paramount role in the elaboration, and dissemination, of conceptions of the nation as what became known as the 'family state'. It was argued that, through their ancestry from the gods and goddesses, all Japanese were related to each other and the supreme patriarch, the emperor. Acts of filial piety towards one's parents were an expression of patriotism (and vice versa). The children's story, *A Sailor's Mother*, made the point.

> It was the time of the War of 1894–95. One day on our ship, the *Takachiho*, a sailor was weeping as he read a letter written in a woman's handwriting. . . . [It read]:
> 'You said you did not fight in the battle of Feng-tao, and you did not accomplish much in the August 10ᵗʰ attack at Weihaiwei either. I am very disappointed in you. Why did you go into battle? Wasn't it to sacrifice your life to

repay the emperor? The people in the village are good to me and offer help all the time, saying kindly: "It must be hard on you having your only son off fighting for the country. Please don't hesitate to tell us if there is anything we can do." Whenever I see their faces, I am reminded of your cowardice and I feel as if my heart will break. So every day I go to the shrine of [the god] Hachiman and pray that you will distinguish yourself in battle. Of course, I am human, too, and cannot at all bring myself to hate my own child. Please try to understand my feelings as I write this letter . . .'

An integral part of the ethics curriculum, *A Sailor's Mother* was retold time and time again and memorised by generations of schoolchildren before the Second World War.[27]

Each revision of the curriculum saw a shift from individualism and internationalism towards patriotism and the family. In accordance with the resolution passed by the 1918 Extraordinary Commission on Education, the aims of Japanese education were to be redirected:

Since the Restoration Japan has been so intent upon the importation of Western science and systems that she has failed fully to consider the merits and demerits before adopting them. . . . Although . . . her civilization has been enhanced and her national wealth and strength have witnessed a considerable growth, the indiscriminate adoption of Western science and systems has had the effect of disturbing the popular sentiments and seriously impairing the fine traditions of the country. In removing these evils of the day, nothing is more important than to fix a common goal for which the people shall strive, and such a goal may be found in an endeavor to develop and protect Japan's peculiar civilization.[28]

The responsibility for inculcating nationalistic ideals assumed greater prominence still during the 1930s and early 1940s. Teaching concentrated upon Japan, with even young pupils subjected to a considerable volume of militaristic material. It has been calculated that, by this period, 8 to 10 per cent of the reading matter used in the lower classes of elementary schools dealt with military themes. It usually took the form of stories about the armed forces, the Greater East Asia Co-Prosperity Sphere and the occupied territories of Manchukuo and South-East Asia, and carried titles such as 'Flag signals', 'The Classification of Warships', 'Playing at Soldiers' and 'My brother goes off to the front'. The final examination of a 1941 ethics course asked:

Why are loyalty and filial piety united in our country?
. . .

Discuss the necessity for overseas expansion.
Why is Japan's constitution superior to those of other nations?
What kind of spirit is required to overcome the present difficulties facing the nation?

As Buruma explains, 'Even geography lessons were harnessed to the imperial cause.' In one textbook, the shape of Japan was described as 'not without significance. We appear to be standing in the vanguard of Asia advancing bravely into the Pacific. At the same time we appear ready to defend the Asian continent from outside attack.'[29]

Such efforts had their effect. In fact, some of those who attended school and university during the 1930s and early 1940s have attempted to evaluate the relationship between militaristic education and popular ideology in the light both of their personal experiences and their academic training. Iritani, for example, was a schoolboy during the Second World War, and found himself evacuated to Nagano, in the centre of Honshû, between the summer of 1944 and the beginning of 1945. Forty-five years later, the publication of his book, *Group Psychology of the Japanese in Wartime*, marked the culmination of his attempts to understand how it was that his contemporaries could have behaved as they did. His conclusion is that the work of the elementary schools was of crucial significance. 'Education in prewar Japan imbued the people with nationalist fervour. They believed themselves to be blessed because they belonged to the "Great Japanese Empire".'[30]

Ienaga agrees. The best-known of all campaigners against the silences and distortions of Japanese textbooks, he has fought for more than thirty years to assuage the guilt he feels for not protesting when his pupils went off to fight during the war. He too is convinced about the relationship between education and nationalism. He recalls the story about a schoolboy who was squeamish about having to dissect a live frog. 'Why are you crying about the lousy frog?', demanded his teacher. 'When you grow up you have to kill a hundred, two hundred Chinks.' The conclusion he reaches is that,

> In modern Japan, when everybody was able to receive compulsory education, and its contents were totally uniform, there was no escape from the fact that a greater part of the people were inculcated with a uniform way of thinking . . .
>
> Moreover, in prewar Japan, when the majority of the people started their lives after finishing elementary school, the fact that the textbooks used at elementary schools were authorized by the government was an extremely serious matter.[31]

Those familiar with developments in other parts of the world will not be surprised – though they may be shocked – by the cynicism and determination with which the rulers of Japan used education as a means of pursuing their broader political, military, economic and social objectives. They will recognise that the modern Japanese state's interest in mass education, like the early Victorian obsession with working-class education in Britain, is best understood as a concern about authority and power, about the assertion and re-assertion of control.

> This concern was expressed in an enormously ambitious attempt to determine, through the capture of educational means, the patterns of thought, sentiment and behaviour of the working class. Supervised by its trusty teacher, surrounded by its playground wall, the school was to raise a new race of working people – respectful, cheerful, hard-working, loyal, pacific and religious.[32]

Religion

Even those familiar with developments in other parts of the world may well be taken aback by the cynicism and determination with which the rulers of Japan attempted to adapt religious practices to secular ends. Of course, the study of religion, religious belief and religious behaviour invariably raises issues that are extremely difficult to disentangle. There are several ways, after all, of defining a religion, several ways in which it is possible to belong to a religious organisation, and several functions that a religious organisation can perform for its members other than providing them with access to the supernatural. These are issues which, it will be seen, can prove particularly difficult to deal with in the case of late nineteenth and early twentieth-century Japan.

Nonetheless, considerable progress can be made. It can certainly be shown that those who were in power between 1868 and 1945 did their best to create a new religious tradition that was designed deliberately to further the aims of the state. Moreover, it can be suggested with some confidence that, although they were far less successful than in their educational initiatives, the new religious tradition they invented helped to shape the ways in which the Japanese thought about themselves and about the world in which they lived.

Shinto and State Shinto

The rulers of the Meiji state were determined to use religion, like education, as a means of binding together the nation in obedience to the emperor and those acting on his behalf. The vehicle they selected was State Shinto. It is not difficult to see why: Shinto was hundreds of years old and seemed to provide the one indigenous belief system that could be used to effect and enforce national unity (whereas Buddhism emphasised the rewards of the next life). Moreover, in the century preceding the Meiji Restoration, an influential (if elite) intellectual tradition known as 'nativist studies' grew in sophistication, emphasising both the divinity of the emperor and the racial and cultural homogeneity of the Japanese people. The eighteenth-century nativist scholar Motoori explained nationality in spiritual terms:

> I suggest that one first cleanse oneself of any defiled notions one may have acquired from reading Chinese texts, and then, holding fast to one's pristine Japanese heart, study our ancient texts well. If one does this, one will automatically learn about the Way that should be adopted and practised. To know these things is to adopt and practise the Way of the Gods.[33]

The idea that Japan should purge herself of all foreign influences made Shinto an attractive vehicle for the dissemination of ideas of national unity.

The power of Shinto could, and still can, be seen in its tens of thousands of shrines across the country, each of them marked by a *torii* gateway, and each of them dedicated to a deity: the sun goddess, an emperor, an ancestor or a natural phenomenon such as the sun, a stretch of water, a tree, a rock or a mountain. Unconcerned with the afterlife, Shinto easily accommodated itself to other faiths, settling into a congenial, albeit subordinate, relationship with Buddhism, whereby Shinto shrines often became linked administratively to Buddhist monasteries.[34]

This comfortable coexistence was undermined, from different directions, by the decline of Buddhist fervour and the spread of aristocratic dissatisfaction with the rule of the *shôgun*. With Shinto centred increasingly around reverence for the emperor, it strongly influenced the movement which opposed the Shôgunate and culminated in the Restoration of 1868. The leaders of 1868 had two aims when it came to religion: they were determined to separate Shinto from Buddhism, and then to transform it into what eventually became known as State Shinto.[35]

State Shinto was an 'invented tradition', a potent mixture of religion, ethics and nationalism which was separate, initially at least, from the folk religion of the shrines. The leaders of the Restoration signalled their involvement in religion with the Great Promulgation Campaign of 1870–84, an undertaking whose purpose was to create a state religion that would transcend – and subsume – the ideological differences that divided Shinto from Buddhism. They established a Department of Divinity, the emperor proclaimed 'the unification of rites and government', and for the first time in a thousand years he worshipped at Shinto's premier shrine, Ise close to Nagoya.[36]

The authorities put in place a system of state support for existing shrines, which were now ranked into an official hierarchy and required to bring their practices into line with those at Ise. They also established new shrines with avowedly nationalist purposes. The two best known were both in Tokyo. Immediately following the Restoration, the Yasukuni Shrine, near the imperial palace, was dedicated to the souls of those who had sacrificed their lives in defence of the country; and, fifty years later, the Meiji Shrine was dedicated to the memory of the Emperor Meiji, who gave his name, of course, to the years between 1868 and 1912.[37]

State Shinto provided the ideological and symbolic legitimisation that the new imperial order required. In both its teaching and its ritual it encapsulated the links between religion, the emperor and the state. These interrelationships could be observed on any number of occasions. When the 'Three Great Teachings' were promulgated in 1872, they expounded the virtues of paying one's taxes, sending one's children to school, complying with the conscription laws and supporting the policy of enriching the country and strengthening the military. Erwin Baelz was not unsympathetic.

> The artificial revival of this cult . . . is based on the perfectly sound idea that it will be to the advantage of Japan to preserve in certain respects things that distinguished it clearly from other nations, to have institutions that unite all the Japanese and are found among no other people in the world.[38]

Indeed, it was the issue of unity which enabled Shinto, in particular, and religion in general, to survive attacks from influential groups of modernisers during the early and mid-Meiji periods. In 1908, for example, the emperor issued a 'thrift and diligence' rescript – ostensibly to commemorate the fortieth anniversary of the Meiji Restoration – which the government hoped would counteract what it saw as a breakdown in the unity of purpose and national solidarity that had enabled Japan to emerge victorious against Russia only a few years earlier. Reconstituting the goal of modernising the country within religious and moral boundaries, the rescript stated explicitly that, 'it is now desired . . . that the shrines will be utilised in promoting the *unification* and *administration* of the country'.[39]

It was during the following two decades that the emperor was transformed from an officially sanctioned, but abstract, notion of a 'manifest deity . . . the living representative of a divine imperial line' into a figure to be worshipped as a 'living god'. The result was that, when Emperor Hirohito was enthroned in 1928, he was involved in several weeks of Shinto ceremonies. He attended banquets, immersed himself in river water, underwent periods of contemplation and participated in a series of purificatory rites. Indeed, so sacred were the proceedings that, 'after the whole thing was all over, all the artefacts involved, as well as the buildings in which the ceremonies had taken place, were ceremonially burnt'. The links between Shinto, the emperor and the state were constantly reinforced. For example, when the country celebrated the 2,601st anniversary of the founding of the Japanese empire in 1941, there were religious ceremonies and a parade of 120,000 schoolchildren, factory workers and 'representatives of national organizations' who marched past the emperor for hour after hour as he returned their salutes.[40]

But how effective were these initiatives? What part did State Shinto play in persuading the Japanese people to accept totalitarianism, dictatorship and emperor-worship, and to support overseas adventures and imperial expansion? Did State Shinto really encourage millions upon millions of families to work hard, spend cautiously and save assiduously? Even to pose these questions in such stark terms is to expose the difficulty of answering them satisfactorily. If the link between state, religion, popular attitudes and popular behaviour is to be established, two things need to be done: it has to be shown first that State Shinto changed people's attitudes, and secondly that these changed attitudes determined people's behaviour.

It is exceptionally difficult to demonstrate that State Shinto changed the attitudes of the Japanese people. It is never easy to allocate cause and effect in spiritual and intellectual matters, and it proves particularly challenging in the case of an ideology such as State Shinto which did not even attempt to lay exclusive claim to its adherents' attitudes and beliefs. This then is a subject fraught with complexity and uncertainty. But there are at least three reasons for doubting that government initiatives had a great deal of impact on this aspect of the nation's life. The effectiveness of the Shinto enterprise was undermined by its own internal divisions, by misguided government-led reforms, and by the resilience of what are often seen as Shinto's major spiritual and intellectual rivals, Buddhism, Confucianism, the so-called 'New Religions' and, to a lesser extent, Christianity.

Internecine conflict, government errors, Buddhism, Confucianism, 'New Religions' and Christianity

Internecine conflict cost State Shinto a good deal of support in the 1870s and 1880s. As Hardacre has shown, the priesthood was an insular and disparate group, with a small and fractious administrative elite ranged against a much larger, and much less well educated, rank and file. For a

considerable time, she argues, personal and doctrinal differences milit-
ated against either consensus or the adoption of a concerted course of
action. Some priests felt that they should adopt a pastoral and doctrinal
role, others that their primary function should be to administer the
shrine rites that constituted the core of Shinto's public ceremonies. It
was not until the end of the century that the latter view prevailed, with
the priesthood as a body finally promoting the notion that it was a
citizen's 'patriotic duty' to participate in the newly standardised rites and
prayers that were performed at Shinto shrines.[41]

Just as deleterious to the cause of State Shinto was the attempt made
by bureaucrats ignorant of folk culture to rationalise parish administration by merging into one all the shrines in a village or a town. Although
their efforts met with some success, there was a heavy price to be paid
'in ripping shrines from their natural hamlet matrix'. As a priest at Ise
explained,

> I feel . . . that it was a mistake to try to merge all shrines in each village, as it
> was not emotionally right for the villagers. From ancient times their daily life
> had centred in the small hamlets. . . . And [with] their tutelary *ujigami* [pro-
> tective deity] taken from them, the people were left with a great feeling of
> loneliness. With shrines, emotion comes first.

The feelings of the villagers affected tended to be more succinct: 'Our
kami-san [protective deity], who had his own place right here, has had to
go out and live in borrowed quarters.'[42]

The effectiveness of State Shinto was undermined just as seriously –
and for considerably longer – by the resilience of its major rivals,
Buddhism, Confucianism, the 'New Religions' and Christianity. Buddhism
first came to Japan in the sixth century and, like Christianity in Europe
it served as a vehicle for the transmission of high culture, and went on
to assume wide political, economic and social influence during the
fifteenth and sixteenth centuries. Thereafter its power began to decline,
and those who led the Restoration of 1868 launched a vehement attack
upon what remained of its authority. Nonetheless, Buddhist teaching
retained a considerable attraction, particularly as many of its rituals were
deeply embedded in popular practices, especially those concerning death.
Moreover, Buddhist leaders, sensing the failure of their initial attempts
to portray their religion as a 'native' Japanese faith, turned towards institutional reform and the expansion of charitable activity at home and
missionary work in the colonies. Their efforts paid dividends for it seems
that, by the end of the nineteenth century, State Shinto began to look

upon Buddhism less as a threat than as an integral component of Japanese culture.[43]

Confucianism was an ethical philosophy rather than a religion. It had no deity, no priesthood and very little ritual. It stressed that man was part both of a rational natural order and of a social order based upon a unified state, strict ethical rules and government by men of superior education and wisdom. Its emphasis upon loyalty to one's superiors helped to legitimate the social hierarchy: those in authority were to guide and nurture their dependants with benevolence, while those in subordinate positions were to respect their superiors and be grateful for the favours bestowed upon them.

Although Confucianism's intellectual domination did not survive the reforming zeal of the Meiji state, its philosophy continued to exert considerable influence. It was seen in the discussion above that the 1890 Imperial Rescript on Education urged the people of Japan to be 'filial' to their parents, respect the constitution, observe the laws and, in an emergency, offer themselves 'courageously' to the state. Confucian political ethics, which stressed the relationship between a benevolent ruler educating his people, even informed Yoshino's 'liberal' formulations of democracy within a Japanese context. These principles, it will be recalled, not only remained in place until the end of the Second World War, but were reiterated time and time again during the late 1930s and early 1940s. So it was that obedience and resignation continued to be considered virtues, and duties and obligations to be regarded as more important than individual rights. It is true that Confucianism as a discrete intellectual discipline was regarded as out of tune with the designs of many of Japan's leaders. The *genrô* Itô complained in 1879 that

> Today's students are usually trained in Chinese learning and, whenever they open their mouths, it is to argue political theory and discuss public affairs. Thus, when they read Western books, they are unable to set about their tasks with calm and cultivated minds but plunge themselves instead into the radical schools of European political thought. In a whirlwind of empty theory, they fill city and countryside with political talk.

Nevertheless, Confucian attitudes, with their emphasis on age, status and hierarchy continued to permeate popular attitudes and assumptions. As one local leader complained when not shown the respect that he felt was his due, 'Whether in moral repute or property, in this village there is no one who can compare with me. And I am older, too. To call me "*Gicho, gicho*" ["chairman"], without the "*-san*" [honorific title], is the height of outrage.'[44]

Influential too were the 'New Religions', which combined millenarian calls for 'world renewal' with faith-healing, magic and miracles by 'living gods' (some of whom were women). Because many of the 'New Religions' incorporated major elements of traditional Shinto doctrines (making them eligible for state sponsorship), they were able to inspire religious fervour, channel dissatisfaction with the authorities and largely escape government censure during the 1930s. Generally emerging in times of crisis such as famine or war, the first wave of 'new religious' fervour occurred in the early to mid-nineteenth century and was influential in the political and social upheavals of the 1860s and 1870s. A second wave of fervour emerged between the late 1910s and the 1930s. According to a Ministry of Education survey in 1924 there were 98 'new religions': four were Christian-based, 29 were affiliated to Buddhism and 65 were attached to Shinto. Ten years later, there were 1,029: some of the larger groups claimed millions of adherents, though most were centred around one geographical location where they met the needs of the local population.[45]

There were also spontaneous outbursts of popular religious energy such as mass pilgrimages to the shrine at Ise. The 'what the hell' movement is of particular interest. On the eve of the Restoration, large numbers of people around the country flooded onto the streets where they danced orgiastically. On the surface, it appeared to be 'the nonsense attendant on restoration history' or little more than a Shinto-style supplication to the gods.

> But, then, it was a frightfully bad year [1866] and is best forgotten. Thanks to the *kami* [gods] we shall dance, right? Right. Right on! Remaking the world of Japan is right, too, no? Yes. Go for it? Congratulations are due on the good fortune of a bountiful harvest this year, so let's dance on it.

Nevertheless, 'what the hell' activity also included breaking into, and looting the houses of landlords and officials which suggests that its insurrectionary potential was far greater than is usually assumed. In all events, such forms of agitation continued to irritate the authorities throughout the early decades of the Meiji period, though it appears that the energy behind them was directed increasingly into modern forms of social and political protest and/or subsumed by the all-encompassing ideology of State Shinto.[46]

Christianity too is sometimes linked with Shinto, Buddhism and Confucianism as one of Japan's leading religions. However, this is seriously misleading. Introduced to Japan by the Jesuits in the mid-sixteenth century, it was suppressed so ruthlessly that a hundred years later only a few tiny communities known as the 'hidden Christians' survived in the areas around Nagasaki. Fears of a Christian threat with its God that transcended all earthly political authority once again emerged with the opening up of the country. Immediately following the Restoration, the government issued an anti-Christian proscription, that offered rewards for information leading to the discovery of any traitorous Japanese practising this 'pernicious sect'. Despite the protests of the foreign community, some 500 'hidden Christians' were exposed and executed during the persecution that took place. 'The question just now, perhaps, which most excites the serious attention of residents in Nagasaki, is the destination or ultimate disposal of the cargoes of native Christians departing from this port within the past few days', explained the *Nagasaki Express* in 1870.

> What becomes of them eludes us. – These facts we know. . . . More than a thousand have been arrested and carried hence: some with wife and children – others alone. We know what has been done with the Christians of a bygone age. Is this a continuance of the barbarity? Surely the embarkation *here* is done to outrage us. Will no Consul step forward and take the responsibility of unveiling this business, when his war-ship is in port? . . . We would we could make clear this Christian question. It is one demanding our keenest watching and regard.[47]

Despite these grave setbacks, the Christian religion has more claim to our attention than this bare narrative would lead one to suppose. In the years following the persecution, Christian missionaries and converts, who mostly came from the educated middle and upper classes, played a major part in fostering female and secondary education, and during the early years of the twentieth century they played a central role in the promotion both of Christian Socialism and of social work.[48]

State Shinto, attitudes and behaviour

How effective then was State Shinto in changing public attitudes? To what extent is it possible to come to a conclusion which is convincing enough to have some hope of convincing the sceptical? It is tempting, it must be admitted, to hedge one's findings with so many cautions and qualifications that it begins to look suspiciously like obfuscation. How is one to generalise helpfully about the attitudes of millions and millions of people? How is one to show that State Shinto changed, rather than simply reflected, the attitudes of these people? And how is one to isolate State Shinto from all the many other influences – both spiritual and secular – that crowded in upon them during the three-quarters of a century of unprecedented political, economic, social and intellectual change that forms the subject of this book?

One clear finding does emerge. It can be said that, insofar as State Shinto changed public attitudes, it did so much more towards the end of the period than it did towards the beginning. It has been seen that the movement's early years were plagued by internal divisions: in fact, claimed the movement's opponents, these quarrels were more likely to drive people to Christianity than they were to Shinto. It can be shown too that the Great Promulgation Campaign of 1870–84 generated a good deal of opposition and bad feeling. The sermons given by Shinto priests were boring, it was maintained, their teachings were unbelievable and nobody liked their funerals. Critics did not mince their words: the evangelists of the new movement, it was alleged in the mid-1870s, were ridiculous jackasses who were unfit to serve the nation.[49]

The situation changed significantly towards the turn of the century. The movement's internal divisions were more or less resolved and as Hardacre explains, the country's wars with China (1894–95) and Russia (1904–05) provided the opportunity for the state to tap into what she calls 'Japan's oldest and most affectively laden area of religious life, the cult of the dead and the ancestors'. It proved a shrewd strategy. The years following the Russo-Japanese War saw an aggressive campaign to promote the 'rites of empire'. Great use was made of the two new shrines in Tokyo which, it has been seen, had been established with avowedly nationalist purposes. The Yasukuni shrine, which was dedicated to the war dead, and the Meiji shrine, which was dedicated to the late emperor, joined the Grand Shrine at Ise as the central pillars of State Shinto.[50]

The campaign to make State Shinto supreme reached its height, as might be expected, during the late 1930s and early 1940s. Throughout the latter half of the 1930s, the government attempted to crack down on, and eliminate those religions whose interpretations of the role of the emperor and state differed even slightly from those of State Shinto. By the close of the decade, the government had introduced the Religious Organisations Law which aimed to ensure that 'religion participated in the war objectives and conformed to the needs of the government in this wartime state of emergency'. Speaking before a Diet committee in 1939, prime minister Hiranuma explained that the cult of the emperor needed to assume absolute primacy: 'Let me emphasize that all religions must be one with the ideal of our national polity; they cannot be at odds with the spirit of our Imperial Way.' The Konoe cabinets of 1940–41 did their best to translate such rhetoric into policy and practice. After years of denying that State Shinto was a religion, they declared that it was *the* religion, and they revised the Peace Preservation Law so that it could be used to eliminate any groups which 'blasphemed the dignity of the Grand Shrine of Ise or the Imperial House'.[51]

It is impossible to plot the impact of State Shinto upon popular attitudes with anything remotely approaching statistical precision. Yet it does not seem unreasonable to conclude that the significant, and increasing, efforts which were made to promote State Shinto had a significant, and increasing, impact upon the ideas and beliefs which were put before the Japanese people, and upon the ways in which the Japanese people thought about the world in which they lived. This, at any rate, is the conclusion of those who have studied the issue most closely. Hardacre believes, for example, that the fourteen years of the Great Promulgation Campaign were 'highly influential in creating a popular awareness and understanding of "Shinto" as an independent entity'. Garon concludes that 'The relationship between state and religion in prewar Japan was not simply one of antagonism but often involved efforts by the religious bodies themselves to use state power to their advantage.'[52]

There is one further complication when attempting to trace the relationship between religion, attitudes and behaviour. It is impossible to plot with any sort of precision the impact that State Shinto had upon the behaviour of those who were exposed to it. Indeed, the relationship between attitudes and behaviour is always exceptionally difficult to disentangle. There is inevitably the temptation to use the behaviour which one can observe as evidence of the attitudes which one cannot; and once this has been done, it becomes impossible, of course, to distinguish behaviour from attitudes in the way which is necessary if one is to attempt to establish the existence of a causal relationship between them.

Nevertheless, it is commonly accepted that the efforts made to promote State Shinto were part of the state's broader – and successful – campaign to encourage emperor-worship, nationalism, military aggression and, it seems, the work ethic. It can be suggested, though it cannot be proved, that it became increasingly difficult for the Japanese people to avoid the state's propaganda, and increasingly difficult therefore to escape the pressures to conform which were placed upon them.

There is little doubt that the influence of State Shinto was on the increase. Certainly, the Ise shrine came to assume considerable influence in Japanese popular culture. More and more households enshrined its talismans, more and more schools organised tours of the shrine, and more and more of the population made pilgrimages to it. The statistical

indicators of Ise's prominence are extremely telling. It has been calculated, for example, that by the early 1940s, eleven or twelve million Ise
talismans were distributed each year, that nearly two million children
(from nearly 20,000 schools) visited on organised excursions, and that
almost eight million people paid tribute at the shrine.[53]

Foreigners living in Japan were struck by the pervasiveness and ex-
tremism of propaganda extolling the emperor system. John Morris noted
in the mid-1940s, for instance, that 'the myth of divinity has played an
exceedingly important part in the expansion of nationalist feeling, and
the leaders of Japan have cleverly exploited it to gain their ends'.

> It has been built up by methods similar to those employed by advertising
> agents, that is to say it has been constantly brought to the notice of the people.
> It is the method adopted by Dr Goebbels for misleading the German people,
> also that employed by the manufacturers of soap and toothpaste, but the
> Japanese thought of it first.

The Japanese, he stressed, were no more susceptible to such propaganda
than any other nationality. 'They do not necessarily believe it, but since
they are never for one moment allowed to forget it there comes a time
when all but the intelligent and sceptical tacitly accept the myth.' Others
like Leslie Johns, likened emperor-centred patriotism to fanaticism.

> Recognizing none of the moral forces of the Western world, the Japanese, if
> they mean to attain a definite objective, will do so, brushing aside anything in
> their path, realizing none of their obligations to the rest of the world, adhering
> only to their own code of honour and aiming to achieve their object whatever
> the cost. Japanese pride of race amounts almost to fanaticism at times of
> national crisis. . . . When fighting between Japan and China broke out, so dis-
> appointed were some men on being classed as unfit for army duty, that they
> cut off fingers, sent them to the War Office, and with this token of their sincerity,
> begged to be permitted to die for their country.[54]

Twenty-five years earlier, when Japan was seen as a committed member of the Western international order through her alliance with Britain,
such patriotism was considered one of the country's most valuable and
laudable characteristics. On a visit to Japan in the 1900s, Lady Lawson
offered nothing but praise.

> They can still teach us lessons; and it is in the sphere of patriotism, which we
> have been too apt to regard as something peculiarly our own, that Japan has
> lessons to give. The last few years have revealed the land and the people as
> possessing a spirit that is worth preserving to humanity – valorous in the field
> and active in solving social questions at home. A lofty patriotism still shines in
> every corner of the Empire, and one and all are as ready to-day to lay down

their life for their military ideals as they were in the old romantic days of feudalism . . .

We cannot do better than copy the example of Japan in bringing every influence to bear on the rising generation, so as to encourage the old natural warrior spirit which is their heritage, and which should not be allowed to degenerate.[55]

The Japanese themselves recognised the pressure which they were under to accept State Shinto, the emperor system and all that went with them. The trouble is that such testimony is often open to the same charges of hindsight and self-justification that can be levelled at the evidence about education which was discussed in the previous section of the chapter. Nonetheless, it seems perverse to deny that by the end of the period, State Shinto, and the emperor system with which it was so closely associated, had a considerable effect upon the ways in which the Japanese people conducted themselves.

It is helpful to turn to the work of scholars such as Edgerton and Iritani. Edgerton has attempted to solve the riddle of what he describes as 'Japan's sudden transformation from a country that epitomized military chivalry to one that embodied the depths of armed depravity'. Part of the explanation, he believes, is to be found in the principles and practices of State Shintoism and the emperor system.

Unlike Western soldiers who often professed to believe that God or Christian doctrine were moral authorities standing above their officers or political leaders, most Japanese recognized no moral authority higher than the emperor. When officers told their men that they must act brutally in the name of the emperor, as they often did, few Japanese would resist the order.[56]

Iritani's work has already been discussed. His book, *Group Psychology of the Japanese in Wartime*, is the result, it will be recalled, of the attempt to understand Japanese behaviour in the late 1930s and early 1940s. His conclusion is remarkably similar to that reached by Edgerton.

Japanese leaders used the absolute authority of the Emperor to stir up the people so that they would go to war. Their weapon was the fanatical theory that Japan was a divine country and should be proud of it. They were successful in uniting people of all generations into a homogeneous unit and made them push forward in the cause of preserving the nation's prosperity.[57]

The complexities of studying late nineteenth and twentieth-century religion are not easily resolved. Nonetheless, two clear conclusions emerge from the analysis which has been carried out. It has been shown that those who were in power between 1868 and 1945 invented a religious tradition, State Shinto, which they designed, along with education, to make the people revere their emperor, respect their leaders and support their governments' initiatives. It has also been suggested, though it has not been proved, that the rulers of Japan were successful in this policy of turning religious practices to secular ends. State Shinto played a part, along with education, in persuading the Japanese people to think and act in the ways that their leaders wished them to.

The media

One might possibly imagine therefore that there was unlikely to be government pressure on the media to persuade the people of Japan to think and behave in the ways that those in authority desired. It might be supposed that those in power would be satisfied that their educational and religious policies were doing all that was necessary to inculcate the values they wished among a receptive and increasingly acquiescent popu-lation. On the one hand, Japanese newspapers today are accused of docility and a 'distressing uniformity in coverage and treatment'. On the other hand, the press during the Meiji and Taishô periods was described in the words of one journalist, as 'the script writers of real politics'. 'On one point – the journalists' sense of the press as a defender of the public interest', writes Huffman, 'there was never much wavering. The earliest editors took up the brush as a cudgel, to defend the nation . . . against the usurping Meiji "rebels".'

> By early Meiji, they were talking about themselves as society's 'uncrowned kings', not so much because they sought personal power as because they saw newspapers as tools for shaping political policy. 'Newspapers are teachers . . . the new kings of the imperial court and friends of all people. They make trouble for the former samurai . . . and make light of the nobility . . .' And the press leaders kept on saying such things, with obvious conviction, to the end of the era . . . no one, not even the most commercial of editors, stopped insisting that journalists must guard the public trust.[58]

Such contradictions need to be considered in more detail. Accordingly, it is intended that these issues be explored by taking as our starting point Huffman's claim, quoted at the beginning of the chapter, that 'no single institution did more to create a modern citizenry than the Meiji newspaper press'. The analysis will be undertaken in three stages. It will be shown first that those in power made considerable efforts to bend the press, and later the radio and the cinema, to their own ends. It will be shown next that the press, and later the radio and cinema, responded as compliantly to these demands as those in power could reasonably have wished. It will be suggested finally, though much more cautiously, that the press, and later the radio and cinema, probably played some part in persuading the Japanese people to revere the emperor, respect their leaders, support government initiatives and adopt other officially sanctioned attitudes.

Regulation, accommodation and incorporation

There was a long tradition of government attempts to curb the media. For several centuries before the Restoration, the Tokugawa regime had displayed a determination to maintain the tightest possible control over its subjects. In their never-ending struggle to prevent challenges to the political, social, religious and moral hierarchy, the authorities did their best to control the production of everything from books and popular drama to puppet theatre and woodblock printing. Between the mid-seventeenth and the mid-nineteenth centuries, those who breached government controls were fined, jailed, banished, executed or forced to commit suicide. There can be no mistaking the authorities' determination. According to Yamamoto, 'the traditional communications policy of the ruling class in Japan' was, 'Let them serve you, but keep them ignorant'. According to Huffman, 'Even the bravest and most independent pre-1868 writers operated in an environment suffused with regulations, threats, and prohibitions designed to maintain the existing regime and prevent subversive ideas.'[59]

This repressive environment did not change a great deal in 1868. After a few months of press freedom, the authorities reasserted their control. By the end of the year, the government had imposed a series of Tokugawa-like licensing regulations which permitted the publication of journals and newspapers only if the authorities believed that they would encourage good order, maintain traditional moral standards and promote national well-being. Thereafter, government policy changed remarkably little. There persisted, explains Marshall, a 'remarkably unwavering obsession with limiting political debate in the popular press'.

> Over the almost eight decades from the Meiji Restoration to the last months of the Pacific War, there seems seldom to have been much rest for those cabinet ministers, Diet politicians, civil and military bureaucrats, and self-appointed vigilantes who saw it as their civic duty to protect the public from dangerous ideas.[60]

Those who were in power between the Restoration and the Second World War left little to chance in their dealings with the media. They knew precisely what they were attempting to achieve. What they wanted was an acquiescent but enthusiastic press, reinforced by an acquiescent but enthusiastic radio and cinema, regaling an acquiescent but enthusiastic population with a diet of officially sanctioned opinions and information. The likelihood of Japanese politicians, bureaucrats and 'self-appointed vigilantes' succeeding in their endeavours was strengthened by the fact that they were prepared to be flexible with regard to the means, if not the ends, which they employed.

Immediately following the Restoration, the Meiji government set about its task by encouraging the establishment of new publications which were ready to publicise the government's reforms and fill their pages with official notices and ordinances. But within a few years, these (and other) papers grew less responsive to official pressure, and the authorities decided that they needed to change their tactics. They became a great deal more selective in the support which they offered to individual papers, and in the summer of 1875 they passed two far-reaching laws which, it has been said, 'closed the door forever on any kind of thorough-going press–government cooperation'. The new legislation included regulations which prohibited newspapers from reviling 'existing laws' or confusing 'the sense of duty of the people', and which insisted that writers found guilty of provoking a crime were to be considered 'equally guilty with the person who had been caused to commit it'.[61]

However, the authorities did not rely simply on closer regulation. They also began to accommodate – and incorporate – the media in ways which have become well known, widely criticised and regarded some-how as being quintessentially Japanese. From the 1890s onwards, politicians and officials encouraged the formation of press clubs, small groups of journalists which were attached to, and dependent upon, government ministries, the Diet and the headquarters of the political parties. The result, critics claimed from early in the new century, was the stifling of journalistic initiative, the neutralisation of editorial independence and consequently the almost complete emasculation of the press.

> All the 'journalistic vassals' attached to any one ministry are given exactly the same news materials, which makes it impossible for one reporter to scoop another. Now any idiot can join a press club and if he shows up every day he'll get exactly the same news as the smartest veteran in the bunch.

'And if, on occasion, a spunky reporter should do a piece that made the government look bad', the president of his club would 'immediately take steps to isolate him, see that a million stumbling blocks were put in his path, and generally give him a hard time'.[62]

The clubs multiplied rapidly between the wars, spreading out from Tokyo and Osaka to centres such as Nagoya and the prefectural capitals, and at the same time they began to specialise, some of them, in politics, economics or local news. Yet they proved no more independent than their predecessors. Indeed, the few signs of independence which did emerge were stifled in the militarisation of the 1930s. According to Yamamoto, 'as fascist control increased, the press clubs became part of the state's propaganda machine, taking on the function both in name and in fact of "guiding public opinion, conveying the will of those above to those below"'.[63]

The outbreak of war served only to intensify the authorities' anxieties. Jazz was banned, cinemas were forbidden to show British and American films, and imported expressions like *nyûsu* (news) and *anaunsaa* (announcer) were excised from the nation's officially sanctioned vocabulary. However, it was the press which remained the primary concern. When Japan went to war with China in 1937, the authorities classified news about the economy and foreign relations as state secrets which could be published only with prior consent; when she went to war with America and the allies in 1941, those in power prescribed severe penalties for the publication of any information which might assist the nation's enemies.[64]

Opposition, submission and collusion

How successful were these efforts? How did the press, and later the radio and the cinema, respond to the efforts that were made to influence, accommodate and incorporate them? It will be clear by now, of course, that such questions are a great deal easier to ask than they are to answer satisfactorily. It is never easy to attribute cause and effect, and it does not follow that, when there was a coincidence between what the authorities demanded and what the media did, it was the former which caused the latter. Nevertheless, it will be suggested, and with some confidence, that the press, radio and cinema responded as compliantly to the inducements and pressures placed on them as even the most authoritarian politician or 'self-appointed vigilante' could reasonably have wished.

This is not to suggest that the Japanese media were mere cyphers prepared to do anything that was demanded of them. This was certainly not the case. In fact, it has been seen already that the discussion of patronage and coercion reveals the limits, as well as the power, of government initiatives. It has been shown that within a few years of the Restoration the press began to chafe against official pressure, and that by the turn of the century there had emerged passionate and articulate criticism of the role that was played by the press clubs.

There were many other challenges to the consensus that those in power were seeking to establish. In the 1870s, three hundred newsmen were imprisoned for violating the newspaper law of 1875. In his serialised commentaries, Fukuzawa reported that

> The government is as despotic as before, and Japanese subjects continue to be stupid, spiritless and powerless. The slight progress made is out of all proportion to the energies and money spent for it. In the last analysis, this is because the civilization of a nation cannot be made to advance solely through the power of the government.[65]

In the late 1880s, the press complained that the cabinet, dominated by 'the indolent soldiers of *Satsuma* and *Chôshû*' had forged national stability not through 'unity' but 'almighty power'. The press could be just as scathing in its condemnation of government foreign policy. In the mid-1890s (prior to the Sino-Japanese War), most newspapers castigated what they saw as the Itô government's 'caution on top of caution' in the face of Chinese 'lawlessness' and 'lack of principle'. Ten years later (in the wake of the Russo-Japanese War), it was the press that led the opposition, once again over the government's vacillating diplomatic efforts.

> We say to the government, why is it necessary to maintain the current situation in Korea! If we desire the eradication of the intrigues of the Russian faction in Korea and to protect and expand our rights and interests, there is nothing more urgent than at this opportunity, openly and without delay, to send a large force to Korea, quelling Korean apprehension, and hence, maintain peace and order.[66]

There were also some publications that condemned the war altogether. In 1903, the *Yorozu Chôhô* published a series of 'Miscellaneous Thoughts' by a Christian pacifist. In his first article, he condemned the general phenomenon of war, declaring, 'Peace is not cowardice, it is courage'. By the third article, his attacks had sharpened: 'Those who chant advocacy for starting war are most definitely not patriots. The enemies of humanity are humans. The enemies of Japan are the Japanese.' Another newspaper, the *Heimin Shinbun*, devoted itself – virulently – to the pacifist cause. 'The time has come!', it believed.

> For the sake of truth, for the sake of correct principles, for the prosperity of the world's masses, the time has come to scream out 'end war'. We repudiate war to the bitter end. Morally, it is a dreadful sin. Politically, it is a most dreadful poison. Economically, it is a dreadful loss.[67]

Even when there was no major issue or crisis, the mainstream press could be exceptionally critical of the authorities. In 1910, for example, the *Tokyo Mainichi* published an editorial that castigated the entire political establishment.

> It is our opinion that while the achievement of constitutional government is urgent, the 750 members of both the upper and lower Houses are far in excess and that as representatives of the current Imperial Diet, 30 or 40, even 80, in fact, are sufficient to debate the affairs of state.

It did not mince its words. 'We feel the masses of rank and file, wriggling like maggots, are superfluous and completely useless . . . The party men, vainly dreaming of forming a party cabinet, neglect regularly their moral cultivation. How dangerous!'[68]

It is not surprising, therefore, that Huffman concludes his study of the press in Meiji Japan with the observation that the newspapers' relationship with the authorities was characterised, not by consensus, but by unending conflict.

> On the one side stood the government. . . . On the other side stood the journalists, government critics who, in the popular mind, were true to their profession only when they were 'registering dissent, decrying abuse, and awakening the people to alternative and generally more liberal, policies and programs for modernization' than those of the officials.[69]

This independent voice was not silenced for another twenty years. The press was highly critical, for example, of the government's handling of the 'rice riots' which took place in 1918; and more than 300 representatives from 139 newspapers in the Osaka area demanded the resignation of the Terauchi cabinet for violating the 'sanctity of the constitution' when it prevented them from reporting on the disturbances. Four years later, the country's nine leading papers signed a joint statement entitled, 'We Demand the Immediate Enactment of Universal Suffrage', and the press continued to voice their complaints during the mid-1920s when cabinets were formed without representation from the political parties.[70]

It is easy perhaps to misunderstand the meaning of these incidents. They point, most of them, not just to the independence of the press, but also to the struggle which was necessary to maintain that independence. The pressure to conform, though often hidden, was intense, increasing, and often highly effective. As students of the press are at pains to explain, 'the threat of being banned, fined, or even jailed under one or more of the publishing regulations led authors, editors and publishers to practice self-censorship, sacrificing passages, sections, chapters, or even whole works rather than face another round with the authorities'. Indeed, the press seemed at times overly amenable to government arguments and in some cases, endorsed the need for censorship. On the day after the commencement of hostilities with China in 1894, for example, the *Tokyo Asahi* published an editorial supporting censorship so long as it was not wasteful of reporters' time. Even in times of normality when there were no internal or external exigencies encouraging exceptional demands for national unity, it seemed, to some at least, that the press was incapable of initiating meaningful debate and lodging constructive criticism. Many concluded, not surprisingly, that such acquiescence undermined press independence, fragile as it was at the best of times. The *Japan Weekly Chronicle* put it like this in 1920:

> in no other country does the Government exercise such control over the press as in Japan. This is obtained in two ways – negatively by forbidding the publication of news and positively by inspiring both news and comment.[71]

The pressure to conform became all but irresistible during the 1930s. It was the Manchurian Incident, it is generally agreed, that marked the decisive turning point. While there were some voices calling for the withdrawal of troops, it is true that the press in general did not need much persuading to support the army's actions in 1931, and that no paper apparently felt it necessary to investigate the official version of events with which they were presented. The *Tokyo Asahi*, for instance, reported on this 'highly regrettable' event.

> In regards to the facts of the matter, it is after all as public reports have stated. . . . It was most definitely not an event that coincidentally occurred. In order for the Chinese to remove the rights and interests of our Empire from Manchuria and Mongolia, they ignored treaties, brazenly committed illegal acts and all manner of persecutions, and recently, their anti-Japanese [views] have conspicuously changed, becoming scorn for our Empire, and in the end, reaching the extent of an attitude of provocation.

It was critical only insofar as it wanted to know why it took the cabinet so long to offer its support to the armed forces: 'once the army took an action, it is the action of the Imperial Army. . . . The people both inside and outside the country should not be given the impression that there is a gulf or difference between the military and the government.' The *Osaka Mainichi*, far from critically investigating the event, called for unity, declaring that, in regards to China, 'our country is subject to an inevitable fate in which we must show a hardened attitude'.

> Should we bend [our] insistence on justice at this time, our empire will not only be subjected to scorn from without, but will fail to reach its conception of national progress. Our countrymen facing such a destiny must be one in their resolution.[72]

Thereafter, coercion reinforced collusion. It has been seen, of course, that criticism of those in power had only ever been tolerated within closely defined limits. 'Before the 1930s', explains Lee, 'the oppositional press simply backed down whenever threatened by the government, and after the rise of militarism they hardly resisted the harsh control imposed on them.' For the remainder of the 1930s and the early 1940s, the media enjoyed very little room for manoeuvre, and faced little choice but to metamorphose into what one commentator has called 'the dutiful mouthpieces of the government'.[73]

Those who have examined the stance adopted by the authorities towards film-makers and broadcasters (not to mention book and magazine publishers) are in no doubt that the pressure applied to these branches of the media proved just as effective as that exerted over the country's newspapers. The cinema was certainly subjected to strict control. The Motion Picture Film Inspection Regulations of 1925 required the inspection of all films before they were released – and as one would expect the censors were particularly concerned about anything that might undermine the constitution or 'desecrate the sanctity of the imperial family'. Although the system generally worked smoothly with self-censorship reinforcing state censorship, the authorities were not prepared to take any chances.

> Emperor Hirohito's visit to Kansai in 1929 was preceded by a list of injunctions to local film inspectors: no errors in script or film headings, especially in the specialized language used to describe the imperial family; no mistakes in the order of events on the Emperor's schedule; no films making it appear that the Emperor's attendants are moving forward parallel to them; no shots showing the exhaust from the bodyguards' side car; nothing out of focus, and so forth.[74]

The radio was controlled just as closely, with governments using the new medium to promote their own policies while denying their critics the right of reply. (On one occasion, the Communications Ministry banned the reporting of a temporary breakdown in the telephone network in the wake of a series of thunderstorms.) However, according to Kasza, radio censorship was usually 'a cooperative endeavor of state and radio personnel'. This co-operation can be seen, he explains, in national radio's adoption of the circuit-breaker system. 'There was always the danger that live shows would stray from the authorized script onto illegal ground, so in December 1926, the Communications Ministry ordered *Nihon Hôsô Kyôkai* [NHK – the national broadcasting company] to equip its transmitting stations with circuit breakers that could stop a program in progress.'

There were two sound monitors in the inspector's room, one carrying the transmission and one a studio monitor. If a speaker wandered from the script, the inspector turned a key, halting transmission. He continued to follow the program on the studio monitor, and when the illegal material ceased he restored transmission power.

The result was that the programmes put out by the NHK were so strictly censored that 'nothing that might harm the interests of the country and its people is allowed to go on air'. According to John Morris, government control was so deeply entrenched that 'Even before the outbreak of war it was impossible to broadcast the proceedings of the Diet or any political speeches without authorisation.'[75]

However, the way in which coercion was used to reinforce collusion can be seen most clearly by examining government–media relations during the late 1930s and early 1940s. Controls were tightened, and tightened again. It was not too difficult, of course, to secure the dissemination of 'positive' news so long as the war was going well: in fact, papers vied with one another in heaping praise upon the country's military and diplomatic achievements. 'The War of Great East Asia is not a war of destruction', explained the *Nichi nichi* in late 1941. 'There has never been a more constructive war than this. Every bullet fired from the guns of the Japanese forces carries the destruction of the old order and helps to bring a new and better one.'[76]

It was more difficult to ensure favourable coverage of military reverses. Yet a good deal could be done. Journalists were forced to rely upon the military for their information and, when the tide began to turn in favour of the allies, the media colluded with the government to deny, delay and sanitise the news that came in from the front. The defeat at the battle of Midway in the summer of 1942 was presented as a victory, the death of Admiral Yamamoto in the spring of 1943 was not made public for five weeks, and the launch of *kamikaze* attacks in the autumn of 1944 was hailed as an example to the nation. 'All of us should learn from the serene spirit of these youths', claimed the *Mainichi*. 'If the same spirit that imbued them characterized our other actions, there would be no obstacle that we could not surmount.'[77]

It is clear then that the authorities worked hard, and with increasing success, to secure the sort of media coverage which they desired. Although they faced more obstacles than they did when dealing with education and religion, they experienced less difficulty than they might have expected in bending the mass media to their will. When the Emperor Meiji died in 1912, the struggle between government and media was well and truly joined; when Manchuria was seized twenty years later, the struggle was more or less over. Whether it was from fear or conviction – or some pragmatic combination of the two – the press, the cinema and the radio were all persuaded to collude in the government's management of the news.

Readers, viewers and listeners

There is one further issue that needs to be addressed before it can be agreed that the press, cinema and radio played a part in persuading the Japanese people to think and behave as those in authority wished them to. It has to be demonstrated not just that the media urged their readers, viewers and listeners to revere the emperor, respect their leaders and so on, but that their readers, viewers and listeners accepted what they were told, and acted upon it.

One is reminded of prime minister Tôjô's comments about the power of propaganda. 'The general public is foolish', he maintained. 'If we tell the truth, it will break the public's spirit. . . . If we carry out a policy by saying that "red" is "white", they will follow us.' But were the public really so malleable? Is it possible to plot cause and effect quite so simply? Is it not likely that different groups reacted in different ways, at different times, to different messages, from different branches of the media? It is this more nuanced approach which will be adopted here. It will be suggested that, although there is little doubt that the influence of the media increased hugely between 1868 and 1945, it is an influence that remains remarkably difficult to substantiate in any systematic fashion.[78]

The number of newspaper readers, film-goers and radio-listeners increased dramatically between the Restoration and the Second World War. In the early years of the period, there was no radio or cinema, of course, and newspaper sales were still exceedingly modest. Indeed, even when allowance is made for the fact that readership exceeded circulation – and for the possibility that the readership might have been unusually impressionable – it is difficult to make the case that newspapers affected the behaviour of the mass of the population. In 1875, for example, the country's six major papers sold fewer than 32,000 copies – and this in a country of 35 million people.[79]

It was not until the end of the century, with literacy rising, that individual papers began to sell in significant numbers: in 1895, the *Osaka Asahi* had a circulation of over 100,000, the *Chûô* just on 80,000, the *Osaka Mainichi* nearly 70,000, and the *Yomiuri* nearly 16,000. Thereafter, sales grew apace. The *Yomiuri*, for instance, increased its circulation from

21,500 in 1903, to 55,000 in 1924, 670,000 in 1935 and a million or so in 1938. When a new president took over in 1924, he decided that he 'wanted to make an interesting paper or a paper the people felt pleasure in reading', and he 'adopted, for example, a policy to print big photographs of women in order to make such a paper'. By the late 1930s, the *Yomiuri* was selling a million copies a day, and the country's most popular daily paper, the *Asahi shimbun,* two-and-a-half times that number. The result was that, whereas in 1895 the country's fifteen leading papers had a circulation of under 700,000, forty years later the press as a whole had a circulation of nineteen million copies a day – a figure equivalent to more than one newspaper for every household in the country.[80]

When the cinema and radio became available, they too proved highly popular. The cinema arrived in Japan at the end of the nineteenth century, and as elsewhere attendances grew apace. In 1926, for example, the 'typical' Japanese citizen – whether man, woman or child – visited the cinema more than two and a half times during the course of the year. The first radio programme was not broadcast until 1925, but by the end of the 1930s there were nearly four million radios in the country, a figure which meant, the *Japan Times Weekly* calculated, that there were probably some twenty million listeners. Corroboration, albeit of a distinctly jaundiced kind, is provided by Morris's memories of wartime Tokyo. By the early 1940s, he recalls, there was 'hardly a household that does not own a set'.

> The programmes start at six o'clock in the morning and continue until eleven at night, and during the whole of these seventeen hours nearly all the radio sets in the country are kept going at full blast. Radio is, in fact, one of the major curses of living in Japan. There is no escape from the noise; it assaults one from all directions.[81]

But what evidence is there that this growing body of newspaper readers, radio listeners and film-goers were susceptible to the messages, whether overt or covert, to which they were subjected? The evidence, by its very nature, tends once again to be anecdotal rather than statistical, suggestive rather than conclusive. However, it is certainly robust enough to show how misleading it would be to accept the view, still current in some quarters, that the Japanese were little more than mindless automatons prepared to do whatever they were bid.

The readers of the country's newspapers certainly had their own opinions. It has been suggested, for example, that by the end of the nineteenth century, 'the people had . . . begun to have as much impact on the press as the papers did on the people . . . they now expressed tastes and interests to which the editors had to pay attention, at the risk of survival itself'. It has been seen, too, that readers were able to choose between newspapers promoting different political views – and it is striking that for many years papers opposed to the government of the day enjoyed larger circulations than those which offered their support.[82]

Even in the 1930s and early 1940s, some readers, viewers and listeners retained their critical edge. 'These days radio is uninteresting', wrote one dissatisfied listener in 1932. 'I'm getting tired of it.'

> One restraint after another is imposed by state officials who are like obstinate swine and have no comprehension of things. The best thing would be to liberate it from these restrictions and make it free, but even within the limits of present restraints, one can think of numerous methods preferable to those being used now.[83]

When the authorities banned jazz as decadent, the owners of the tea and coffee shops that played the music soon realised that they could continue doing so because, they claimed, the police were unable to distinguish between Mozart and Duke Ellington. In fact, 'the degenerate American jazz music' survived in the most unlikely circumstances: a *kamikaze* pilot describing the hours before his final flight, pointed out 'how funny' it was 'to listen to jazz music on the night before going out to kill the jazzy Americans'.[84]

In a fascinating study entitled 'Sensational rumours, seditious graffiti, and the nightmares of the thought police', Dower examines the way in which the morale of the country declined during the course of the war. He suggests that, 'contrary to the public rhetoric of one hundred million hearts beating as one, police records from as early as 1942 convey a picture not merely of demoralization and mounting defeatism, but of growing contempt for existing authority extending even to the emperor himself'. He argues, for example, that 'whispered rumours' began 'to supplant broadcast pieties as the people's touchstone of belief'. He cites the case of a Kyoto journalist who reported that as the war turned against Japan, the two hundred or so letters a day received by his paper included 'much denouncing of officials and the military for their alleged failure to share the people's hardships'. He reproduces examples of graffiti collected by the Thought Police between late 1941 and early 1944: 'Kill the Emperor', they read. 'Her Majesty the Empress is a lecher', 'No rice. End the War', 'Ridiculous to be a soldier – 35 *sen* a day'.[85]

The difficulty, of course, is to know how much weight to afford such evidence. It will never be possible to know for certain how to strike the balance between private doubts and public support, between what was thought, what was said, and what was written. Indeed, the supposed success of Japanese news management should not be misunderstood. It was a tribute not to the gullibility of the Japanese people, but to the determination of the country's rulers and the knowledge and skill of her editors, broadcasters and film-makers.

It is possible to discuss properly the impact only of what was printed in the press. There is no doubt that the newspapers exerted considerable power – and it does not seem unreasonable to suggest that the radio and cinema probably did the same. In fact, it has been suggested that press influence was the almost inevitable result of the changes taking place in the newspaper industry. By the 1890s, explains Huffman, the 'growing closeness between the papers and their readers touched off something of a circular process'. The capital investment necessary to produce papers attractive enough to sell in large numbers meant that they had to sell in large numbers in order to justify the capital investment which had been made. This meant, in other words, that the papers needed their readers as much as the readers needed their papers. The symbiosis which this created, claims Huffman, served only to reinforce the political and social impact of the press. 'The late-Meiji papers did more than pander to the masses, however; they also led them, sometimes in tumultuous directions.'[86]

The press continued to set the agenda and guide public opinion during the 1920s and 1930s. There seems little doubt – though it is impossible to prove – that the press was successful both in rousing opposition to, and in marshalling support for, those who were in power. It will be recalled from the discussion of international relations and imperial expansion that the failure to secure better terms in 1905 at the end of the Russo-Japanese War led to a great deal of domestic criticism, two days of rioting in Tokyo and the resignation of prime minister Katsura. 'Flags draped in black crêpe appeared around Tokyo', reports Edgerton. Leaflets 'denounced the government, newspapers bordered in black openly called for the assassination of cabinet members'. It will be recalled too that in 1931, the Wakatsuki government was afraid of provoking a *coup d'état* if it disciplined those responsible for the Manchurian Incident. The press did not confine their efforts to the printed page. Papers like the *Asahi* collected gifts and donations, organised lectures and exhibitions, produced news films like *The Shining Imperial Army* and *Let's Defend Manchuria and Mongolia*, and arranged to show them to some ten million viewers. 'In short, concludes Edgerton, 'the papers were enthusiastic and active in mobilizing the Japanese people on behalf of the military occupation of Manchuria.'[87]

Propaganda, susceptibility and persuasion

There is no denying the difficulty of determining the effect that education, religion and the media had upon popular attitudes and behaviour – and there is no question of claiming that these difficulties have now somehow been resolved. Nonetheless, it is believed that considerable progress has been made during the course of the chapter. It has been shown that education and the press, and later the radio and cinema, made serious, and increasingly determined, efforts to promote the ideas and values that those in power deemed to be desirable; and it has been suggested that it became increasingly difficult for students and readers and later listeners and viewers, to avoid being exposed to them. The result, it has also been suggested, was that, although the Japanese people were not especially susceptible to propaganda, the educational system, the press, radio and cinema played an important role in persuading their students and readers, their listeners and viewers to worship the emperor, support the government and behave in other respects as the authorities wanted.

Notes

1. **J. Hunter**, *The Emergence of Modern Japan: An Introductory History since 1853*, Longman, 1989, p. 183; **J.L. Huffman**, *Creating A Public: People and Press in Meiji Japan*, University of Hawaii Press, 1997, p. 2.

2. **M. Fletcher** in *Journal of Japanese Studies*, 23, 1997, p. 224; **A. Waswo**, *Modern Japanese Society 1868–1994*, Oxford University Press, 1996, pp. 26–33; **W.G. Beasley**, *The Rise of Modern Japan: Political, Economic and Social Change since 1850*, Weidenfeld and Nicolson, 1990 (2nd ed. 1995), p. 82. Also **A. Narusawa**, *Gendai nippon no shakai chitsujo*, Iwanami Shoten, 1997, pp. 31–3; **Y. Takeuchi**, *Risshin shusse shugi*, Nippon Hôsô Shuppan Kyôkai, 1997, pp. 155–65; **T. Hirota**, *Nipponjin no shitsuke wa suitai shitaka*, Kôdansha, 1999, pp. 8–48, esp. pp. 30–6.

3. Tokyo University was established in 1877 (and renamed Tokyo Imperial University in 1886), followed by Kyoto Imperial University in 1897, and Keiô (developed from Fukuzawa's school in 1858) and Waseda Universities in 1918. **C. Simmons**, *Growing Up and Going to School in Japan: Tradition and Trends*, Open University Press, 1990, p. 36; **D. Roden**, *Schooldays in Imperial Japan: A Study in the Culture of a Student Elite*, University of California Press, 1980; **B.K. Marshall**, 'Growth and Conflict in Japanese Higher Education, 1905–1930', in **T. Najita** and **J.V. Koschmann** (eds), *Conflict in Modern Japanese History*, Princeton University Press, 1982, pp. 276–7.

4. **B.K. Marshall**, *Learning to be Modern: Japanese Political Discourse on Education*, Westview Press, 1994, pp. 51–89; Beasley, *Rise*, p. 95; **Y. Fukuzawa**, *An Encouragement of Learning*, **D.A. Dilworth** and **U. Hirano** (trans.), Sophia University, 1969, pp. 1–2, 22, 30; **E.H. Kinmonth**, *The Self-Made Man in Japanese Thought: From Samurai to Salary Man*, University of California Press, 1981, pp. 50–7.

5. Fukuzawa, *Encouragement*, p. 24.

6. Fukuzawa's views influenced the preface to the Fundamental Code of 1872. Fukuzawa, *Encouragement*, pp. 6, 14, 23.

7. At least one teacher was burnt to death while trying to save an imperial portrait from a fire (*Japan Chronicle*, 10 February 1927). Although the Rescript has been interpreted as the ultimate statement of modern Confucian piety, Marshall comments that it 'was a compromise aimed at bridging the gap between traditionalists and modernizers'. At the same time that national morality was firmly grounded in the imperial institution ('a concrete symbol of uniquely Japanese customs and mores') it prevented 'renewed efforts to establish Confucianism as a moral orthodoxy or "national doctrine".' Marshall, *Learning to be Modern*, pp. 58–9. Simmons, *Growing Up*, pp. 30–1, 34–5. **D.J. Lu** (ed.), *Sources of Japanese History*, vol. 2, McGraw-Hill, 1974, pp. 70–1. **J.E. Thomas**, *Modern Japan: A Social History since 1868*, Longman, 1996, p. 258; **W.M. Fridell**, 'Government Ethics Textbooks in Late Meiji Japan', *Journal of Asian Studies*, August 1970.

8. One observer commented that, 'with the substitution of the stars and stripes for the emperor, the methods of moral education in Japan might well be translated to American soil'. **C. Gluck**, *Japan's Modern Myths: Ideology in the Late Meiji Period*, Princeton University Press, 1985, p. 146. **P. Brooker**, *The Faces of Fraternalism: Nazi Germany, Fascist Italy and Imperial Japan*, Clarendon Press, 1991, pp. 249–55; interview with Mrs N. Nakagama, Lethbridge, Canada, 24 May 1999. Cf. **Y. Soeda**, *Kyôiku chokugo no shakaishi*, Yûshindôkôbunsha, 1997, pp. 210–12, 229–33.

9. *Japan Chronicle*, 27 July 1933. For attempts to control the universities, see *Japan Chronicle*, 3 March 1927, 3 August 1933; *Japan Weekly Chronicle*, 6 March, 17 April 1930, 4 July 1935.

10. *Japan Times Weekly*, 26 January 1939; Thomas, *Modern Japan*, p. 262; Hunter, *Modern Japan*, p. 176; **T. Iritani**, *Group Psychology of the Japanese in Wartime*, Kegan Paul International, 1991, pp. 163–4.

11. It is well known that during the 1870s, the Ministry of Education sent Tanaka Fujimaro, Izawa Shûji, Takamine Hideo and others to Europe and the United States to learn from Western educational systems. **H. Passin**, *Society and Education in Japan*, Columbia University Press, 1956, pp. 88–92; Simmons, *Growing Up*, pp. 31–2; **E. Baelz**, *Awakening Japan: The Diary of a German Doctor: Erwin Baelz*, Indiana University Press, 1974, p. 360; **J. Morris**, *Traveller from Tokyo*, The Book Club, 1945, p. 47.

12. *Daughters of Changing Japan* is an intriguing account of ten women's experiences and attitudes in the years before and after the Second World War. Not strictly a translation, it is a narrative reconstruction based on the life stories of these women who wrote their histories specifically for the author's use. **E.H. Cressy**, *Daughters of Changing Japan*, Victor Gollancz, 1955, pp. 68–72; 76–7.

13. Iritani, *Group Psychology*, p. 191. Also pp. 176–80, 192–4; *Japan Chronicle*, 20 July 1933; **I. Buruma**, *Wages of Guilt: Memories of War in Germany and Japan*, Vintage, 1995, pp. 191–2.

14. Simmons, *Growing Up*, pp. 26–7, 39. However, an official investigation suggested that in 1930 200,000 and more children were not at school. See *Japan Weekly Chronicle*, 17 April 1930. For popular disinterest in, and opposition to education, see Takeuchi, *Risshin shusse shugi*, pp. 143–5; Hirota, *Nipponjin no shitsuke*, pp. 40, 50–74.

15. However, the system continued to be based less upon nurturing individual ability than upon the reproduction of existing economic and social structures. **T. Liesner**, *One Hundred Years of Economic Statistics*, Economist Publications, 1989, pp. 262–3;

W.O. **Lee**, *Social Change and Educational Problems in Japan, Singapore and Hong Kong*, Macmillan, 1991, pp. 148–9; **D.B. Smith**, *Japan since 1945: The Rise of an Economic Superpower*, Macmillan, 1995, p. 50; Marshall, 'Growth and Conflict', pp. 276–9. Also **I. Amano**, *Gakureki no shakaishi – kyôiku to nippon no kindai*, Shinchôsha, 1992, pp. 146–8.

16. By the time of the Sino-Japanese War, Tokutomi had become highly nationalistic. **D. Irokawa**, *The Culture of the Meiji Period*, **M.B. Jansen** (ed. and trans.), Princeton University Press, 1985, pp. 299–300.

17. *Japan Times*, 23 March, 21 April, 22 April 1897; Thomas, *Modern Japan*, p. 46.

18. Uchimura supported the Sino-Japanese War but opposed the Russo-Japanese War. *YC*, 26 September 1903.

19. *Japan Chronicle*, 3 February 1927, 10 August 1933; *Japan Weekly Chronicle*, 11 July 1935.

20. Marshall, *Learning to be Modern*, p. 102; *Japan Weekly Chronicle*, 9 September 1920; 2, 30 January, 27 February 1930; Morris, *Traveller*, p. 48; Cressy, *Daughters of Changing Japan*, pp. 114–15. For the universities, see Marshall, 'Growth and Conflict'.

21. Iritani, *Group Psychology*, pp. 192–3; *South China Morning Post*, 29 August 1997. Also **H. Gold**, *Unit 731: Testimony*, Yenbooks, 1996, pp. 245–6, 250; Waswo, *Modern Japanese Society*, p. 64; Huffman, *Creating a Public*, pp. 226, 312–13.

22. **K. Tsurumi**, *Social Change and the Individual: Japan Before and After Defeat in World War II*, Princeton University Press, 1970, pp. 272–3.

23. There were a number of other agencies involved in the inculcation of patriotic values and the cultivation of military discipline. Organisations like the Greater Japan Youth Association and the Imperial Military Reserve Association were established to 'plug the obvious gap in the male indoctrination system – the period of adolescence between the ending of compulsory elementary schooling and conscription into the armed forces'. Although their influence was important particularly in the 1930s, there was a conspicuous discrepancy between (high) rural and (low) urban membership rates. If the cities were underrepresented, females were hardly targeted at all, although female youth clubs and groups were established around the nation independent of government sponsorship. Brooker, *Faces of Fraternalism*, pp. 259–66. Further discussion is found in **R.J. Smethurst**, *A Social Basis for Prewar Japanese Militarism*, University of California Press, 1974.

24. *Japan Weekly Chronicle*, 6 March 1930; **I. Hall**, *Mori Arinori*, Harvard University Press, 1973, p. 344.

25. Mori was assassinated while Minister of Education. **G. Letendre**, 'Guiding Them On: Teaching, Hierarchy, and Social Organization in Japanese Middle Schools', *Journal of Japanese Studies*, 20, 1994, p. 42; **R.G. Edgerton**, *Warriors of the Rising Sun*, Norton, 1997, p. 306.

26. Gluck, *Japan's Modern Myths*, pp. 135–6; *JS*, 29 June 1894; *KS*, 10 August 1894.

27. Irokawa, *Culture of the Meiji Period*, pp. 305–6.

28. Marshall, *Learning to be Modern*, p. 107.

29. **S. Ienaga**, *The Pacific War: World War II and the Japanese, 1931–1945*, Pantheon books, 1978, pp. 107–9; Buruma, *Wages*, pp. 191–2; Passin, *Society and Education*, pp. 191–2.

30. Iritani, *Group Psychology*, pp. 166, 193; *South China Morning Post*, 29 August 1997.

31. Buruma, *Wages*, pp. 172–3, 189–201.

32. **R. Johnson**, 'Educational Policy and Social Control in Early Victorian England', *Past and Present*, 49, 1970, p. 119.

33. **J. Dower**, *Japan in War and Peace: Essays on History, Race and Culture*, HarperCollins, 1995, p. 273; **K.B. Pyle**, *The Making of Modern Japan*, Heath, 1996 (2nd edition), p. 50; **A.C. Underwood**, *Shintôism: The Indigenous Religion of Japan*, Epworth Press, 1934; **H. Hardacre**, *Shintô and the State, 1868–1988*, Princeton University Press, 1989, pp. 4–5; **S. Murakami**, *Japanese Religion in the Modern Century*, **H.B. Earhart** (trans.), University of Tokyo Press, 1968, pp. 4–10. For the debate over whether Shinto was a religion, see Hardacre, *Shintô*, pp. 39, 115, 256. Other general discussions of Shinto and Japanese religions include **I. Hori**, *Folk Religions in Japan*, Chicago University Press, 1968; **J. Kitagawa**, *On Understanding Japanese Religion*, Princeton University Press, 1987.

34. *Japan Times Weekly*, 6 October 1938; Reischauer, *Japanese Today*, pp. 207–9; Hardacre, *Shinto*, p. 14.

35. *Japan Weekly Chronicle*, 19 August 1920; *Japan Times Weekly*, 23 October 1938; Reischauer, *Japanese Today*, p. 209; Hardacre, *Shintô*, pp. 59, 124.

36. Hardacre, *Shintô*, pp. 43–4, 50. Two important articles on the interrelationship of Shinto, politics and the Restoration are **J. Breen**, 'Shintôists in Restoration Japan (1868–1872): Towards a Reassessment', *Modern Asian Studies*, 24, 1990; **J. Breen**, 'The Imperial Oath of April 1868: Ritual, Politics, and Power in the Restoration', *Monumenta Nipponica*, 1996.

37. Hardacre, *Shintô*, pp. 38, 90–2, 128–9; **H. Hardacre**, 'Creating State Shinto: The Great Promulgation Campaign and the New Religions', *Journal of Japanese Studies*, 12, 1986, p. 43; Buruma, *Wages*, p. 219ff.

38. Baelz, *Awakening Japan*, p. 354.

39. **W.M. Fridell**, *Japanese Shrine Mergers, 1906–1912: State Shintô Moves to the Grassroots*, Sophia University, 1973, p. 45.

40. *Japan Times Weekly*, 6 October 1938; Hardacre, 'Creating State Shintô', p. 45; **E. Behr**, *Hirohito: Behind the Myth*, Penguin, 1990, pp. 95–8, 242; Hardacre, *Shintô*, pp. 32–3, 38, 59, 124. Also *Japan Weekly Chronicle*, 20 February 1930; Gluck, *Japan's Modern Myths*, pp. 142–3.

41. Even today, Shinto shrines play a preeminent role in the rites of passage including marriage, birth and the important stages (the third, fifth and seventh year) of a child's life. Hardacre, *Shintô*, pp. 44–5, 60, 110–11; Hardacre, 'Creating State Shintô', p. 46. Also *Japan Times Weekly*, 6 October 1938.

42. Fridell, *Shrine Mergers*, pp. 102, 82–3.

43. *Japan Weekly Chronicle*, 19 August 1920; Reischauer, *Japanese Today*, pp. 265–7; Hardacre, 'Creating State Shintô', p. 44; **H. Cortazzi**, *Modern Japan: A Concise Survey*, Macmillan, 1993, p. 183; **C. Holland**, *Things Seen in Japan*, Seeley, Service, 1912, p. 204; Gluck, *Japan's Modern Myths*, pp. 132–8. An excellent overview of the threat to Buddhism in the Meiji period and its attempts to accommodate itself to the new circumstances is **M. Collcutt**, 'Buddhism: The Threat of Eradication', in **M.B. Jansen** and **G. Rozman** (eds), *Japan in Transition: From Tokugawa to Meiji*, Princeton University Press, 1986, pp. 143–67.

44. Waswo, *Modern Japanese Society*, p. 16; Reischauer, *Japanese Today*, pp. 203–4; Cortazzi, *Modern Japan*, p. 76; Gluck, *Japan's Modern Myths*, pp. 107, 111; Passin, *Society and Education*, pp. 97–101.

45. Murakami, *Japanese Religion*, pp. 10–18, 70–91. A concise guide to the major 'new religions' and their doctrines is **H. Thomsen**, *The New Religions of Japan*, Charles E. Tuttle, 1963.

46. G. **Wilson**, 'What the Hell! *Ee ja nai ka* Dancing as a Form of Protest', in G. **Wilson** (ed.), *Patriots and Redeemers in Japan: Motives in the Meiji Restoration*, University of Chicago Press, 1992, pp. 105, 111; S. **Vlastos**, '*Yonaoshi* in Aizu', in Najita and Koschman (eds), *Conflict*, pp. 164–75. S. **Takamoto**, '*Ee ja nai ka*', Kyôikusha, 1979, pp. 208–34.
47. 31,000 people were transported from Nagasaki – and 1,500 returned without abandoning their belief in Christianity. Breen, 'Shintoists', pp. 579–602; *The Nagasaki Express*, 1, 15 January, 20, 28 May 1870. S. **Turnbull** examines the history of the 'hidden Christians' in *Kakure Kirishitan of Japan: A Study of their Development, Beliefs and Rituals to the Present Day*, Japan Library, 1998.
48. Beasley, *Rise of Modern Japan*, p. 97. Surveys of Christianity in modern Japan include **J.L. Van Hecken**, *The Catholic Church in Japan since 1859*, **J. Van Hoydonck** (trans.), Heder Agency, 1963; A. **Lande**, *Meiji Protestantism in History and Historiography*, Uppsala University, 1988; O. **Cary**, *A History of Christianity in Japan*, 2 vols, Curzon Press, 1993.
49. Hardacre, *Shintô*, pp. 22–6; Hardacre, 'Creating State Shintô', p. 46; **S.M. Garon**, 'State and Religion in Imperial Japan, 1912–1945', *Journal of Japanese Studies*, 12, 1986, p. 277.
50. Hardacre, *Shintô*, p. 161.
51. *Japan Times Weekly*, 6, 20 October 1938; Garon, 'State and Religion', pp. 300–1; Brooker, *Faces*, pp. 244–6.
52. Hardacre, 'Creating State Shintô', p. 41; Garon, 'State and Religion', p. 276.
53. *Japan Weekly Chronicle*, 23 January 1930; 6, 20 October 1938; *Japan Chronicle*, 3 August 1933; Hardacre, *Shintô*, pp. 25–6, 91, 109–10.
54. Morris, *Traveller*, p. 49; **L.W. Johns**, *Japan: Reminiscences and Realities*, Stanley Paul, 1939, p. 12.
55. **Lady Lawson**, *Highways and Homes of Japan*, T. Fisher Unwin, 1910, pp. 264–5.
56. Edgerton, *Warriors*, p. 312. Also Buruma, *Wages*, p. 173.
57. Iritani, *Group Psychology*, p. 161.
58. Huffman, *Creating a Public*, pp. 371–2; Reischauer, *Japanese Today*, p. 220.
59. T. **Yamamoto**, 'The Press Clubs of Japan', *Journal of Japanese Studies*, 15, 1989, p. 375; Huffman, *Creating a Public*, pp. 14, 17.
60. **B.K. Marshall**, review of **R.H. Mitchell**, *Censorship in Imperial Japan*, Princeton University Press, 1983, *Journal of Japanese Studies*, 11, 1985, p. 223; Huffman, *Creating a Public*, pp. 44–5.
61. The extent of press censorship is hotly debated. Akita, who asserts that the oligarchy was 'force-feeding liberalisation', claims that 'suppression' was light. Sims agrees claiming that censorship was 'unsystematic' and that it was possible to discuss 'fundamental issues' like the best form of government. G. **Akita**, *Foundations of Constitutional Government in Modern Japan: 1868–1900*, Harvard University Press, 1967, pp. 2, 174; **R.L. Sims**, *A Political History of Modern Japan: 1868–1952*, Vikas, p. 53; Baelz, *Awakening Japan*, p. 20; Huffman, *Creating a Public*, pp. 68–77; **J.B. Lee**, *The Political Character of the Japanese Press*, Seoul National University Press, 1985, pp. 13–14.
62. Yamamoto, 'Press Clubs', pp. 375–6.
63. Yamamoto, 'Press Clubs', pp. 371–4, 382, 387.
64. **B.-A. Shillony**, *Politics and Culture in Wartime Japan*, Clarendon Press, 1981, pp. 93, 144.
65. Fukuzawa, *Encouragement*, p. 22; Baelz, *Awakening Japan*, p. 21; Lee, *Political Character*, pp. 14, 16, 28–9, 32.

66. *JS*, 29 July 1894; *OM*, 29 January 1904.

67. *HS*, 17 January 1904; *YC*, 25–27 September 1904; Mitchell, *Censorship*, pp. 135–9.

68. *TM*, 5 January 1910.

69. Huffman, *Creating a Public*, p. 373.

70. *OM*, 12 August 1918; *Japan Chronicle*, 17 April 1919, 17 March 1927; *Japan Weekly Chronicle*, 12 February 1925; *OM*, 16 August 1918; Lee, *Political Character*, pp. 35–8; **T. Yamamoto**, review of **G.J. Kasza**, *The State and the Mass Media in Japan, 1918–1945*, University of California Press, 1988, in *Journal of Japanese Studies*, 16, 1990, p. 189. See also *JS*, 16 August 1918.

71. *Japan Weekly Chronicle*, 2 September 1920; Marshall, in *Journal of Japanese Studies*, 11, 1985, p. 233; *TA*, 2 August 1894; Fukuzawa, *Encouragement*, p. 25.

72. Lee, *Political Character*, pp. 41–2; *TA*, 20 September 1931; *OM*, 27 September 1931. On press censure of the army, see for example the article by **K. Yokota**, *Teikoku daigaku shimbun*, 5 October 1931; *TA*, 6 October 1931.

73. Lee, *Political Character*, p. 47; Reischauer, *Japanese Today*, p. 221.

74. Kasza, *State*, pp. 55, 59–60, 64–5.

75. Kasza, *State*, pp. 72–3, 78–9, 82–4, 89–96; *Japan Times Weekly*, 9 February 1939; Morris, *Traveller*, pp. 84–6; **R. Benedict**, *The Chrysanthemum and the Sword: Patterns of Japanese Culture*, Charles E. Tuttle, 1996, p. 96; Dower, *Japan*, pp. 33–51, esp. pp. 35, 51.

76. *NN*, 17 December 1941; Shillony, *Politics*, p. 99. Also *Japan Times Weekly*, 1 August 1943; Kasza, *State*, pp. 232–3, 252.

77. Shillony, *Politics and Culture*, pp. 95–7.

78. Reference mislaid.

79. Huffman, *Creating a Public*, p. 386.

80. Huffman, *Creating a Public*, p. 387; Lee, *Political Character*, pp. 12–13, 16, 20–2, 24–6; Shillony, *Politics*, p. 91.

81. *Japan Times Weekly*, 19 January 1939; Morris, *Traveller*, pp. 84–6; Kasza, *Origins*, p. 54.

82. Huffman, *Creating a Public*, pp. 197–8; Lee, *Political Character*, pp. 28–44.

83. Kasza, *State*, p. 96.

84. Shillony, *Politics*, p. 144.

85. Dower, *Japan*, pp. 124–31. See also **R. Mitchell**, *Thought Control in Prewar Japan*, Cornell University Press, 1976.

86. Huffman, *Creating a Public*, pp. 222–3, 330; Lee, *Political Character*, p. 40.

87. Edgerton, *Warriors*, p. 219; Lee, *Political Character*, p. 44.

Individual, family, class and nation

Whatever power they attribute to education, religion and the media, there are many in both East and West who believe that Japanese society was – and remains – virtually unique. It was a society, they contend, which was distinguished by its homogeneity, by the weakness of the individual and the strength of the family, by the weakness of class ties and by the strength of the people's loyalty to the nation. Whether or not it is accepted that these features of Japanese social organisation were imposed by those in authority, it is asserted on every side that they provide an invaluable way of understanding developments in Japanese politics, international relations and economic life which might otherwise remain largely, if not completely, inexplicable.

It is agreed almost without exception that the Japanese, like many others in the East, valued the individual less than the group. In Japan, claims Lee, 'individualism has always been subordinated to family and group loyalty'. Macpherson agrees. 'Most important was the subjection of the individual to the group, originally the *ie* or household later transferred to the company or firm.' Even today, the Japanese, it is maintained, 'are much more likely than Westerners to operate in groups or at least to see themselves as operating in this way'.

> Whereas Westerners may at least put on a show of independence and individuality, most Japanese will be quite content to conform in dress, conduct, style of life and even thought to the norms of their group.[1]

There is much less agreement about the consequences of the homogeneity that results from valuing the individual less than the group. Those from the East tend to take a positive view. Lee, for example, believes that 'Industrial growth and efficiency have been enormously facilitated by the possibility of transferring these traditional life-long loyalties to the firm and corporation'. Ozaki too places great emphasis upon the importance of group consciousness in the country's culture.

To approach one's work strictly as a contractual matter makes many Japanese uncomfortable. It is too dry and inhuman. To report to work no earlier than is required, to go home as soon as the official work hours for the day are over, even if there is an unfinished job lying on the desk . . . seems to indicate, to the Japanese eye, that you do not identify yourself with your company.[2]

Those from the West tend to be more divided about the consequences of favouring the group so highly. Some are extremely critical, feeling that lack of individuality is tantamount to lack of humanity. In the early 1990s, when trade disputes with Europe over cars were at their height, French prime minister Edith Cresson criticised the Japanese as

little yellow men . . . who spend all night thinking of ways to screw us [in their] absolute desire to conquer the world. . . . [They] work like ants, live in little flats and take two hours to commute to work. . . . We [the French] cannot live like that, I mean, in those tiny flats, with two hours of commuting to get to work. . . . We want to keep our social security, our holidays, to live like human beings as we have always lived.

Of course, such racist vitriol is not that common, at least in public statements. Nevertheless, even seemingly 'objective' arguments concerning the merits and demerits of group-centredness *vis-à-vis* Western individualism frequently smack of ethnocentrism. 'If democracy means the rule "of the people, by the people and for the people",' maintains Woronoff, 'then what passes for democracy in Japan certainly does not qualify.' Others suggest that the emphasis placed upon the group helped – and helps – to create a dedicated workforce, a loyal citizenry and a crime-free society. Because 'the self-esteem of the ordinary Japanese depends upon his identification with the group', explains Christopher, 'the withdrawal of group approval' provides a 'powerful deterrent to crime in Japan'. In fact, he concludes, 'any Japanese who has once suffered the psychic torments of social disapproval or rejection is unlikely to risk facing that experience again'.[3]

Such arguments remain, of course, enormously difficult either to substantiate or to repudiate. It is dangerously unhistorical to take the claims made about Japanese society since the Allied Occupation and apply them to the years before it. There is also something ahistorical about the claims made for the homogeneity and group consciousness of Japanese society between 1868 and 1945. It will never be possible to delineate unequivocally the relationships which existed between millions and millions of individuals, the families in which they were brought up, the classes in which they found themselves, and the country to which they belonged.

Nonetheless, it is believed that considerable progress can be made. It will be suggested that the generalisations commonly made about the homogeneity of Japanese society between the Restoration and the Allied Occupation stand in need of substantial modification. It will be argued that it is necessary to look beyond the easily recognisable examples of group consciousness and national homogeneity to take account of the less obvious, but perhaps little less significant, instances of individualism, family tension, class consciousness and heterogeneous behaviour. Only then will it be possible to judge with any confidence the true nature of Japanese society between 1868 and 1945.

Individualism

Nobody would deny that Japanese society changed enormously between the Restoration and the Allied Occupation. It would hardly be surprising therefore if there were changes in the relationships which developed between individuals, the families in which they were raised, the classes in which they found themselves and the country to which they belonged. Accordingly, it is the purpose of this section of the chapter to begin to explore these issues by examining the role of the individual in Japanese society. It will be shown that, although the position of the individual changed very significantly, it did not do so in the simple, linear fashion that common sense might lead one to suppose.[4]

The undermining of the individual

Given the developments in politics, international relations, economic life and education, religion and the media which have been discussed in earlier chapters, there are obvious grounds for supposing that the political, economic and social power of the individual was weakened significantly between 1868 and 1945. It has been seen that, particularly at times of internal crisis and war, the state and its agents made determined, and increasingly successful, efforts to impose their will in virtually every sphere of national life. Indeed, what has not been stressed as strongly as it might have been is that many of these efforts were directed, either directly or indirectly, towards the undermining of the individual, and the promotion of the group.

It is important to make clear that many of the reforms enacted in the years immediately following the Restoration were designed, *inter alia*, to foster loyalty to the family and obedience to the emperor in order to provide the nation with unifying symbols in the face of what was seen as a serious threat from the West. We know that 'the Government encouraged through [the Constitution], the educational system and State Shinto, a belief in the emperor as a symbol of Japan's divine origins and destined greatness'. It is clear too that persuasion was reinforced by coercion.

> Individuals were guided towards the ideals of service and loyalty through a centralized system of compulsory education and military conscription, but for those whose individualism survived these processes, a comprehensive local police force used repression to eradicate dissent.[5]

It is also important to make clear that such efforts were intensified during the late 1930s and early 1940s. In 1938, the Foreign Affairs Association – under the supervision of the Bureau of Information – stressed that the Japanese had 'no conception of the individual as opposed to the State'. The Association went on to explain that Western ways of thinking about the relationship between individuals and the state were fundamentally flawed. 'All human beings who are actually living in this world are entities which, while having their respective independent life and existence, depend, in a deeper sense, upon the whole and live in coordinated relationship with one another.'

> They are, in reality, born from the State, sustained by the State, and brought up in the history and traditions of the State. In other words, individual men can exist essentially only as links in an infinite and vast chain of life which is called the State.[6]

The state used whatever groups it could – the family, the company, youth leagues, women's groups and neighbourhood associations – to control individual behaviour and, insofar as it was possible, individual thought. The neighbourhood associations are of particular interest. By September 1940, there were more than a million such associations in existence, each of them normally consisting of between ten and twenty families. They were used for both administrative and political purposes. They 'disseminated official instructions, usually by means of a *kairanban*, or "circulating bulletin board", reported on compliance with them, distributed rations, collected taxes and contributions, and performed a number of similar services'. These strategies, it is claimed, proved highly successful. 'The multiplicity of groups to which each individual was obliged to belong placed further constraints on his or her activities, and discouraged the expression of independent thought even among close friends or relatives.'[7]

The resilience of the individual

Such views have the ring of truth. When one considers the range of institutions that were used to control the behaviour of the individual, it seems almost perverse to doubt the effectiveness of state influence. Yet as has been seen so often in the course of this book, generalisation is dangerous and governments did not necessarily achieve all that they wished. It is prudent to be sceptical: public responses must not be mistaken for private beliefs.

It is important to recognise that not all the reforms enacted in the aftermath of the Restoration were designed to foster loyalty to the family and obedience to the emperor. They were intended, some of them, to promote the individual. They promoted the individual, others of them, even though this was not the primary intention of those introducing them. The abolition of the feudal system, the restructuring of taxation, the reform of education and the introduction of conscription combined, in their different ways, to assert the importance of the individual as well as of the group.

Education certainly played a part. 'Merely by setting foot in Meiji classrooms,' it has been said, 'youngsters found themselves in an achievement-oriented setting in which performance, not wealth or image, counted.' The military too had an impact. For, despite the emphasis which the army laid upon discipline and co-ordinated action, it also placed considerable responsibility upon the individual soldier. 'What mattered was what the conscripts themselves could do, not the status of their families, and they were rewarded, or punished, according to their own achievements.'[8]

Moreover, as Dower has been at pains to point out, the efforts made by the state to contain signs of independence were themselves testimony to the resilience of the independence and individualism that the authorities distrusted so strongly. It was not the case, he argues, that even during the Second World War, 'the Japanese people were, in actuality, homogeneous and harmonious, devoid of individuality and thoroughly subordinated to the group'.

> Indeed, the government deemed it necessary to draft and propagate a rigid orthodoxy ... precisely because the ruling classes were convinced that a great many Japanese did not cherish the more traditional virtues of loyalty and filial piety under the emperor, but instead remained attracted to more democratic values and ideals.[9]

The difficulty, of course, is to decide how to measure the ways in which individuals thought and the ways in which they interacted with those around them. There is no shortage of anecdotal evidence. But it is hard to know how much weight to accord, for instance, to the 'civilisation and enlightenment' thinkers whose conceptions of the individual 'consisted in the main of British liberalism, or utilitarianism based upon it, French notions of people's rights, German nationalism, and, one might add, American sects of Christianity'. How are we to interpret the behaviour of eccentrics who flew in the face of convention, individuals who opposed the government of the day and women's groups which challenged existing social and political assumptions?

Can we take it for granted indeed that readers interpreted the writings, thoughts and deeds of such outstanding 'individualists' in the ways that were intended? It is possible, for example, that the theme of individual self-reliance that is found in *Self Help* may have been read as a Tokugawa-style Confucian treatise extolling the relationship between individual character, the Way of Heaven and the nation. 'National progress is the sum of individual industry, energy and uprightness, as national decay is of individual idleness, selfishness and vice.' Similarly, Fukuzawa's groundbreaking treatise, *An Encouragement of Learning*, was not, as Dore explains, 'simply introducing a startling new Western idea; [it] was succinctly summarizing a current of thought long since developing in Tokugawa society'. In short, there is the danger, with which we are all now familiar, of mistaking the visible for the normal, the intriguing for the important, the unusual for the usual.[10]

What is needed, it is not difficult to see, is some quantitative measure of individual attitudes and the individual's relationship to society. If a suitable measure could be found and reliable evidence collected, it could be used to construct an index of 'individuality' between 1868 and 1945. The problem, of course, is that there is no generally accepted and readily available measure of political, economic and social individuality. Nor is there ever likely to be. Nevertheless, it is believed that there are three measures which may prove of some value as we attempt to chart the individual's position in Japanese society. The first is the birth rate, the second is the age of marriage and the third is the suicide rate.

The birth rate was obviously the product of many factors other than the individual's relationship to society. However, it is believed that the examination of this aspect of demographic history will prove to be more helpful than one might imagine. This is because of the possibility that fertility was related inversely to individuality. It may be the case, in other words, that an increase in fertility represented a decrease in individualism, and a decrease in fertility an increase in individualism.

Reliable national statistics are not available until well into the twentieth century, but it seems likely that the birth rate changed little during the last thirty years of the nineteenth century. Thereafter, however, the birth rate declined by 16 per cent between 1920 and 1935, and by a further 9 per cent between 1935 and 1950 (though it possibly increased during the Pacific War). If one accepts the possibility of a link between fertility and individuality, these figures acquire considerable significance. They suggest that the decline in the birth rate after the First World War reflected not just rising standards of living, improving health and the increasing availability and acceptance of contraception, but also a change in women's aspirations for themselves, and some change too in men's and women's aspirations for their children. The connection, tenuous though it may seem, is certainly intriguing.[11]

According to some theorists, the decline in the birth rate was connected to, and perhaps caused by, a long-term increase in the age at marriage from the turn of the century. In 1910, the average age at which men and women married was 26.94 and 22.92 respectively. By 1940, these ages had increased to 28.95 and 24.61.

> The prewar trend towards later marriage (which was more marked in rural than in urban prefectures, reflecting a levelling between town and country) may be attributed to . . . the following factors . . . the extension of opportunities for higher education and employment of women – the former affecting upper- and the latter lower-class girls, and . . . less tangibly, an increasing reaction against the attitude expressed in the traditionally accepted reason for early marriage: that a girl should be married off as young as possible while she was still immature and malleable and so able to adapt herself easily to her position in her new home as her mother-in-law's servant-in-chief.[12]

The connection between suicide and individuality may be just as tenuous. But it is just as intriguing. Of course, the suicide rate, like the birth rate and the age of marriage, was the product of many factors other than the individual's position in society. (It may well be, for example, that fluctuations in the suicide rate were associated with fluctuations in people's sense of economic well-being – and almost certain that the decline in the rate after 1930 was associated with the pressure on people to dedicate their lives to the emperor.) Nonetheless, it is believed that the examination of this aspect of demographic history too will prove of some value when attempting to understand Japanese individualism. This is because of the possibility, first raised by Durkheim at the end of the nineteenth century, that there was an inverse relationship between suicide and the individual's sense of integration into the society to which he or she belonged.[13]

It has been reported that the suicide rate increased by 40 per cent between 1884 and 1913, declined by 6 per cent between 1913 and 1930, and by a further 34 per cent between 1930 and 1942. If one accepts the existence of a correlation between suicide and alienation, these figures too acquire considerable significance. However, they do not make the task any easier, for they point to a conclusion very different from that suggested by the demographic data which were considered above. On the one hand, the decline in the birth rate and the increase in the age of marriage indicates, if anything, that there was an increase in individualism between 1920 and 1935. On the other hand, the rise and subsequent decline of the suicide rate suggest, if anything, that there was an increase in alienation/individualism between 1884 and 1913, a modest decrease between 1913 and 1930, and a substantial decrease between 1930 and 1942. Suicide was romanticised, not in the tradition of the *samurai* ethic of loyalty, but as an ultimate expression of individuality. In 1903, an eighteen year old student destined for Tokyo Imperial University struck a chord when he committed suicide at Kegon Falls, not far from Tokyo. Before jumping, he carved in the trunk of a tree a poem, 'Thoughts upon the Precipice', which became a best-selling pamphlet and which inspired over the next five years, it is said, more than a hundred suicide attempts at Kegon Falls alone.

> The philosophy of Horatio
> What means it in the end?
> All the truth is but one word –
>   Unfathomable.
> Anguished, I think of this.
> In the end, I decide on death.
> Quiet. Quiet.[14]

It is difficult to know what to make of such contradictory propositions. Paradoxically, however, there is something revealing about the very difficulty of reconciling the three sets of data. It reminds us to be circumspect when generalising about individual attitudes and the individual's position in society. It alerts us to the need to be cautious, if not sceptical, when considering the confidence with which some observers and analysts feel able to comment upon individuals, individualism and individuality. It suggests, perhaps, that individualism and group loyalty co-existed more readily than is often supposed. There are good reasons for believing that the position of the individual in Japanese society changed, and changed significantly between 1868 and 1945. But there are no reasons at all for supposing that it did so in some simple, linear fashion which can be quickly identified and easily described.

The family

Such contradictions and cautions serve as a warning too against accepting too readily the claims which are made for the persistence, power and prestige of the Japanese family. The family, of course, took many forms:

from the so-called 'traditional' family comprising a husband and wife, married children, relatives and servants; to the 'modern', nuclear family consisting of a husband, wife and unmarried children. If it is accepted that society changed greatly between 1868 and 1945 and that the role of the individual probably changed with it, it would be extremely surprising if the family remained unaffected by what was going on within it and around it. Accordingly it is the purpose of this section of the chapter to examine the position of the family in Japanese society. It will be shown that, although the power and prestige of the family must never be overlooked, it does not follow that its dominant position remained universal, unchallenged or unchanging.

The rural family

The 'traditional', close-knit family had its roots deep in rural society. Indeed, it is sometimes suggested that it was the mountainous nature of the country and its susceptibility to earthquakes and typhoons that encouraged mutual dependence and collective action. It is much more commonly accepted that the cultivation of rice depended heavily upon family and/or communal methods of cultivation. Once the site for a paddy-field was selected, it had to be levelled and an irrigation system constructed; once the rice was planted, it had to be transplanted, weeded, harvested, threshed, winnowed and polished. 'All these things require an intensive team effort, none more so than the levelling of the ground necessary to grow the rice (the ground must be absolutely even, or part of the crop will be dry and part saturated by water), the building of low banks of water around the paddy-fields, and the irrigation of the field to replace water lost through evaporation, leakage or in transit.'[15]

Material imperatives were reinforced by ideological encouragement. It was seen in the previous chapter that Confucianism had always laid great emphasis upon family loyalty and obedience to one's superiors. This meant that those who found themselves in subordinate positions in the social hierarchy were expected to respect their superiors and be grateful for any favours that were bestowed upon them. Gender and age were both important: wives were expected to respect their husbands, children their parents, sisters their brothers and younger brothers their elder brothers. A woman, it was said, 'was thrice without a home': she was dependent first upon her father, then upon her husband and, if she outlived her husband, finally perhaps upon her son.[16]

The result, it seems to be agreed, was that the family constituted an integral part of the pre-Restoration system of authority, deference and obedience. It was a system, some even go so far as to claim, which 'was among the most elaborately and fiercely repressive the world had ever seen'.

> There were at least four levels of oppression: the hierarchy within the family, the hierarchy within the village, the hierarchy of economic dependence – usually between landlord and tenant – and the hierarchy of central government over local community.[17]

The reinforcing of the family

One could be forgiven for thinking that the last thing that the institution of the family needed was any reinforcing. However, the authorities were not prepared to take risks with so valuable an institution. So although the family was deeply entrenched, especially in rural society, they did their best to ensure that it – or certain aspects of it – survived the changes brought about by economic growth, industrialisation and urbanisation. Nor were they tilting at windmills. It was seen in chapter 4 that the Japanese economy was growing, growing fast, and from the First World War onwards growing faster than those of her major competitors. It must not be forgotten that this impressive economic performance was accompanied by, and dependent upon, the rapid growth of the urban population. As Figure 15 indicates, the proportion of the population living in (incorporated) cities was growing, and growing fast. It grew almost seven times between the early 1890s and 1940, increasing from 10 per cent in 1891, to nearly 17 per cent in 1913, just under 24 per cent in 1930 and 38 per cent in 1940.[18]

In fact, the authorities took such pains to protect, reform and elevate patriarchal values and women's domesticity from threats such as these that some believe that the 'traditional' family was the creation of the Meiji state. Although this is an exaggeration, the conception of the family that evolved in these years differed significantly from its pre-modern counterpart. One of the first tasks the Meiji authorities set for themselves was the reform of sexual morality, with concubinage, common-law marriage, pre-nuptial sex, extra-marital trysts and liberal attitudes towards 'bisexual' activity – none of which were necessarily inconsistent with Confucian ethics – early victims of the government's intervention.[19]

The leaders of Meiji Japan then turned to codifying the new morality concerning the family, gender and sexual practice. The new educational system treated boys and girls very differently, the Constitution of 1889 excluded women from the political process, and the Civil Code of 1898 enshrined patriarchy and patrilinealism. As Waswo points out, 'Only

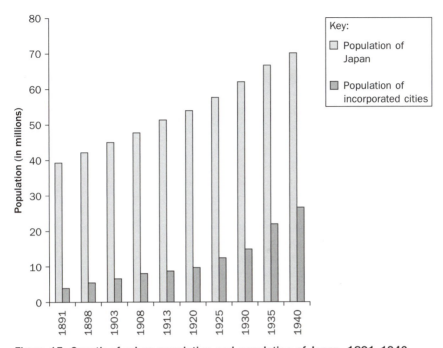

Figure 15: Growth of urban population and population of Japan, 1891–1940

Source: Compiled from T.O. Wilkinson, *The Urbanization of Japanese Labor, 1868–1955*, University of Massachusetts Press, 1965, p. 45; *Sôrifu tôkeikyoku*, Nihon tôkei nenkan.

men were legally recognised persons; women were classified in the same category as the "deformed and mentally incompetent" and needed their father's or husband's consent before entering into a legal contract.'

A husband was free to dispose of his wife's property as he wished; only a wife's adultery constituted immediate grounds for divorce; in the event of divorce, the husband or his parents took custody of the children.[20]

The ministry of education always took a gendered view of its responsibilities. It announced at the end of the century that the purpose of female education was to create 'good wives and wise mothers'. Immediately afterwards, it issued a 'morals' textbook which set out in detail what was required. In a passage which is worth quoting at some length, it stressed how differently girls and boys needed to be brought up. 'Girls must be gentle and graceful in all things. In their conduct and manner of speech, they must not be harsh.' But the ministry foresaw difficulties.

Loquacity and jealousy are defects common among women, so care must be taken to guard against these faults. When a girl marries she must serve her husband and his parents faithfully, guide and educate her children, be kind to her servants, be frugal in all things, and work for the family's prosperity. Once she marries, she must look upon her husband's home as her own, rise early in the morning, go to bed late, and devote all her thoughts to household affairs. She must assist her husband, and whatever misfortune befalls the family she must not abandon it.[21]

Such policies had their effect, even in what were regarded as the most enlightened of establishments. Kimi Hara claims, for example, that the First Girls' High School of Tokyo, which she attended from 1928 onwards, 'placed great confidence in the young women's abilities and characters. . . . Unlike girls' high schools generally, these students were never treated as not equal to boys.' However, it was a strange sort of equality that was practised.

> There were also special Etiquette Rooms, one Japanese and the other Western, in which girls learned how to behave in their daily lives. In the Japanese Room students sat straight on the tatami mat floor and practiced repeatedly how to sit, stand, walk, and bow according to the Japanese style. Also, they learned how to behave when invited as guests and how to entertain guests as hostesses as well as how to drink green tea and eat Japanese cakes.[22]

Policy and practice, the public and the private

The difficulty, yet again, is to distinguish between policy and practice, to decide whether, and to what extent, the rules laid down by the Meiji state determined the ways in which Japanese families functioned between 1868 and 1945. But will it ever be possible to understand the workings of families fifty, a hundred and a hundred and fifty years ago? Will it ever be possible to know how husbands and wives, parents and children, brothers and sisters, younger brothers and older brothers treated one another and thought about one another? There is the temptation, which we have discussed so often before, to mistake the unusual for the usual, the public for the private. 'A Japanese wife who walks deferentially behind her husband on a city street may have scolded him vigorously half an hour before.'[23]

It goes without saying that during the past twenty years or so, the worldwide surge of interest in women's history has done an enormous amount to enrich our understanding of the past. However, it has not entirely eradicated the 'great woman' approach to the study of late nineteenth and early twentieth-century Japanese family life. The result is that we know a good deal about the tiny minority of women who publicly rejected the domestic, maternal role which was traditionally assigned to them. In the 1880s and 1890s, for example, Tsuda pioneered higher education for women and went on to found the college that bears her name. In 1911, Hiratsuka began the Bluestocking movement, a small literary group of women graduates who shocked the establishment with the inaugural lines to their new publication, *Bluestocking*.

> In the beginning, woman was the sun.
>   An authentic person.
> Today, she is the moon.
>   Living through others.
>   Reflecting the brilliance of others . . .
> And now, *Bluestocking*, a journal created for the first time with the brains and hands of Today's Japanese women, raises its voice.

In the 1920s and 1930s, activists like Oku campaigned to improve women's economic conditions and political rights, while writers like Uno outraged her more conventional contemporaries by wearing Western dress, bobbing her hair, and not only having a series of love affairs but also chronicling them in the fiction which she produced.[24]

The courage, independence and foresight of these women is not in question. But neither, almost certainly, is their unrepresentativeness. The problem remains: what can the experiences of a tiny minority of activists tell us about the lives of millions upon millions of women whose behaviour aroused no controversy and left little, if any, mark upon the historical record?

If we are to have any hope of separating the unusual from the usual, the public from the private, we must begin by recognising the limits of state influence. The authorities faced real difficulties in protecting patriarchal values and women's domesticity. No matter how determined they were, it was difficult to deal with the contradictions which arose from attempting simultaneously to promote economic growth and protect traditional gender roles. For example, when the post office was established in the early 1870s, the regulations proposed for its new postal savings scheme applied to both men and women. Officials in the justice ministry were so concerned that this would undermine the authority of husbands over their wives and daughters that they required account-holders to obtain the approval of the head of the household in which they lived.[25]

As time went by, the authorities were prepared to concede publicly that both industrial growth and the demands of war had the tendency to remove women from their traditional domestic environment. Throughout the Taishô and Shôwa periods, therefore, the political establishment was forced to respond to the 'familial disintegration' that women's employment supposedly effected. Initially, it attempted to render female employment unnecessary and undesirable by reducing male unemployment and rationalising home economics through programmes like the 'Daily Living Improvement Movement'. Following the outbreak of war with China, the government, needing to mobilise the entire population for the war effort, acknowledged the contribution made by women's employment by enacting the Motherhood Protection Law of 1938. All the legislation did, however, was to limit working hours and control the kinds of places in which they could be employed.

> While many feminists sought a motherhood protection that *facilitated* women's access to work by removing impediments to mothers' employment (which would help them carry out their socially defined role as supporters of their children), male social reformers and politicians sought to *deny* access to some types of work to protect the bodies of potential mothers.[26]

Good wives and wise mothers

There was little outward sign of women challenging their officially sanctioned domesticity and inferiority. Rather the reverse. Insofar as it is possible to plot changes in Japanese family life, it appears that 'traditional' arrangements not only survived but became more widely adopted. It seems that arranged marriages became more common, that the divorce rate fell, that the illegitimacy rate declined and that women concentrated more and more upon being 'wise mothers and good wives'.[27]

Arranged marriages grew more common between the Restoration and the First World War. Industrialisation and urbanisation meant that young men and women were more likely to travel, more likely to meet new people, and more likely therefore to choose their partners from families which did not know one another. In these circumstances, an increasing number of families felt it sensible to adopt the *samurai* practice of using a go-between to collect the information needed to allow them to judge the economic and social suitability of their children's choice of marriage partner. By the turn of the century, this way of doing things was recognised, in both principle and practice, as the 'true Japanese way' of conducting courtship. Indeed, an opinion poll carried out just after the end of the Second World War revealed that even at this late date, 20 per cent of male respondents still felt that parents should choose their children's marriage partners, with twice as many believing that parents and children should consult one another about the decision to be made.[28]

Those disenchanted with Western ways of doing things may be tempted to link the spread of arranged marriage with the decline in the divorce rate. And there is no doubt that a comparison of family breakup in Japan and the West provides Western readers with considerable pause for

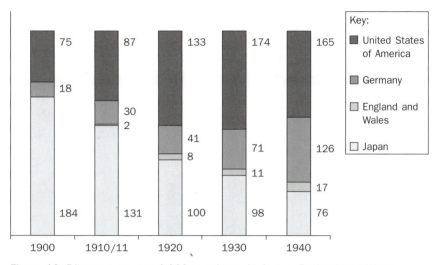

Figure 16: Divorce rates per 1,000 marriages in Japan, England and Wales, Germany and the United States of America, 1900–40

Note: Figure for England and Wales unavailable for 1900.

Source: W.J. Goode, World Revolution and Family Patterns, Free Press, 1963, pp. 82, 359.

thought. Figure 16 suggests that between 1900 and 1940, divorce in Japan became a good deal less common, whereas in Western countries it became a great deal more so. Whatever the reasons, the divorce rate decreased by almost 60 per cent in Japan, but increased by 120 per cent in the United States, by 600 per cent in Germany, and by almost 675 per cent in England and Wales.

However, it does not follow that the decreasing likelihood of Japanese marriages ending in divorce can be attributed to the increasing likelihood that they had been arranged by parents and go-betweens. There is simply no way of establishing a causal relationship between marriage breakup/survival and the way in which courtship had been conducted. The divorce rate was affected too by demographic shifts, changes in attitudes and changes, not least, in the ways in which marriage breakup was recorded. (And, if the decline in the divorce rate cannot be linked to the spread of arranged marriage, it is even more difficult to argue that a decline in divorce signalled a breakdown in traditional family values.)[29]

Those disenchanted with Western ways of doing things may also point to the decline in illegitimacy which occurred during the late nineteenth and early twentieth centuries. Once again, a comparison of developments in Japan and the West proves most instructive. Figure 17 suggests that between 1890 and 1940, illegitimacy in Japan became a great deal less common, whereas in Western countries illegitimacy rates either

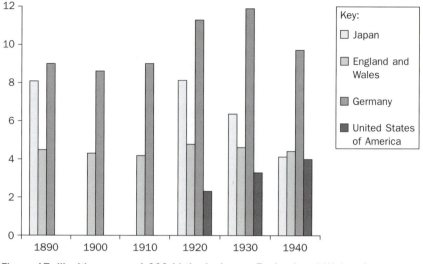

Figure 17: Illegitimacy per 1,000 births in Japan, England and Wales, Germany and the United States of America, 1890–1940

Note: Figures for Japan (1900, 1910) and the United States of America (1890, 1900, 1910) unavailable.

Source: W.J. Goode, *World Revolution and Family Patterns*, Free Press, 1963, pp. 38, 342.

remained stable or increased. The illegitimacy rate decreased by 100 per cent in Japan, but decreased by just 2 per cent in England and Wales, increased by 7 per cent in Germany and increased by 74 per cent (between 1920 and 1940) in the United States of America.

However, it does not follow that the decline in illegitimacy, any more than the decline in divorce, can be explained by the spread of arranged marriage. It is notoriously difficult, after all, to identify, let alone explain, changes in private, and sometimes shaming, aspects of people's sexual relationships. Nonetheless, it is telling that those who have made a close study of the decline in illegitimacy believe that it may very well be related to the spread of so-called 'traditional' family values. Goode is adamant that we should not dismiss the possibility of a causal relationship between declining illegitimacy and the increasing popularity of arranged marriage. However, he believes that the relationship was less straightforward than Western commentators often suggest:

> the spread of the aristocratic family pattern to the rural or to the lower social strata . . . meant essentially that the head of the household obtained much greater control over the behaviour of members of his family – greater supervision as well as the ability to force a quick marriage. Thus, illegitimacy could be forestalled by a speedy marriage.[30]

The difficulties of studying arranged marriage, divorce and illegitimacy appear relatively manageable compared to the complexities of exploring women's reactions to the changes in family life which took place between 1868 and 1945. We must not mistake public deference for private acquiescence. We must never forget that 'the subtleties of social expectation, reward, and punishment in the intimate relations between husband and wife permit the wife to express her objections without openly defying the husband's authority'. So what then did Japanese women think of their officially sanctioned domesticity? Did they welcome it or did they resent it; did they challenge, did they support or did they ignore the increasing pressures which were placed upon them to be wise mothers and good wives?[31]

It is never easy to extrapolate attitudes from behaviour. On the one hand, the spread of arranged marriages, the decline of divorce and the decrease in illegitimacy point, if anything, to growing acquiescence rather than growing resentment. A woman born in 1905 reflected that,

> The twenty years of my married life have been a long, long period of servitude. I tried to do my best to serve my husband, mother-in-law, and sisters-in-law, who did not acknowledge half of what I served them. I felt myself caught up by the love of my four children for me, just as an insect was caught in a spider's web. . . . I have made up my mind to efface myself for the sake of this family and to live solely for the love for my four children to bring them up well. With that single purpose in mind, I endured all the hardships, always gnawing my lips, so to speak.[32]

On the other hand, even a cursory glance at Japanese employment statistics shows how common it was for women to work. For as Figure 18 reveals, even in the shrill ideological climate of the 1930s, very nearly 50 per cent of 'employable' women were reported to be economically active.

It is important, of course, to differentiate between the experiences of different groups of women, in different places, at different periods of time. It appears that in the countryside, working-class wives enjoyed greater autonomy than is usually associated with Japanese women. It was said at the turn of the century, for example, that wives employed in the (still rural) textile industry were renowned for the 'petticoat' government which they conducted. Thirty years later, female labour accounted for 45 per cent of the agricultural workforce, a proportion which increased in a decade to over 50 per cent as men were conscripted into military service. Indeed, it was even claimed at the end of the 1930s, that 'In farm work land and wife are equal', with the result 'that in a farmer's household a woman has a comparatively higher status than in a shopkeeper's home'.[33]

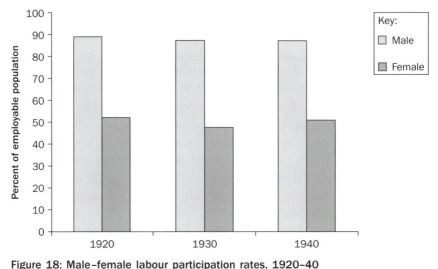

Figure 18: Male–female labour participation rates, 1920–40

Source: R. Minami, *The Economic Development of Japan: A Quantitative Study*, St Martin's Press, 1986, p. 268.

In the cities, too, a significant number of wives worked outside the home. It has been noted that during the Taishô and Shôwa periods, middle-class women found it increasingly difficult to maintain the life-style and status they wanted on a single income. 'It should not be forgotten . . . that the times encouraged women to look to employment as a means of satisfying their desire for economic independence and self-fulfilment . . . [during] this era both private and public employers actively recruited women for white-collar jobs as a cheap source of competent labour.'[34]

It is well known, of course, that many working-class women had little alternative other than to work. It is less well known, perhaps, that their participation in the labour market helped them not only to exert more influence over family budgeting decisions but also, sometimes, to del-egate unwanted household chores to their husbands. These women, it has been said, 'demonstrated their devotion to their husband, children, and/or home by participating in paid employment rather than painstak-ing involvement in domestic work.'[35]

As time went by, the distinctions between rural and urban areas, be-tween working-class, middle-class (and upper-class) women began to break down. Attitudes changed more quickly in the towns than in the country-side – and attitudes everywhere probably changed more quickly than behaviour. The result was that, by the end of the Second World War, wives generally seemed to enjoy freer and more open relationships with their husbands than they had done earlier in the century (with relationships in towns and cities changing more than those in rural areas). But one must not mistake change for emancipation. An NHK poll of 1941 to 1942 revealed that women – not very surprisingly – spent more time than men on housework, and enjoyed less time than men for eating and sleeping.[36]

Parents and children

There are some indications too that children began to chafe at the constraints imposed upon them by 'wise mothers', 'traditional' families and the 'beautiful customs' of rural Japan that these seemed to represent. The *Japan Times*, for example, waged a forceful campaign against the Department of Education, arguing that 'The relations between parents and children have been reversed'. The former it maintained 'have now little authority over the latter.'[37]

It seemed to the authorities that their cherished objective of catching up with the West, a dream that had once unified the nation, was now tending to tear it apart. By the late Meiji period, Japan appeared to be buffeted by a host of undesirable social changes, the so-called 'fevers' of modernity as the press called them. 'Education fever' was certainly a particular concern. At the same time that the education system emphasised filial piety and service to the state, it held out the possibility of personal success, of 'rising in the world'.

> I will be a doctor of laws.
> You a doctor of letters.
> So let's go to the pleasure quarter.
> Our parents in the country are digging yams.[38]

Even more worrying was the emergence of the 'anguished youth', a defeated, despairing, dissolute and world-weary soul who rejected 'wealth, honor, and fame' and 'rising in the world'. There were certainly some signs too of a generation gap developing. Brown, suggests, with some exaggeration, that even before the First World War, 'many Japanese were concerned by mounting evidence that their own society had not entirely avoided the undesirable implications of modernisation'.

> Outbreaks of popular unrest and strikes appeared to threaten the very ethos of national life by challenging existing notions of status and group loyalty. Others detected signs that the effort traditionally exerted on behalf of the group and the nation was being diverted towards personal aggrandisement and acquisitiveness by a hedonistic, younger, post-revolutionary generation.[39]

John Morris, whose observations on daily life in the capital during the late 1930s and early 1940s were used in the previous chapter, suggests that by this time, at least, there were certain signs of youthful independence.

> The young Japanese of the educated classes is not as a rule unduly national-
> istic, and certainly does not believe in the divinity of the Emperor, or his own
> descent from the gods. My pupils would talk quite frankly on these subjects and
> never made any attempt to disguise their dislike of the actual trend of affairs.[40]

Perhaps the most shocking development in the later Taishô and Shôwa eras was the appearance of the 'modern girl'. Wandering around the Ginza area of Tokyo in flapper-style fashions that emphasised her legs and buttocks (and popularising 'erotic-grotesquerie' entertainment styles that celebrated the 'materiality of everyday existence'), the 'modern girl' caused outrage. The 'modern girl' movement not only challenged gender norms prescribing marriage and dependence on men, but also, in its most extreme form, went so far as to advocate sexual equality.[41]

However, these were the exceptions that proved the rule. Indeed, as one observer commented, in some ways the 'modern girl' was a mood rather than a person.

> When we say the Modern Girl exists in our era we are not in particular refer-
> ring to individuals named Miss So-and-so . . . or Mrs Such-and-such. . . . Rather,
> we are talking about the fact that somehow, from the midst of the lives of all
> sorts of women of our era, we can feel the air of a new era, different from that
> of yesterday. That's right; where can you folks clearly say there is a typical modern
> girl? That is to say that the Modern Girl is but a term that abstractly alludes to
> one new flavour sensed from the air of the like of all women in society.[42]

Whether or not young people chafed at the constraints placed upon them, it appears that the overwhelming majority did not rebel publicly in the ways that those from the West would probably expect. Of course, acquiescence and obedience rarely leave as much evidence – or attract as much attention – as resentment and disobedience. Nonetheless, there is little doubt that, whatever the changes going on around them, Japanese children and adolescents remained, at least by Western standards, re-markably uncritical and unthreatening. Morris himself emphasises the power that parents continued to exercise over their children even when they became young adults. 'To marry', he reminds us, 'is considered a duty, and no Japanese, not even the most emancipated, is able to recog-nise any excuse for not marrying.'

> As soon as their child whether it be boy or girl, reaches a marriageable age, the
> parents select a suitable partner, or rather they entrust the matter to a go-
> between, choosing some discreet married man who is an intimate friend of the

family. Information is collected, and a meeting of the prospective bride and groom and their families is arranged.

On return to their respective homes the boy and girl are free to announce their decisions. In theory either is at liberty to object to the proposed marriage, and there the matter ends until a new candidate is produced. In actual practice, however, the young people are very much in their parents' hands; and neither is likely to raise any objection; certainly not the girl, for girls are not supposed to have any minds of their own.[43]

But why did arranged marriages persist so long? Why were young people so accommodating? Why were there so few signs of youthful insubordination? The reason, it is nearly always suggested, lay in the persistence of 'traditional' child-rearing practices and, of course, in the pervasiveness of 'traditional' training in the importance of the group.[44]

The discussion of family loyalty and children's obedience brings us full circle. There is no doubt that it has been helpful to look critically at the claims made for the persistence, power and prestige of the Japanese family. However, it is only proper to concede that the scepticism which was displayed at the beginning of this discussion turns out to have been very largely misplaced. The 'traditional' Japanese family of popular imagination survived, or at least adapted to, the upheavals of late nineteenth and twentieth-century society with a resilience that continues both to intrigue and to impress.

Class

The claims made about class, class consciousness and class action also cry out for examination. As one might expect, such claims are, in many ways, the reverse of those which are made about the strength and resilience of the 'traditional' family. During the late 1860s and 1870s, it is explained, *samurai* privileges were removed, and feudal estates destroyed. The introduction, later in the century, of conscription, state education, the Meiji Constitution and the civil code all tended, it is suggested, to emphasise collective values, to homogenise experiences and to standardise expectations. The gradual spread of mass communications, mass consumption and mass-mediated entertainment during the late Meiji to the Shôwa periods encouraged the emergence of a mass culture that seemed to be smoothing out the divisions within society. The result, claims Eccleston, was that by the 1930s, 'the conception of class interest was overwhelmed by the countervailing pressures for national unity based on loyalty to the Emperor'.[45]

From the time of the Allied Occupation onwards, it became common for Japanese and foreign commentators alike to describe the country as classless. Both 'a sense of class and actual class differences' were 'extremely weak', maintained one observer in the late 1970s: 'In most essential ways, Japan today has a very egalitarian society – more so in fact than those of the United States and many European countries.' Year after year, it was pointed out, between 80 and 90 per cent of those surveyed by the prime minister's office and the economic planning agency defined themselves as middle class. In fact, it was commonly believed that the classlessness cum group orientation of the Japanese was in some contradictory way both unique and exportable. 'Our business and management style is part and parcel of our unique spiritual culture', explained a company president in the late 1980s. 'It's nice to think that it is being adopted in foreign countries too.'[46]

Division, consciousness and action

However, the way in which Japan developed between 1868 and 1945 revealed clear class divisions, a certain amount of class identity and several incidents which smacked suspiciously of class opposition. A great deal depends, of course, upon the ideological stance adopted and the ways in which class, class identity and class opposition are defined. There are some who discern class tension even when there seems to be little overt discontent, and others who deny the existence of class tension even when there appears to be discontent of the most virulent kind. As anybody familiar with the debates between Marxists and non-Marxists will know only too well, the discussion of issues such as class, class identity and class opposition can give rise to intense, acrimonious and utterly irreconcilable differences of opinion.[47]

There were, it seems, irrefutable class divisions in Japanese society. Of course, it is difficult to know whether it is best to define class in Japan – or anywhere else – by economic criteria like occupation and income, by social and cultural criteria like attitudes, behaviour, status and power, or by some elusive combination of them all. Yet even those who believe that class should be defined in social and cultural terms recognise that in practice it is usually possible to identify the class position of large groups of people over long periods of time only by using economic indicators such as employment or income, the evidence for which tends to be available in reasonably accessible form.[48]

If an economic definition of social class is accepted as valid, it is possible to apply it – with appropriate caution – to Japanese society

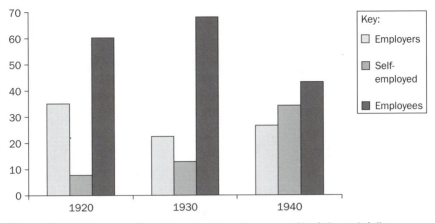

Figure 19: Employers, self-employed and employees as % of the gainfully employed, 1920–40

Source: Hundred-Year Statistics of the Japanese Economy, Statistics Department, Bank of Japan, 1966, p. 52.

between the late nineteenth century and the middle of the twentieth century. When this is done, it confirms that profound differences persisted both in the Japanese people's relationships to the means of production and in the rewards which they were able to secure from the investment of their capital and their labour. It confirms, in other words, that whether one adopts a Marxist or a non-Marxist definition of social class, there are few signs that Japan was becoming a classless society.

Unfortunately, Figure 19 relates only to the years between 1920 and 1940. Nonetheless, it is of considerable significance for the purpose of this discussion. It shows that, although there occurred a substantial decrease in the proportion of the population who were classified as employers, a rapid increase in the proportion classified as self-employed and a significant decrease in the proportion classified as employees, at the end of the period each of the three groups accounted for at least a quarter of the economically active population. Figure 20 relates to the years between 1890 and 1939, and it too is of considerable interest. It shows that, although there was some increase in the proportion of the population receiving the highest incomes, a significant increase in the proportion receiving average incomes and a significant decrease in the proportion receiving the lowest incomes, income differentials remained both persistent and profound. In 1939, the richest 0.6 per cent of the population received 30,000 yen and more a year, the poorest 60 per cent 2,000 yen and less.

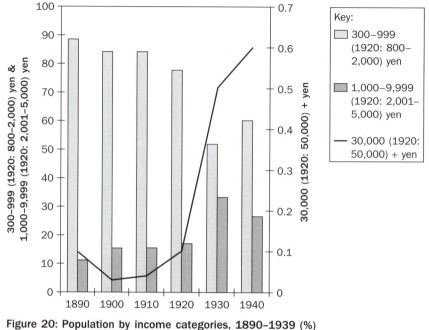

Figure 20: Population by income categories, 1890–1939 (%)

Source: Hundred-Year Statistics of the Japanese Economy, Statistics Department, Bank of Japan, 1966, p. 362.

These different groups/classes displayed a certain amount of class consciousness and became involved in several incidents of class action. Of course, attempting to define class consciousness and class action is almost as difficult as defining class itself. It was possible for different people – and for the same person at different times – to assume a number of contradictory stances: to deny the existence of class, to recognise and welcome its existence, to recognise and accept its existence, to recognise and resent its existence, or to resent its existence so strongly that they sought to overthrow the entire class system in which they found themselves embedded.[49]

It is not difficult to discover evidence of growing middle-class consciousness. However, it has been decided to concentrate here upon working-class consciousness and working-class action, and this makes it possible to call upon the work which has been carried out by the British sociologist Mann. He distinguishes most helpfully between four tiers of class consciousness: class identity – the definition of oneself as working class; class opposition – the perception of employers and their agents as enduring class opponents; class totality – the situation in which class identity and class opposition constitute the defining characteristics of one's existence; and class alternative – the conception of an alternative form of social organisation, 'a goal toward which one moves through the struggle with the opponent'. It is the first two tiers of Mann's four-tier model, class identity and class opposition which, because they were so much more common than the second two, will form the basis of the discussion which follows.[50]

Class identity

In Japan, as in other countries, a growing number of employees began to define themselves as working class. It was seen in chapter 4 that, although women, the unskilled, the casually employed and those working in the traditional sectors of the economy rarely joined trade unions or took strike action, they had other ways of asserting their class identity. It will be recalled that, even before the First World War, the songs sung by women textile workers revealed a good deal about their developing sense of class identity.

> Who dares to say that
> Factory girls are weak?
> Factory girls are the
> Only ones who create wealth.

This growing sense of class identity manifested itself in other, more overt ways. It has been suggested, for example, that by the turn of the century, some working men were conducting themselves in a fashion which suggested that they were proud of – and certainly conscious of – the class position in which they found themselves. They behaved in a provocatively proletarian manner, getting drunk in public, singing in the street, picking fights and pushing into people. It seems that these, and other, working people were able to reinforce their sense of self-worth by devouring the street songs and joke books which ridiculed the hypocrisy and dandyism of the middle class, or by reading the workers' newspapers which railed against the pretensions of the intellectuals. 'How does it happen', demanded one proletarian paper in 1922, 'that people who know nothing of the world control everything?'[51]

Sometimes working people felt that they were superior to their supposed betters. In 1931 when the authorities were placing greater emphasis on national unity, one popular singer was arrested for singing:

> When sons of the poor
> Are shot in Manchuria and
> Die for His Majesty and for the country
> Then the rich buy all the salt up
> And store it for their profit
> Oh what a great life![52]

It was more usual, however, for working people to behave in ways which suggest that they were ashamed, rather than proud, of their position in the class structure. It is known that, by the turn of the century, they were doing their best, some of them, to cultivate the frugality, sobriety, regularity and respectability which they associated with their social superiors. They also did their best, when they could, to conceal the external symbols of their social inferiority. It was common practice, it has been suggested, for factory workers to change out of their work clothes before leaving for home. As one of these workers explained in 1913,

> Because our countrymen despise us, we try to avoid their contempt by dressing outside the plant gate as merchants or students. If all of us were to walk down the street at the same time in work clothes, people would be astonished not only by our numbers but also at our good behaviour.[53]

These twin strands of working-class pride and working-class shame became fused, it seems, when subjected to the pressures that occurred during the 1930s and early 1940s. It is, of course, extraordinarily difficult to know how to interpret the scale and significance of the anti-war and anti-imperial criticisms uncovered by the authorities as the tide began to turn against Japan. Yet there is no doubt that some at least of the discontent reveals a clear, if sometimes rather inchoate, sense of class identity.

> Even if drafted, I don't want to die for the emperor.
> True happiness will not come to Japan until the imperial family is overthrown.
> The emperor is a puppet of those Jews, the *zaibatsu*.

> Socialize the means of production.
> The emperor is an expensive rubber stamp.
> Overthrow the country of the capitalists.
> We are bled white with taxes for the military.[54]

Class opposition

In Japan, as elsewhere, some of the employees who began to define themselves as working class began to become involved in incidents which can be seen as manifestations of class opposition. It has been decided to concentrate here upon the three incidents which have been interpreted most often in class terms: the Rice Riots of 1918, the landlord–tenant struggles of the 1920s and 1930s, and the industrial disputes which occurred at various times throughout the first half of the twentieth century. It will be suggested that consumers' complaints against producers, tenants' struggles with their landlords and employees' disputes with their employers should all be understood, to some extent at least, as expressions of – or related to – working-class identity and working-class opposition.[55]

The Rice Riots of 1918 have usually been seen in class terms. The events themselves are not in dispute. During a two-month period, complaints about the cost of rice swept across the country, the government responded by mobilising the troops, and in the unrest which ensued there were nearly 25,000 arrests and more than 8,000 prosecutions. Thirty people were killed and many more were injured. The *Osaka Asahi* was quick to interpret developments in anti-monarchical and quasi-class terms. 'The age that dazzled the people with majestic brilliance has long passed', it announced: 'who can respect the crown of a monkey? The people suffer in misery; hungry sparrows weep in empty storehouses.' With an eye, no doubt, on the Chinese Revolution of 1911 and the Russian Revolution of 1917, the paper went on to wonder whether 'our great Japan, once so full of flawless pride, is approaching the dreaded final judgement'.[56]

Indeed, the Riots have sometimes been regarded as a failed revolution, as 'an economic struggle based on fixed and clear class relationships' whose potential to unleash class warfare upon capitalist society was thwarted only by the weakness of the country's left-wing leadership. 'According to this long-prevailing view, the handful of Japanese socialist and anarchist thinkers had neither the organization nor the uniform ideology required to transform mass discontent into a fundamental social restructuring.' All that was missing, it is said, was a 'revolutionary vanguard'.[57]

Indeed, it is striking that even those uneasy with this view of events attempt to modify, rather than overthrow, the prevailing Marxist-inspired orthodoxy. They stress, for example, the heterogeneity and autonomy of the rioters: 'because the disputes were spontaneous economic struggles by groups still lacking union leadership, no links could be forged in any organized fashion with the rice riots'. They argue that, 'There was not a universal driving force or a single ideology behind the rice riots' – and those 'hunting for "red" agitators behind the riots always came up empty-handed'. Yet even this avowedly revisionist history of the events of 1918 is at pains to emphasise the importance of the underlying structural changes which were taking place in Japanese society:

> the protests themselves can be seen as symptoms of deeper changes, which had begun before the riots and continued afterward. The transformation altered the public's attitude towards governmental and corporate policies, whether they were explicit (as in the state's legal prohibition of strikes) or implied (as in the gulf separating company profits from worker wages).[58]

The landlord–tenant struggles of the 1920s and 1930s have also usually been interpreted in class terms. Between 1917 and 1930, for instance, there were more than 20,000 disputes, the great majority of them in the rural heartlands of the main island of Honshû. During the 1920s, disputes centred upon the tenant farmers' demands for rent decreases in the wake of poor harvests; during the 1930s, they centred upon the nature of the landlord–tenant relationship. Tenants joined together to negotiate collectively with the landowners, and achieved considerable success by the adoption of tactics such as threatening not to cultivate the land which they rented. Although they did not overthrow the land-lord system, they were able to win a number of concessions: rents were reduced, contracts improved and tenant tenure made more secure.[59]

Those leading the disputes often saw them in class terms. We used to think that 'our existence depended on the grace and favor of landlords', explained one activist, but now we realise that it is 'our labor that en-ables landlords to live'. Others widened the argument. 'The majority of Japanese are farmers, and the majority of farmers are tenants', they pro-tested. 'By their efforts the nation is protected, its land cultivated, and its people fed.' Such arguments had an effect. 'I just received your paper', wrote a subscriber to one tenants' periodical.

> I too am a propertyless tenant farmer. I am a miserable creature who lives at the very bottom rung of capitalist society. The key to our liberation is a class newspaper like yours. By reading this kind of newspaper we get the weapons to break our chains. In that connection, please add my name to your list and lead me to the goal of liberation.[60]

It is an interpretation with which many historians have concurred. During the 1920s, it is explained, the combination of rural poverty, growing economic inequality, the Rice Riots, industrial disputes – and the Russian Revolution – encouraged tenant farmers to think of them-selves not as petit bourgeois but as wage-earners. According to Nakamura, the development of this 'rural proletarian mentality' encouraged rural tenants to join urban workers and radical intellectuals in what amounted to a class struggle against the repressive 'landlord-capitalist-militarist-civil-bureaucratic-authoritarian emperor system'. It was a struggle, Nakamura concludes, which was doomed to failure.[61]

It will come as no surprise to learn that it has also been common to interpret in class terms the industrial disputes that occurred during the first half of the twentieth century. It was seen in chapter 4 that even the much vaunted Japanese system of industrial relations was unable to guarantee loyalty, harmony and goodwill in the workplace. Labour turn-over was high, absenteeism widespread and strikes and lockouts more usual than one would probably imagine. It was shown that, although the incidence of disputes was low by international standards, the number of strikes and lockouts increased steadily during the first forty years of the new century.

It has always been common for those with a particular interest in the history of industrial relations to regard strikes and lockouts as prime examples of class identity and class opposition. During the 1920s and 1930s, left-wing journalists and intellectuals perceived the increase in strike activity – along with the Rice Riots and the surge of tenancy disputes – as evidence of a proletarian awakening. In the years that followed, left-wing scholars continued to propagate the view that the increase in strike activity – like the Rice Riots and the surge of tenancy disputes – represented the stirrings of working-class consciousness. 'Post-war historical treatments have viewed the mass protests as indicative of a crisis of capitalism that pitted the rich against the poor and portended the possible onset of class warfare.'[62]

It will come as no surprise either to learn that the view that strikes can be used as indicators of class identity and class opposition has come in for a good deal of criticism. It is stressed how difficult it is to discover the motives of those who went on strike, and it is pointed out that the behaviour of those involved in industrial disputes often seemed to indicate class division as much as class unity, and occupational solidarity as much as class-based loyalty. Only a small number of workers were involved in disputes, and only a small number of those involved in disputes behaved in ways that can be construed unambiguously as evidence of class identity and class opposition. 'If Japan is taken as a whole', concludes Hastings, 'the labor movement seems soft-spoken – a voice that was scarcely heard before it was silenced in 1940.'[63]

Such views carry considerable weight. But they do not mean that Japan was a classless society. Workers' everyday behaviour, consumers' complaints against producers, tenants' struggles with their landlords and employees' disputes with their employers all point to conflict rather than consensus, to heterogeneity rather than homogeneity. They should all be understood, to some extent at least, as expressions of working-class identity and, to a much lesser extent, as expressions of working-class opposition.

Nation

It is time finally to reconsider the generalisations which are made so often, and so confidently, about the homogeneity of Japanese society and the patriotism of the Japanese people. This is surprisingly difficult.

To do so will involve moving beyond the easily recognisable and constantly cited examples of centralisation, uniformity and acquiescence,
and looking instead for the less obvious – but possibly no less significant
– instances of decentralisation, diversity and dissent. It will entail examining the degree to which Japan's geography and early history, government policies and popular responses to them, undermined the uniformity
of a country which is routinely presented as among the most homogeneous in the world.

Homogeneity

There are good reasons, of course, for supposing that Japanese society
became more, rather than less, homogeneous between 1868 and 1945.
It has been explained at several points in the course of the book that
Japan's geographical position and cultural seclusion had long tended
to foster feelings of isolation, uniqueness and national pride. 'Nation,
language, race and culture are all related but distinct concepts to most
modern peoples,' it has been pointed out, 'but in Japan they all seem
virtually synonymous.'

> The origins of Japan's sense of uniqueness are easily found in its long history
> of isolation, at first natural but later self-imposed, its distinctive culture, its
> unusual type of language, its unique and very difficult writing system, and its
> strong patterns of group organization.[64]

It has also been pointed out on more than one occasion in this book
that those who were in power made conscious, determined and often
ingenious efforts to build upon these feelings of isolation, uniqueness
and national pride. It has been shown that from the earliest days of the
Meiji reforms, Japan's rulers attempted to create not only a literate and
pliable workforce but also a loyal and obedient citizenry whose members
would be committed to the emperor and those who ruled in his name. It
has been shown too that in the years between the wars, the authorities
did more and more to encourage the belief that the Japanese were at
once different from and superior to – not to mention at risk from – the
people of other nations. It has been established that throughout the late
nineteenth and early twentieth centuries, the state did what it could to
encourage rapid economic growth, harmonious industrial relations and,
to a lesser extent, consumer frugality. It has been suggested finally that
those in power between the Restoration and the American Occupation
did all they could to mobilise education, religion and the media and
yoke them to the needs of the state. It was suggested, it will be recalled,

that, although the Japanese people were not particularly susceptible to such pressures, it became increasingly difficult for them to avoid being exposed to government persuasion and official propaganda.[65]

It is this suggestion which brings us to the heart of the matter. In truth, it is not hard to show that those in power worked assiduously to promote political uniformity and social homogeneity. However, it is enormously more difficult to evaluate the success of such policies. If there is one methodological conundrum that has been stressed in this study it is the difficulty of distinguishing between policy and practice, between public rhetoric and private behaviour.

Fortunately, the difficulty is not as crippling as it probably appears. The claim that Japan was becoming more homogeneous does not rest solely upon a belief in the effectiveness of government pressure and official propaganda. It is a claim which can be supported, though not of course proved, by bringing together a number of the arguments which have been propounded at various stages in the course of the book. It will be suggested that there is considerable evidence that Japan was growing more homogeneous – and some evidence too that the Japanese recognised, and welcomed, the fact that their country was developing in this way.

To generalise in terms of what was 'typical' about the Japanese experience is, of course, hazardous in the extreme. To go on to generalise in terms of what was 'typical' about Japanese responses to this growing homogeneity of experience is more hazardous still. Yet there is a good deal of evidence to suggest that the people of Japan embraced the increasing uniformity and exclusivity of Japanese life. The Great Kantô Earthquake of 1923 provides a telling illustration of the way in which they defined themselves by excluding members of 'non-Japanese' minority groups. It will be recalled that, when it was rumoured in the wake of the earthquake that members of the despised Korean minority were robbing, raping, looting and poisoning the water supply, the authorities sanctioned a pitiless witch-hunt by members of the public. 'Thousands were massacred, while police and army units stood by.'[66]

It is possible, or course, that an event like the Hibiya riot of 1905 was 'little more than a blind outburst'. Nevertheless, it cannot be denied that its 'basic orientation was toward nationalistic chauvinism'. Indeed, when the ambassador who negotiated peace terms with the Russians returned to Japan, he was greeted in Tokyo by the 'melancholic gloom' of empty streets stripped of their celebratory decorations and of utter silence rather than the usual congratulatory cries of *'banzai'*. The imperial funerals of 1912 and 1927 were similarly imbued with a patriotic edge. When the

Emperor Meiji died, seven thousand people witnessed his funeral and a further 300,000 lined the streets to watch the procession. One shop-owner described the emperor as 'one who cared for us even more than the gods and Buddha', while a policeman on patrol in a city park re-marked, 'I can't remember a time when I saw the park in such a lonely and sad state . . . even the . . . prostitutes show[ed] deference'. Fourteen years later, when the Emperor Taishô died, 540,000 delegates from 600 organisations applied to watch the four-mile long procession as it made its way from the imperial palace to the Shinjuku Gardens.[67]

There are many other examples of the way in which the Japanese people embraced exclusivity and nationalism. In 1904, for example, the *Yorozu Chôhô* published a letter written by a primary school student who wished to donate his spending money to the war effort. This money, he explained, 'is what I received from time to time – 10 *sen*, 20 *sen* – from my uncle and aunty and grandfather and saved'.

> It is the original amount plus interest. In the ethics class at school, I heard a story about a twelve-year old elementary school student from Osaka Prefecture who saved and gave his money to the Emperor's government at the events of 1894 to 1895 [the Sino-Japanese War]. Even if there is a war, I can't go because I am too small, so I would like this money to go towards buying bullets [so that] the soldiers can fight a great war. When I told my father that I wanted to donate this money I saved to the Emperor's government, [he said] that it was a very good idea. Please accept it.[68]

The most telling examples of exclusivity and nationalism come, as one would expect, from the late 1930s and early 1940s. Some of them ap-pear, at least in retrospect, to border almost on the absurd. In the winter of 1939–40, for instance, a small group of Tokyo residents established the 'No Overcoat Society'. The group had two aims. The first was to distribute leaflets in the Ginza district urging people to send their fur coats to the soldiers of the Imperial Army who were having to cope with the bitterness of the Chinese winter; the second was to 'pledge them-selves to dispense with overcoats to train their bodies and to be in tune with the national policy of conserving such a natural resource as woolen goods and furs'. Absurd or not, there was no mistaking the pressure to conform. Nationalism was growing apace, concluded the *Japan Times Weekly* in 1938. 'Now it has taken the form of an ideology, and its leading protagonists demand that it shall dominate every activity both in the national life and in international relations.'[69]

There is good reason therefore to go along with many of the claims made about the homogeneity of Japanese society and the patriotism of the Japanese people. For, although such claims are often tinged – and more than tinged – by Japanese chauvinism and Western racism, they contain a substantial element of truth. During the period covered by this book, Japan – like most other industrialising countries – grew increasingly homogeneous; and the Japanese people, like those living in most other industrialising countries, grew increasingly proud of the nation to which they belonged.

Heterogeneity

The growing uniformity of Japanese experience and belief should not be underestimated. But neither should it be misunderstood. The centralisation, uniformity and acquiescence with which we are so familiar was accompanied, and sometimes undermined, by variety, diversity and dissent. It will be suggested that, although the demographic, economic and cultural developments discussed above tended in certain respects to be mutually reinforcing and powerfully homogenising, their consistency and strength can easily be exaggerated.[70]

It is true that it became increasingly common for the Japanese to find themselves in urban areas. It was seen earlier in the chapter that the proportion of the population living in cities of 100,000 or more, for example, increased from 6 per cent in 1893, to 11 per cent in 1913, 18 per cent in 1930 and 25 per cent in 1935. This means, however, that even in the mid-1930s, after seventy years or so of rapid economic and social change, three-quarters of the population still lived in villages, or in towns or in cities with fewer than 100,000 people in them.[71]

It may also be the case that many of the developments discussed above affected women in much the same way as they did men. It became increasingly common for women, like men, to live in a city, to work in the modern sector of the economy and to save for the future. Women, like men, were increasingly likely to attend elementary school, to enjoy a number of civil and democratic rights, enter into an arranged marriage, restrict the size of their family, enjoy the radio and cinema, read a newspaper, follow State Shinto, support an aggressive foreign policy and honour the emperor.

However, to present the argument in such stark terms is immediately to reveal its inadequacy. It is always erroneous to suggest that gender was unimportant, and it would be utterly absurd to adopt such a stance in the light of the evidence which has been brought forward in the course of the book. Girls, it has been seen, were less likely than boys to attend school, and most certainly did not follow the same curriculum as the boys who were taught alongside them. The purpose of female education, it will be recalled, was to create 'good wives and wise mothers', with special care being taken to guard against women's ingrained tendency towards 'loquacity and jealousy'.

It has been seen too that, when they grew up, women were less likely than men to work in the high-wage, modern sector of the economy, less likely to join a trade union and less likely to go on strike. When planning to get married, women faced more pressure than men to accept their parents' choice of a partner; and once married they were expected to accept unquestioningly their inferior domestic and maternal role. Married or single, there was never any question of them enjoying the same civic and democratic rights as their fathers and brothers – or even as their grown-up sons. Japan remained, as it always had been, a highly patriarchal society.

What has not yet been made fully clear is the paradoxical nature of the relationship between uniformity and diversity, between homogeneity and heterogeneity. The Japanese people's belief in the growing homogeneity of their society rested, in large measure, upon their refusal to recognise its persistent heterogeneity. The Japanese people's sense of what it was to be Japanese depended decisively upon the exclusion and marginalisation of minorities. However, these minorities were more common than one might imagine: there were the Ainu from the northern island of Hokkaidô, the Okinawans from the islands to the south of Kyûshû and the *burakumin* who were to be found in segregated communities all over the country.[72]

The Ainu, indigenous to Hokkaidô, were discriminated against on the basis of their supposedly primitive culture. When the Meiji government initiated policies for the development and colonisation of Hokkaidô, the Ainu were forced to abandon hunting and take up farming, usually on land that was too small in size to sustain them. As a result, they fell into conditions of dire poverty. Their numbers declined drastically and their culture was undermined by the policies of assimilation pursued by the Japanese government. Despite the authorities' attempts at assimilation, the Okinawans guarded their culture and dialect while the majority population despised them for their supposed cultural, educational and economic 'inferiority'.[73]

The unliberated *burakumin*, some two to three per cent of the population, suffered severe social discrimination, despite being granted full legal equality in 1871. Since contact with *burakumin* was considered by the prejudiced to be defiling, they were segregated unofficially into ghettos in the Kansai district and scattered communities elsewhere. By the turn of the century, *burakumin* self-help organisations had been formed and in 1922, the movement became fully politicised with the creation of the Levelling Society whose political, social and economic agenda called for an end to all discrimination. The Society played an important role in the proletarian movement (getting its leader elected to the Diet in 1936).[74]

The Koreans living in Japan were also stereotyped and marginalised. Colonialism, prejudice and resentment reinforced one another in ways which developed into a brutal self-fulfilling prophecy. Korea, it will be recalled, became a Japanese colony in 1910, and thereafter hundreds of thousands of Koreans crossed the Genkainada Straits in search of work. Unskilled and discriminated against, the immigrants were able to find employment only by accepting 'the dirtiest, lowest-paying, and least desirable jobs' that were on offer. Even so, they were hit disproportionately hard by the layoffs of the early 1930s, and during the war, when labour shortages became acute, they were forced to come to Japan to work in mining and munitions.[75]

The way in which the Japanese people's sense of what it was to be Japanese drew upon the exclusion and marginalisation of minorities is most instructive. It helps to explain both the country's reputation for homogeneity and the ways in which its leaders were able to contain diversity and dissent. Japanese society was growing ever more homogeneous, but it remained more heterogeneous than many observers have supposed.[76]

Homogenisation and heterogeneity

The difficulty, of course, is to strike the balance between homogenisation and heterogeneity. On the one hand, there is no doubt that those in power between 1868 and 1945 made increasing efforts to foster family loyalty, national uniformity and patriotic enthusiasm; and there seems little doubt that their initiatives had a significant impact upon the ways in which the Japanese people behaved and thought about themselves. On the other hand, there is no reason for supposing that family loyalty and national uniformity were necessarily compatible, let alone mutually reinforcing; and although there is good reason for believing that the 'traditional' family remained very strong, the position of the individual was changing and class consciousness was becoming more powerful. The conclusion, anodyne though it may seem, must surely be that late nineteenth and early twentieth-century Japanese society was characterised both by increasing homogenisation and by persistent heterogeneity.

Notes

1. **J.E. Hunter**, *The Emergence of Modern Japan: An Introductory History since 1853*, Longman, 1989, pp. 64, 74; **J. Woronoff**, *Japan As – Anything But – Number One*, Macmillan, 1990, pp. 114–15, 275–8; **W.J. Macpherson**, *The Economic Development of Japan 1868–1941*, Cambridge University Press, 1995, p. 4; **E.O. Reischauer**, *The Japanese Today: Change and Continuity*, Belknap Press, 1988, p. 128; **W.O. Lee**, *Social Change and Educational Problems in Japan, Singapore and Hong Kong*, Macmillan, 1991, p. xi; **D.W. Plath**, 'Resistance at Forty-Eight: Old-Age Brinkmanship and Japanese Life Course Pathways', in **T.K. Hareven** and **K.J. Adams** (eds), *Ageing and Life Course Transitions: An Interdisciplinary Perspective*, Tavistock, 1992, pp. 118–19.
2. Lee, *Social Change*, p. xi; **R.S. Ozaki**, *The Japanese: A Cultural Portrait*, Charles E. Tuttle, 1978, pp. 203, 218.
3. *The Independent*, 24 May, 20, 21 July 1991; *The Times*, 12 January 1990, 23 June 1991; Hunter, *Modern Japan*, p. 64; Woronoff, *Japan*, pp. 124–6; Macpherson, *Economic Development*, pp. 4–5; Reischauer, *Japanese Today*, p. 128; **A. MacFarlane**, 'Law and Custom in Japan: Some Comparative Reflections', *Continuity and Change*, 10, 1995.
4. **H.D. Harootunian**, 'Introduction: A Sense of an Ending and the Problem of Taishô', in **B.S. Silberman** and **H.D. Harootunian** (eds), *Japan in Crisis: Essays in Taishô Democracy*, Princeton University Press, 1974, pp. 12–14.
5. Hunter, *Modern Japan*, pp. xiii–xiv; **J. Dower**, *Japan in War and Peace: Essays on History, Race and Culture*, HarperCollins, 1995, p. 274; Macpherson, *Economic Development*, p. 4; **B. Eccleston**, *State and Society in Post-War Japan*, Polity, 1989.
6. *Tokyo Gazette*, March–April 1938, pp. 2–3.
7. According to Bestor, 'Neighborhood associations developed while urban Japan, particularly Tokyo was experiencing unprecedented growth and upheaval; economic, social, and political disruption accompanied the era's industrial growth.' Despite their emergence in the 1920s, it was only during the wars with China and America that the government fully incorporated them into the programme of national mobilisation. The neighbourhood associations became one of the most effective ways of disseminating 'traditional' rural values of communalism and co-operation. **T.C. Bestor**, 'Tradition and Japanese Social Organisation: Institutional Development in a Tokyo Neighborhood', *Ethnology: An International Journal of Cultural and Social Anthropology*, 24, 1985, p. 125; Hunter, *Modern Japan*, p. 75; **K. Steiner**, *Local Government in Japan*, Stanford University Press, 1965, reproduced in **J. Livingston**, **J. Moore** and **F. Oldfather** (eds), *The Japan Reader*, vol. I, *Imperial Japan 1800–1945*, Penguin, 1976, pp. 448–9.
8. *Japan Weekly Chronicle*, 19 August 1920; **A. Waswo**, *Modern Japanese Society 1868–1994*, Oxford University Press, 1996, p. 65. Westney deals with the development of modern meritocratic values in **D.E. Westney**, 'The Military', in **M.B. Jansen** and **G. Rozman** (eds), *Japan in Transition: From Tokugawa to Meiji*, Princeton University Press, 1986, pp. 168–94.
9. **J. Dower**, *War Without Mercy: Race and Power in the Pacific War*, Faber & Faber, 1986, p. 31.
10. **C. Sugiyama**, *Origins of Economic Thought in Modern Japan*, Routledge & Kegan Paul, 1994, pp. 2–3; **E.H. Kinmonth**, *The Self-Made Man in Meiji Japanese Thought: From Samurai to Salary Man*, University of California Press, 1981, pp. 26–43 (cf. **E.H. Kinmonth**, 'Nakamura Keiu and Samuel Smiles: A Victorian Confucian and a Confucian Victorian', *American Historical Review*, 84, 1980; **R.P. Dore**, *Education in*

Tokugawa Japan, University of California Press, 1965, p. 312; **O. Yoshitake**, 'Generational Conflict after the Russo-Japanese War', in **T. Najita** and **J.V. Koschmann** (eds), *Conflict in Modern Japanese History*, Princeton University Press, 1982, pp. 197–8; Reischauer, *Japanese Today*, p. 129; **K.B. Pyle**, *The Making of Modern Japan*, Heath, 1996 (2nd edition), p. 91.

11. **C. Mosk**, 'The Decline of Marital Fertility in Japan', *Population Studies*, 33, 1979; **C. Mosk**, 'Demographic Transition in Japan', *Journal of Economic History*, 37, 1977, esp. pp. 663–4; **Y. Morita**, 'Estimated Birth and Death Rates in the Early Meiji Period of Japan', *Population Studies*, 17, 1963, p. 52.

12. The age of marriage had been increasing for several centuries. **R.P. Dore**, 'Japanese Rural Fertility; Some Social and Economic Factors', *Population Studies*, 7, 1953–54, esp. pp. 62–4.

13. *Japan Weekly Chronicle*, 20 March 1930; **M. Pinguet**, *Voluntary Death in Japan*, Polity, 1993, pp. 21–9.

14. Pinguet, *Voluntary Death*, pp. 16–18. Cf. **M. Iga**, *The Thorn in the Chrysanthemum: Suicide and Economic Success in Modern Japan*, University of California Press, 1986; Kinmonth, *The Self-Made Man*, pp. 207–11, 213–14, 222–3, 277–9.

15. **R. Harvey**, *The Undefeated: The Rise, Fall and Rise of Greater Japan*, Macmillan, 1994, pp. 57–8; Eccleston, *State and Society*, pp. 9–11. See also **A. Fuse**, *Kekkon to kazoku*, Iwanami Shoten, 1993, pp. 72–85.

16. Harvey, *The Undefeated*, p. 59; **J. Lebra**, 'Women in Service Industries', in **J. Lebra, J. Paulson** and **E. Powers** (eds), *Women in Changing Japan*, Westview Press, 1976, p. 107.

17. Harvey, *The Undefeated*, p. 58.

18. The growth in the urban population was related directly to the decline of the extended family, an agency that helped perpetuate communal solidarity. By 1920, as many as 73.1 per cent of urban households and 56.9 per cent of rural households were identified as nuclear. **T. Koyama**, *The Changing Social Position of Women in Japan*, UNESCO, 1961, p. 35; **G.C. Allen**, *A Short Economic History of Modern Japan 1867–1937*, Allen & Unwin, 1946, p. 163.

19. **E. Seidensticker**, *Low City, High City: Tokyo from Edo to the Earthquake*, Alfred A. Knopf, 1983, pp. 37–9; Dore, 'Japanese Rural Fertility', pp. 69–71; **T. Watanabe** and **J. Iwata**, *The Love of the Samurai: A Thousand Years of Japanese Homosexuality*, Gay Men's Press, 1989. See also **E. Ochiai**, 'Kindai kazoku o meguru gensetsu', in *'Kazoku' no shakaigaku*, Iwanami Shoten, 1996, pp. 23–53; **Y. Nishikawa**, 'Kindai kokka to kazoku, in *'Kazoku' no shakaigaku*, Iwanami Shoten, 1996, pp. 79–99.

20. **M. Ohinata**, 'The Mystique of Motherhood: A Key to Understanding Social Change and Family Problems in Japan', in **K. Fujimura-Fanselow** and **A. Kameda** (eds), *Japanese Women: New Feminist Perspectives on the Past, Present, and Future*, The Feminist Press, 1995, pp. 199–203. A history of how the ideas of 'good wife and wise mother' changed is found in **S. Koyama**, *Ryôsai kenbo to iu kihan*, Keisô Shobô, 1993, pp. 233–40.

21. **K. Hara**, 'Challenges to Education for Girls and Women in Modern Japan: Past and Present', in Fujimura-Faneslow and Kameda (eds), *Japanese Women*, p. 93.

22. Hara, 'Challenges', pp. 100–1.

23. **W.J. Goode**, *World Revolution and Family Patterns*, Free Press, 1963, p. 345.

24. **S.L. Sievers**, 'The Bluestockings', in **S.L. Sievers** (ed.), *Flowers in Salt: The Beginnings of Feminist Consciousness in Modern Japan*, Stanford University Press, 1983, pp. 163–88. Hiratsuka believed that 'The time has come today for women to demonstrate fully their special qualities as women in social reconstruction. . . . [Just] as family

requires the power of women – especially a mother's love – society, too, needs the essential elements of women, which are different from those of men, for healthy cultural development.' **S. Garon**, 'Women's Groups and the Japanese State: Contending Approaches to Political Integration, 1890–1945', *Journal of Japanese Studies* 19, 1993. Obituaries in *The Guardian*, 12 June 1996; 24 July 1997; Hunter, *Modern Japan*, pp. 140–4. See also **S.J. Pharr**, *Political Women in Japan: The Search for a Place in Political Life*, University of California Press, 1981; **D. Robins Mowry**, *The Hidden Sun: Women of Modern Japan*, Westview Press, 1983; **M. Hane**, *Reflections on the Way to the Gallows: Rebel Women in Prewar Japan*, University of California Press, 1988; **E.K. Tipyon**, 'Ishimoto Shizue: The Margaret Sanger of Japan', *Women's History Review*, 6, 1997. One of Japan's first suffragettes, Ichikawa Fusae, and the pre-war Japanese women's movement are discussed in **P. Murray**, 'Ichikawa Fusae and the Lonely Red Carpet', *The Japan Interpreter* 10, 1975; **D.A. Vavich**, 'The Japanese Women's Movement: Ichikawa Fusae – A Pioneer in Women's Suffrage', in *Monumenta Nipponica*, 10, 1975, esp. 405–23.

25. *Japan Times Weekly*, 8 September 1938.
26. **M. Nagy**, 'Middle Class Working Women During the Interwar Years', in **G.L. Bernstein** (ed.), *Recreating Japanese Women: 1600–1945*, University of California Press, 1991, pp. 200, 214–15; **Y. Miyake**, 'Doubling Expectations: Motherhood and Women's Factory Work under State Management in Japan in the 1930s and 1940s', in Bernstein (ed.), *Recreating Japanese Women*, pp. 267–95; **B. Molony**, 'Equality versus Difference: The Japanese Debate over "Motherhood Protection", 1915–50', in **J. Hunter** (ed.) *Japanese Women Working*, Routledge, 1993, esp. pp. 122–32.
27. Goode, *World Revolution*, pp. 329–31; **E.F. Vogel**, 'The Japanese Family', in **M.F. Nimkoff** (ed.), *Comparative Family Systems*, Houghton Mifflin, 1965, p. 293; **T. Kawashima** and **K. Steiner**, 'Modernization and Divorce Rate Trends in Japan', *Economic Development and Cultural Change*, 9, 1960, p. 216.
28. Arranged marriages were encouraged both by the Meiji Civil Code (which demanded the agreement of the head of the household) and by the rise in the standard of living after the First World War (which stimulated economic calculation in the choice of marriage partner). The statistics of illegitimacy, divorce and so on are notoriously fallible. See, for example, Kawashima and Steiner, 'Modernization and Divorce Rate Trends'.
29. Goode, *World Revolution*, pp. 358–65; Vogel, 'Japanese Family', p. 299.
30. Goode, *World Revolution*, p. 342.
31. For infanticide, female crime and domestic arguments, see *Japan Chronicle*, 8 May 1919; *Japan Weekly Chronicle*, 26 August 1920, 4 July 1935; *Japan Times Weekly*, 23 March 1939.
32. **K. Tsurumi**, *Social Change and the Individual: Japan Before and After Defeat in World War II*, Princeton University Press, 1970, p. 266.
33. Cited in Miyake, 'Doubling Expectations', pp. 282–3; **J.F. Embree**, *Suye Mura – A Japanese Village*, University of Chicago Press, 1939, p. 97; cf. Goode, *World Revolution*, pp. 344–5.
34. Nagy, 'Middle Class Working Women', p. 209.
35. **K. Uno**, 'One Day at a Time: Work and Domestic Activities of Urban Lower Class Women in Early Twentieth-Century Japan', in Hunter (ed.), *Japanese Women Working*, esp. pp. 41–2, 50–9.
36. Embree, *Suye Mura*; Koyama, *Changing Position*, p. 55.

37. *Japan Times*, 23 March 1897; **C. Gluck**, *Japan's Modern Myths: Ideology in the Late Meiji Period*, Princeton University Press, 1985, p. 159.

38. Cited in Gluck, *Japan's Modern Myths*, pp. 163–74.

39. Goode, *World Revolution*, pp. 347–8. Also Vogel, 'Japanese Family', pp. 295–6; *Japan Weekly Chronicle*, 2 September 1920, 4 July 1935; *Japan Chronicle*, 3 March 1927.

40. **J. Morris**, *Traveller from Tokyo*, The Book Club, 1945, p. 50.

41. Seidensticker, *Low City, High City*, pp. 265–7; **M. Silverberg**, 'The Modern Girl as Militant', in Bernstein (ed.), *Recreating Japanese Women*, pp. 239–66.

42. Cited in Silverberg, 'The Modern Girl', p. 250.

43. Morris, *Traveller*, pp. 70–1; **S. Linhart**, 'From Industrial to Postindustrial Society: Changes in Japanese Leisure-Related Values and Behavior', *Journal of Japanese Studies*, 14, 1988, pp. 288–9.

44. Goode, *World Revolution*, pp. 352–3; **E.H. Cressy**, *Daughters of Changing Japan*, Gollancz, 1955, pp. 114–16. Also *South China Morning Post*, 2 November 1997.

45. **H.I. Martin**, 'Popular Music and Social Change in Prewar Japan', *The Japan Interpreter: A Quarterly Journal of Social and Political Ideas*, 3–4, 1972, esp. pp. 332–4; Eccleston, *State and Society*, pp. 140, 162; Reischauer, *Japanese Today*, pp. 150–1. The emergence of mass media and their relationship with the state is analysed in **G.J. Kasza**, *The State and the Mass Media in Japan, 1918–1945*, University of California Press, 1993.

46. **K. Yoshino**, *Cultural Nationalism in Contemporary Japan: A Sociological Enquiry*, Routledge, 1992, p. 126; Reischauer, *Japanese Today*, p. 150; **G. Honda**, 'Short Tailors and Sickly Buddhist Priests: Birth Order and Household Effects on Class and Health in Japan, 1893–1943', *Continuity and Change*, 11, 1996, p. 282.

47. For a discussion of class and strata, see **J. Hara** and **K. Seiyama**, *Shakai kaisô – yutakasa no naka no fubyôdô*, Tokyo Daigaku Shuppankai, 1999, pp. 197–230, esp. pp. 213–15. **J. Benson**, *The Working Class in Britain, 1850–1939*, Longman, 1989, pp. 141–2, 151–2; **P. Duus**, Introduction, in **P. Duus** (ed.), *The Cambridge History of Japan*, vol. 6, *The Twentieth Century*, Cambridge University Press, 1988, p. 3.

48. Benson, *Working Class*, pp. 3–4.

49. Benson, *Working Class*, pp. 151–2.

50. **L. Young**, 'Marketing the Modern: Department Stores, Consumer Culture, and the New Middle Class in Interwar Japan', *International Labour and Working-Class History*, 55, 1999; **M. Mann**, *Consciousness and Action Among the Western Working Class*, Macmillan, 1973, p. 13. See also: Seidensticker, *Low City, High City*; **E.H. Kinmonth**, 'The Impact of Military Procurements on the Old Middle Classes in Japan, 1931–1941', *Japan Forum*, 4, 1992; **S. Okamoto**, 'The Emperor and the Crowd: The Historical Significance of the Hibiya Riot', in Najita and Koschmann (eds), *Conflict*, p. 260; **H.D. Smith II**, 'Tokyo as an Idea: An Exploration of Japanese Urban Thought Until 1945', *Journal of Japanese Studies* 4, 1978.

51. *Japan Weekly Chronicle*, 12 August 1920; **T.C. Smith**, 'The Right to Benevolence: Dignity and Japanese Workers, 1890–1920', *Comparative Studies in Society and History*, 26, 1984, p. 591.

52. Martin, 'Popular Music', pp. 344–5.

53. Smith, 'Right to Benevolence', pp. 591–2.

54. Dower, *Japan*, p. 144.

55. Okamoto, 'Emperor'.

56. **M. Lewis**, *Rioters and Citizens: Mass Protest in Imperial Japan*, University of California Press, 1990, p. xvii; *TA*, 7 August 1918; *TA*, 8 August 1918; **J.L. Huffman**,

Creating a Public: People and Press in Meiji Japan, University of Hawaii Press, 1997, pp. 366–7; **P. Duus** and **I. Scheiner**, 'Socialism, Liberalism, and Marxism, 1901–1931', in Duus (ed.), *Cambridge History of Japan*, p. 683; *CH* 17 August 1918; **J. Hashimoto** and **Y. Ôsugi**, *Kindai nippon keizaishi*, Iwanami Shoten, 2000, p. 211. On the housewives' riots, see *OM*, 5 August 1918; *TA*, 8 August 1918, *JS*, 9 August 1918.

57. Lewis, *Rioters*, pp. xxii–xxiii. See, for example: *OM*, 20 August 1918; *CS*, 22 August 1918; **G.M. Beckmann** and **G. Ôkubo**, *The Japanese Communist Party, 1922–1945*, Stanford University Press, 1969; **P. Duus** and **I. Scheiner**, 'Socialism, Liberalism, and Marxism, 1901–1931', in Duus (ed.), *Cambridge History of Japan*, pp. 654–710; **S. Katayama**, *The Labour Movement in Japan*, Charles H. Kerr, 1918; **S.S. Large**, *Organized Workers and Socialist Politics in Interwar Japan*, Cambridge University Press, 1981; **R.A. Scalapino**, *The Japanese Communist Movement, 1920–1966*, University of California Press, 1967; **K. Taira**, *Economic Development and the Labor Market in Japan*, Columbia University Press, 1970; **G.O. Totten**, *The Social Democratic Movement in Prewar Japan*, Yale University Press, 1966.

58. Lewis, *Rioters*, pp. xxii, 244.

59. *Japan Weekly Chronicle*, 8 July 1920, 11 July 1935; **A. Waswo**, 'The Transformation of Rural Society, 1900–1950', in Duus (ed.), *Cambridge History of Japan*, p. 585; **R.J. Smethurst**, *Agricultural Development and Tenancy Disputes in Japan, 1870–1940*, Princeton University Press, 1986, p. 5; **A. Waswo**, 'In Search of Equity: Japanese Tenant Unions in the 1920s', in Najita and Koschmann (eds), *Conflict*; Hashimoto and Ôsugi, *Keizaishi*, p. 213.

60. Waswo, 'Search', p. 392. Also *Japan Chronicle*, 10 March 1927; *Japan Weekly Chronicle*, 27 March 1930.

61. As might be expected, such views have come in for considerable criticism. In the introduction to his controversial study, *Agricultural Development and Tenancy Disputes in Japan, 1870–1940*, Smethurst makes explicit the revisionist purposes of his research.

> I intend in this book to break out of the tradition within which Nakamura . . . write[s], and to make two 'heterodox' points. First, the growth of a market economy between 1870 and 1940 brought Japanese farmers, rich and poor alike, great benefits. . . .
>
>   Second, the tenant farmers' movement in the 1920s *and* the 1930s, especially in the commercial areas where farmers were better off, was both entrepreneurial and reformist in nature and highly successful.

He goes on to argue that tenant farmers were 'potential petit bourgeois entrepreneurs' rather than wage-earners, that the tenants' movement was evolutionary rather than revolutionary, and that it should be regarded therefore as a success rather than as a failure. Smethurst, *Agricultural Development*, pp. 8–10, 19, 29, 32–3. See Y. Nishida, 'Growth of the Meiji Landlord System and Tenancy Disputes after World War I: A Critique of Richard Smethurst, *Agricultural Development and Tenancy Disputes in Japan, 1870–1940*, *Journal of Japanese Studies*, 15, 1989; Smethurst, 'A Challenge to Orthodoxy and its Orthodox Critics: A Reply to Nishida Yoshiaki', *Journal of Japanese Studies*, 15, 1989.

62. *Japan Weekly Chronicle*, 24 April 1930; Lewis, *Rioters*, p. xxi; Waswo, *Modern Japanese Society*, p. 71; Duus and Scheiner, 'Socialism', pp. 691–2; Totten, *Social Democratic Movement*, in Livingston, Moore and Oldfather (eds), *Japan Reader*, p. 330. See also: *NN*, 3 August 1917; *OM*, 16 January 1919; *CS*, 22 October 1919; *TA*, 18 December 1919.

63. S.A. **Hastings**, *Neighbourhood and Nation in Tokyo, 1905–1937*, University of Pittsburgh Press, 1995, pp. 134–45,158; **M.J. Haynes**, 'Strikes', in **J. Benson** (ed.), *The Working Class in England 1875–1914*, Croom Helm, 1985, pp. 90–1; Hunter, *Modern Japan*, pp. 244–5.

64. Reischauer, *Japanese Today*, pp. 395–6.

65. Hunter, *Modern Japan*, pp. 70, 74.

66. E. **Behr**, *Hirohito: Behind the Myth*, Penguin, 1990, p. 70; *NN*, 3 September 1923. Also Dower, *Japan*, p. 272.

67. *TA*, 14 September 1912; *OM*, 17 October 1905; *Japan Chronicle*, 27 January 1927, 17 February 1927; Okamoto, 'Emperor', p. 275; **T. Kawahara**, *Hirohito and his Times: A Japanese Perspective*, Kôdansha International, 1990, pp. 20–1. See also *OM*, 7 February 1927.

68. *YC*, 23 January 1904.

69. *Japan Chronicle*, 3 August 1933; *Japan Times Weekly*, 22 September 1938, 19 January 1939.

70. Kinmonth, 'Impact'; **J. Crump**, 'Anarchist Opposition to Japanese Militarism, 1926–1937', *Japan Forum*, 4, 1992.

71. Waswo, *Modern Japanese Society*, p. 57.

72. Yoshino, *Cultural Nationalism*, chs 2 and 3; Dower, *Japan*, p. 277; **I. Neary**, *Political Protest and Social Control in Pre-War Japan: The Origins of Buraku Liberation*, Manchester University Press, 1989; Thomas, *Modern Japan*, pp. 27–42. There are a number of valuable studies of minorities in Japan including: G. **DeVos** and **W. Wetherall**, *Japan's Minorities: Burakumin, Koreans, Ainu, and Okinawans*, Minority Rights Group, 1974; **M. Weiner**, *Race and Migration in Imperial Japan*, Routledge, 1994; **F. Dikotter** (ed.), *The Construction of Racial Identities in China and Japan: Historical and Contemporary Perspectives*, Hurst, 1997; **M. Weiner** (ed.), *Japan's Minorities: The Illusion of Homogeneity*, Routledge, 1997.

73. However, some of the Ainu have managed to preserve their culture. See **S. Takakura**, *The Ainu of Northern Japan: A Study in Conquest and Acculturation*, **J.A. Harrison** (trans.), American Philosophical Society, 1960; **R. Siddle**, *Race, Resistance and the Ainu of Japan*, Routledge, 1996. The history of Okinawa is dealt with in **G.H. Kerr**, *Okinawa: The History of an Island People*, C. E. Tuttle, 1958.

74. See **G. DeVos** and **H. Wagatsuma** (eds), *Japan's Invisible Race: Caste in Culture and Personality*, University of California Press, 1966; **H. Wagatsuma** and G. **DeVos**, 'The Outcaste Tradition in Modern Japan: A Problem in Social Self-Identity', in **R. Dore** (ed.), *Aspects of Social Change in Modern Japan*, Princeton University Press, 1967; **G. DeVos**, *Japan's Outcasts: The Problem of the Burakumin*, Minority Rights Group, 1971.

75. The number of Koreans in Japan grew from 30,000 in 1920, to 300,000 in 1930 and about 2.5 million in 1945. **S. Garon**, review of Weiner, *Race and Migration*, in *International Review of Social History*, 41, 1996, p. 97. On the Korean minority, see **E.W. Wagner**, *The Korean Minority in Japan, 1904–1950*, Institute of Pacific Relations, 1951; **R.H. Mitchell**, *The Korean Minority in Japan*, University of California Press, 1967; **C. Lee** and G. **DeVos**, *Koreans in Japan: Ethnic Conflict and Accommodation*, University of California Press, 1982; **M. Weiner**, *The Origins of the Korean Community in Japan 1910–1923*, Manchester University Press, 1989.

76. B.-A. **Shillony**, *Politics and Culture in Wartime Japan*, Clarendon Press, 1991, pp. 126–9.

7

Epilogue: the Allied Occupation, 1945–52

If one event confirmed Japan's defeat in 1945, it was the Allied Occupation. Never before in her entire history had Japan been occupied by a foreign army and it was with ambivalence, if not fear, that the Japanese people greeted the Occupation forces.

> [All] kinds of rumours about the Americans had begun to spread among the people. There was a general belief that the occupying troops, filled with vengeful hatred of the Japanese, would be virtually unrestrained in their behaviour towards life and property. Many people – women especially – thought it prudent to leave Tokyo and Yokohama before the Americans moved in.

It was against this background that the Occupation forces (or 'Occupationaires'), set about, in the words of an American brigadier general, 'stamping out the bad, stamping in the new'.[1]

In many ways, it seemed that Japan had come full circle. A century of efforts to extricate herself from her weakness and inferiority *vis-à-vis* the West had placed her in a position to be dominated once again. Her institutions and way of life were to be remodelled once more along Western lines. Of course, there were differences from what had happened during the Meiji years. Instead of Japan going to the West to learn, the West came to Japan to teach – and, where this failed, to impose the lessons they felt she should learn. Instead of Japan being at liberty to choose from any number of foreign exemplars, the authorities in post-war Japan were provided with reforms which they were instructed to adopt and implement.

An American Occupation

In principle, the administrative structure of the Occupation was highly complex. The Far Eastern Commission, which sat in Washington and included representatives from all thirteen countries that had fought against Japan, was established in 1946 to formulate basic principles. The Allied Council for Japan was set up in the same year and was charged with assisting in the development and implementation of surrender terms, and the subsequent administration of the country. It consisted of representatives from the USA, the USSR, Nationalist China and the British Commonwealth. Although both bodies were active initially, they were rendered largely ineffectual due to their unwieldy decision-making processes, disagreements between the national delegations (especially the USA and USSR), and the obstructionism of General Douglas MacArthur who headed the Supreme Command for the Allied Powers (SCAP).[2]

In practice, SCAP, the executive authority of the Occupation, essentially ruled Japan from 1945 to 1952. And since it took orders only from the US government, the Occupation became primarily an American affair. Indeed, as a former Japanese minister of education pointed out, SCAP's military personnel and civilian advisors came predominantly from America and had little experience or knowledge of Japan.

> The idea that a group of people who came to Japan with not even a child's knowledge about the Japanese education system could – in just 24 days in the country – get a grasp on how the system really works and propose a set of reforms is simply unbelievable. . . . My theory is that the whole [1946 US] Education Mission was just a trick of the Occupation.

Such ignorance need not necessarily have been a major handicap since the Occupation forces were never intended to exercise direct rule: reform was to be transmitted rather through existing, albeit reformed, Japanese administrative structures. The Japanese, it has been said, were impressed by the professionalism of the Occupationaires. However, it has also been claimed that the reformers – many of them reliant on American-born, second-generation Japanese translators – were 'bamboozled by deceit or corrupted by flattery', their plans undermined and changed as they were being implemented.[3]

The Occupationaires' lack of knowledge about Japan was more than compensated for by their zeal, particularly in the early years. Many of the 'New Dealers' viewed the country and its culture as a laboratory; the 22 year-old Beate Sirota, for example, believed that she and her colleagues in the Civil Rights Committee, had 'the responsibility to effect a social revolution in Japan'.[4]

Disarmament, demilitarisation and the ultranationalist purge

The Occupation programme was revolutionary and involved a two-pronged approach. First, the Americans sought to dismantle the direct cause of the war – the military. In order to ensure that Japan would 'not again become a menace to the United States or to the peace and security of the world,' SCAP set about realising the 'disarmament and demilitarization of Japan, with continuing control over Japan's capacity to make war'. This involved the destruction of military supplies and installations, the demobilisation of over five million Japanese soldiers and the thorough discrediting of the military establishment.[5]

The International Military Tribunal for the Far East established a military court in Tokyo. Charged with trying as class 'A' criminals those in the military and the government accused of being responsible for the war, the Tokyo War Crimes Trial, as it came to be known, began in May 1946 and lasted for two and a half years. Of the 25 found guilty, seven (including Tôjô) were sentenced to death, sixteen to life imprisonment, one to seven years imprisonment and one to twenty years. It has been claimed, of course, that the trial was an expression of revenge rather than of justice, but it represented an important stage in helping the West to understand how 'Japan dar[ed] to attack both the United States and Great Britain, having the unfinished war with China on her hands, and preparing an attack on the Soviet Union'.

> These men [the accused] were supposed to be the elite of the nation, the honest and trusted leaders to whom the fate of the nation had been confidently entrusted. . . . With full knowledge they voluntarily made their choice for evil. . . . With full knowledge they voluntarily elected to follow the path of war, bringing death and injury to millions of human beings and hate wherever their forces went. . . . For this choice they must bear the guilt.[6]

In addition to the trials in Tokyo, a purge was conducted of all who were deemed to have actively promoted the cause of war and/or the ultranationalist agenda. While some of the 200,000 purged were selected following an examination of their personal records, most were identified by their job or by having fallen into disfavour with the Occupation authorities. It was for this reason that men like Ishibashi, one of pre-war Japan's foremost liberals and opponent of expansion into China, found themselves unjustifiably purged.[7]

As part of the drive to rid Japan of its ultranationalist elements, an attack was also launched on the *zaibatsu* and the families associated with them, both of which were widely perceived as bearing a responsibility for the rise of aggressive militarism. The enactment in 1947 of the Anti-Monopoly Law and the Law for the Exclusion of Excessive Concentrations of Economic Power resulted in the dissolution of some *zaibatsu*. However, there were those, both in Japan and America, who felt that Japanese business was being damaged unduly and this prevented the anti-big business sentiments of the Occupationaires from being fully realised.[8]

Once those directly responsible for the war had been dealt with, the Occupationaires turned to address what they felt were the deep-seated causes of Japanese aggression – the country's tenacious 'feudalism' and lack of democracy, or as the Americans interpreted it, her lack of individualism. In an effort to prepare the foundations for a 'peaceful and responsible government . . . which will respect the rights of other states', every area of national life was reviewed. Its 'feudal' elements were identified, and policies implemented which would result in the 'strengthening of democratic tendencies and processes in governmental, economic, and social institutions; and the encouragement and support of liberal political tendencies'.[9]

The Constitution of 1947

The first step in this process was the creation of a new constitution. Unlike the Meiji Constitution which took over a decade to produce, the 1947 Constitution was written and promulgated within two years. Having rejected initial Japanese drafts which left the position of the emperor largely untouched, SCAP took it upon itself to compose its own constitution and force it through a reluctant Diet. Coming into effect in May 1948, the new constitution was passed technically as an amendment to the Meiji Constitution. Nevertheless, it was a radical document that undermined, or at least modified, all that had preceded it. Like many subsequent reforms, it reflected in both tone and substance the idea that foreign models could be transplanted to Japan with little or no modification.

> *Preamble.* We the Japanese people, acting through our duly elected representatives in the National Diet, determined that we shall secure for ourselves and our posterity the fruits of peaceful cooperation with all nations and the blessings of liberty throughout this land . . . do solemnly proclaim that sovereign power resides with the people and do firmly establish this constitution. Government is a sacred trust of the people, the authority for which is derived from the people, the powers of which are exercised by the representatives of the people, and the benefits of which are enjoyed by the people. . . . We reject and revoke all constitutions, laws, ordinances, and rescripts in conflict herewith.[10]

The most far-reaching provision concerned the relationship between the emperor and the people. The people were made sovereign, and the emperor a 'symbol of the state and the unity of the people, deriving his position from the will of the people in whom resides sovereign power'.

Because the emperor now possessed fewer powers than European constitutional monarchs, some have gone so far as to say that Japan became 'a republic in fact if not in name'. Yet, the retention of the emperor was, in fact, a compromise that suited both those who wanted to preserve the essence of the nation for the sake of stability and those who demanded that the emperor system, though not necessarily the emperor, should be expunged.[11]

In line with the democratic spirit of the new constitution, the peerage was abolished and the two-chamber Diet, to which the cabinet was now responsible, became the highest organ of state. The judiciary was made independent and local autonomy was granted in vital areas of jurisdiction such as education and the police. Moreover, the constitution stipulated that 'the people shall not be prevented from enjoying any of the fundamental human rights', that they 'shall be respected as individuals', and that 'their right to life, liberty, and the pursuit of happiness shall . . . be the supreme consideration in legislation'. Its 29 articles guaranteed basic human rights: equality, freedom from discrimination on the basis of race, creed, sex, social status or family origin, freedom of thought and freedom of religion. Finally, in its most controversial section, Article 9, the 'peace clause', Japan 'renounce[d] war as a sovereign right of the nation' and vowed not to maintain any military forces and 'other war potential'.[12]

Democratisation

The attempt to imbue the political system with a thoroughly democratic ethos was only one part of a much broader and comprehensive programme. Society itself required reformation, the Occupationaires believed, if a deep-seated adherence to democratic principles was to grow and flourish: reforms were introduced that touched every aspect of society – the economy, labour, women, young people and the countryside. As we have seen, attempts were made to decentralise economic power and – insofar as domestic competition was stimulated through the dissolution of the zaibatsu – the ideal of 'economic democracy' was encouraged. Yet even before Japan's economic elite were subjected to SCAP's reforming zeal, the Occupationaires addressed the rights of labour. The 1945 Labour Union Law and the 1946 Labour Relations Act guaranteed workers the right to collective activity: within a year, some 34,000 unions representing over 40 per cent of industrial workers, had been established. This was followed, in 1947, by the Labour Standards Law which guaranteed basic standards of work both for men and for women.[13]

In fact, reforms concerned with the status of women were among the most radical introduced since, it was said, they 'went far beyond what Congress, the state legislatures, and many Americans are willing to accept in their own country today'. In accordance with the guarantee of sexual equality in the Constitution, 'the Magna Carta of Japan', the legal institution of the patriarchal household was abolished in the revised Civil Code of 1948. Together with the establishment of the Women and Children's Bureau in the Ministry of Labour and a host of other legislation, there seemed much for women to enthuse over.

> [We] women have special reasons to be proud of [the Constitution] and exultant over it, for it means the complete emancipation of Japanese women from the feudalistic shackles which have been binding women for centuries.... For the first time women are the equals of men before the law. No longer are wives treated as impotent persons like idiots, lunatics, the blind and the deaf and the dumb, incapable of taking care of their own properties and disqualified for legal transactions of business. No longer is marriage considered solely from the viewpoint of the family name, but it is to take place on the mutual consent of both sexes.[14]

The reforms to education were no less significant. The selective, segregated system of the pre-war era was completely dismantled and restructured to mirror the basic principles followed in the United States of America. This introduced the '6-3-3' system of free, co-educational, secular, locally controlled schooling: the '6-3-3' system involved six years of compulsory elementary education and three years of junior high school education, followed by an optional three years at senior high school. (Higher education was also expanded through the establishment of universities around the nation.) More important than structural change was ideological reform. As part and parcel of the general censorship of 'feudal' material in the media and the suspension of the 'most contaminated' courses (history, geography and morals) was the revision of textbooks. In accordance with criteria set out by the Americans, materials were banned if they taught 'The Greater East Asia Co-Prosperity Sphere doctrine or any other doctrine of expansion; the idea that the Japanese are superior . . . and the idea that the Emperor of Japan is superior to the heads of other nations and that the *tenno* system [of imperial sovereignty] is sacred and immutable.' The Education Ministry went further, forbidding among other ideas, the glorification of war, the glorification of dying for the emperor or the idealisation of war heroes. However, the key objective was the cultivation of individualism. Article 1 of the 1947 Fundamental Law of Education stated that

Education shall aim at the full development of personality, striving for the rearing of the people, sound in mind and body, who shall love truth and justice, esteem individual value, respect labour and have a deep sense of responsibility, and be imbued with the independent spirit, as builders of the peaceful state and society.[15]

With women enfranchised and young people being moulded as a guarantee against militarism and ultranationalism, rural Japan was transformed in order to undermine the deleterious effects of class divisions. Although land reform had been discussed before the war, the real impetus came with the Occupation. In 1946, legislation was forced through the Diet. This provided for the purchase of all land held by absentee landlords, allowed resident landlords and owner–farmers to retain a set amount of land (one-third of which they were allowed to let), and required that all remaining land should be sold to the government so that it could be offered to existing tenants. By 1950, the total amount of cultivated land under tenancy agreements had fallen from 46 per cent before the war to less than 10 per cent.

> The long struggle of ordinary farmers against the unequal distribution of wealth and power was now over, and the hamlets in which they lived had become, in comparison with the past, communities of economic, social, and political equals. And that these communities remained important to their residents was now a matter more of choice than of necessity.[16]

The aftermath of war

The economic and social problems that the Japanese faced following their surrender were utterly unprecedented. All major cities, with the exception of Kyoto, had been heavily bombed, with Tokyo levelled for a second time in just over twenty years. The destruction of factories, transport and infrastructure and the crippling of administration meant that decades of economic growth were obliterated with real per capita GNP reduced in 1946 to half the levels of 1934–36. It was the mass of the population, of course, who were hit the hardest. A food crisis saw daily calorific intake drop from 2,400 in the pre-war era to just 1,500: in the cities where conditions were at their worst, a black market emerged and the sight of people scavenging for food became commonplace. There also loomed a population crisis caused by the repatriation of soldiers and civilians (from the empire) – 3.5 million in 1946 alone. The result was that out of a population of 76 million people, 10 million were unemployed.[17]

To physical hardship was added the psychological effects of defeat, particularly popular disillusionment with an ideological and moral system that, as we have seen, had been relentlessly propagated and embraced, outwardly at least, by many, if not most, of the population. Surrender was all the more difficult to comprehend since for weeks the authorities had been nurturing the so-called 'bamboo-spear psychology' – a strategy of spirit over technology – in which every single Japanese was to defend their homeland against an American invasion. 'But what were the results of the fighting operations and the long hours of tiring labor performed by these young men with their noble [sic] and eagerness?', asked one disillusioned observer in 1947.

> They were to face the bitter fact of pitiless defeat. Moreover, the war they so strenuously fought at such great personal sacrifices is now under the trial of world judgement in the name of justice and humanity. They must now realize that the noble lives of hundreds of thousands of promising youths, added to the sacrifices and suffering of the entire population, were all expended merely for the sake of a reckless militarism.[18]

Many women, having devoted themselves to becoming good wives and wise mothers, were forced to accept the fact that those around whom their lives had revolved – their fathers, brothers, husbands and sons – would not be returning from the front. One mother reflected, 'For what purpose did I have to let my son die, now I really wonder?' Another concluded, 'We certainly have been deceived.'[19]

There was a great deal of dissatisfaction, even if it was tempered by relief that years of rigid indoctrination were now over. In the first few months, there spread a very real fear that society was unravelling. 'In this confusion of social order, all past authorities and conventions were denied. Naturally the youth lost the very ground on which they stood, their spiritual and moral guidance crumbled, and they found themselves confronted with a sudden, unwholesome liberty, more akin to license.'

> [The] blind obedience to the military and demand to sacrifice everything for the war has brought about a cultural and intellectual dissolution, leaving Japanese life today in a desert of the most gross materialism.... This excessive indulgence in cheap pleasures naturally accelerates youth's inability to conquer its spiritual and moral disorder, and promotes selfishness and indifference to everything that does not minister to their own pleasures and immediate material needs.[20]

This 'Slough of Despond', as the Imperial Rescript on Reconstruction of 1 January 1946 termed it, was a transitory phase. Once the reconstruction of Japan had commenced, it seems that the people began to face the future and accept the possibilities that the new order offered. One observer concluded in 1948 that 'whether in rural or urban areas, youth today is not satisfied with the old ways. They are interested in blazing new trails. . . . They are willing to be guided along the new paths of a democratic Japan, when they are convinced this is the true way.'[21]

The 'Reverse Course'

In fact, 1948 represented something of a turning point, with a number of international and domestic concerns converging to produce what has been called the 'Reverse Course'. The most important of these was the rise of Mao Zedong in mainland China and the intensification of animosities between the USA and the USSR which erupted into full hostilities in Korea in 1950.

Throughout the late 1940s, US policy focused increasingly on rebuilding Japan as the Pacific region's primary buttress against the spread of Communism. Primarily, this meant the reconstruction of the Japanese economy along mainstream capitalist lines as opposed to the social reformist model advocated by the 'New Dealer' Occupationaires. An Economic Stabilisation Programme was introduced which included a five-year plan to co-ordinate production and target capital by means of the Reconstruction Finance Bank. In 1949, the anti-inflationary 'Dodge Plan' was adopted with its call for balanced budgets, the fixing of the exchange rate at 360 yen to the dollar, and an end to government intervention. In the same year, bureaucratic expertise and co-operation were mobilised by the creation of the Ministry of International Trade and Industry (MITI). It sponsored the formation of conglomerates centred around banks, and in so doing encouraged the re-emergence of a somewhat weaker set of *zaibatsu*, including Mitsui and Mitsubishi. By the end of the Occupation era – and thanks in part to the Korean War – Japan was on the verge of surpassing her 1934–36 levels of economic growth. By 1955, she had entered a fifteen-year period of sustained 'high growth' that reached, and often exceeded, 10 per cent per annum.[22]

Equally important was the rearmament of Japan and Japanese alignment with American foreign policy. Although Japanese public opinion was firmly opposed, the outbreak of the Korean War enabled prime minister Yoshida to agree to US demands for the creation of a 75,000 strong National Police Reserve. By 1952, it had been expanded to 110,000 and was re-named the Self-Defense Force following the inclusion within it of an air force.[23]

The Self-Defense Force was part of the larger process of re-introducing Japan into the international system as a fully committed member of the *Pax Americana*. Since the late 1940s, there had been growing pressure on both sides of the Pacific to end the Occupation. To many Americans, the cost of maintaining forces in Japan and subsidising the Japanese economy seemed a costly venture that brought with it few tangible economic benefits. The Japanese too were eager to end their funding of Occupation salaries and other expenses which took up nearly a quarter of their annual budget. Following a year of bilateral negotiations through diplomatic channels, a peace treaty was signed at a conference of 51 nations in San Francisco in September 1951. With the restoration of Japanese sovereignty, the Occupation was ended.[24]

Although the 'Reverse Course' has been attributed, with some justification, to Cold War politics, domestic politics too played a part. A number of political parties emerged, representing all shades of the political spectrum and a variety of different interests. On the left, the most important were the Japan Socialist Party and the Japan Communist Party. Yet, with the exception of 1947 and 1948 when Katayama, the leader of the socialists, led a weak coalition government, the two parties of the left were relatively ineffective. The two main conservative parties, the Liberals and the Progressives (which would merge after a number of transformations in 1955 to form the Liberal Democratic Party), included many former members of the pre-war Seiyûkai and Minseitô parties despite being hard hit by the purges of 1946 and 1947. Garnering grass-roots support largely through the traditional pre-war network of local notables, the conservatives controlled the Diet, under the leadership of prime minister Yoshida, for all but one year of the Occupation period. The post-war pattern of one hegemonic party dominating the political process was set from very early on.[25]

The re-establishment of conservative politics was of major significance. As the Occupation period progressed, the Americans permitted greater Japanese initiative as power shifted from the reformers to the moderates. In 1949, the purge of the right came under review and many who had been condemned now made a return, if not to the Diet, then to positions of power behind the scenes. At the same time, the Japanese authorities, with the support of MacArthur, began to purge left-wing activists. In June 1950, for example, the central office of the Japan Communist Party and the editorial board of *The Red Flag* were purged.[26]

The gains made by women also seemed to be reversed. Women were elected to eight per cent of available seats in the first election for the lower house in 1946, but to only two per cent of seats in 1952, a trend which was not reversed until the so-called 'Madonna Boom' of the 1980s. Although the number of women voting continued to rise, female politicisation remained more superficial than might be imagined. When a public opinion survey conducted by the Prime Minister's Office in 1950 asked women whether they would vote for a man or woman in the next general election, it found that nearly three-quarters of the 42 per cent who indicated they would vote for a man did so because they felt that 'women were bad'. Other responses included suggestions that 'men's heads are better', 'men are more positive' and 'men are generally more trustworthy and talented'. Only 22 per cent of the women surveyed indicated that their vote was conditional on factors other than gender.[27]

Women's employment too seemed to be little affected by labour legislation. Although women formed nearly 40 per cent of the labour force in 1952, they earned only 45 per cent as much as men. Indeed, women's attitudes towards labour were influenced less by the new ethos of fulfilling individual potential than by traditional attitudes towards family and workplace responsibilities. A 1948 public opinion poll found that just over half of the women questioned worked either to 'support the family' or to 'help out with household expenses'. When asked how long they wished to continue as a 'working woman', 14 per cent responded 'all my life' – and almost 35 per cent 'until marriage'. And, although women claimed that they were generally no longer addressed by their husbands as 'hey you' and that more husbands put away their bed mattresses (*futons*) each morning, almost 70 per cent indicated in a 1950 national opinion poll that their status in the house was low compared to that of their husbands.[28]

In the areas of local autonomy and education, too, substantial modifications were made to the reforms. Because local authorities were not provided with sufficient power to tax, they were unable to realise their (potentially) extensive powers. As a result, they transferred key areas of responsibility back to national jurisdiction. In 1951, for example, 90 per cent of villages and towns placed their police forces under the control of the newly formed National Police Agency. Central control over education was also gradually reasserted. In 1951, for instance, the Yoshida government attempted to re-introduce ethics classes, proposed that textbooks be more tightly controlled by the central government and recommended that local school board elections should be abolished. By the end of the decade, all these changes had been implemented.[29]

Change and continuity

When the Occupation came to a close in 1951, it seemed that the 'Reverse Course' had thoroughly undermined the revolution that the Americans had sought to effect. International events conspired with domestic pressures to prevent the remodelling of Japan in the way that the 'New Dealer' social reformers had envisaged. The idealism with which the Occupationaires attempted to transplant the American way of life into Japan was as inappropriate as the idea that a few hundred men and women could transform Japanese society in less than a decade. In retrospect, it can be seen that the structure and purpose of the Occupation were profoundly contradictory: demilitarisation by a military authority, censorship to protect freedom of speech and thought, the use of men from the pre-war era to create institutions for the post-war period, decentralisation from the centre and, most ironically, 'democracy by decree'.[30]

Yet, change there was. Many of the reforms, modified though they were, did effect change and did address many of the problems that had divided pre-war society. It may be true, as Beasley claims, that under the conservative leadership of Yoshida, there was laid down 'a formulation of a national policy which had considerable public support: implementation of a conservative brand of parliamentary democracy; adherence to the American alliance; a concentration of effort on economic recovery and growth'. That Japan in 1952 failed to reflect the vision of its reformers did not necessarily mean that the Occupation was a failure. In helping to bring stability so that reconstruction could begin, the Japanese were given a chance to look once again to the future and reshape their society without completely rejecting their past.[31]

Notes

1. **R. Storry**, *A History of Modern Japan*, Penguin Books, 1987, first published in 1960, p. 238; Cf. **H. Fukui**, 'Postwar Politics, 1945–1973', in **P. Duus** (ed.), *The Cambridge History of Japan*, vol. 6: *The Twentieth Century*, Cambridge University Press, 1989, pp. 166–9; **R.K. Hall**, 'The Battle of the Mind: American Educational Policy in Germany and Japan', *Columbia Journal of International Affairs*, 2, 1948, p. 63.

2. For general treatments of the Occupation, see **K. Kawai**, *Japan's American Interlude*, University Press of Chicago, 1960; **R. Ward** and **Y. Sakamoto** (eds), *Democratizing Japan: The Allied Occupation*, University of Hawaii Press, 1987; **M. Schaller**, *The American Occupation of Japan: The Origins of the Cold War in Asia*, Oxford University Press, 1985; **R. Finn**, *Winners in Peace: MacArthur, Yoshida, and Postwar Japan*, University of California Press, 1992; **T. Cohen**, *Remaking Japan: The American Occupation as New Deal*, Free Press, 1987.

3. **B.K. Marshall**, *Learning to be Modern: Japanese Political Discourse on Education*, Westview Press, 1994, p. 143; Storry, *History of Modern Japan*, p. 242. On MacArthur,

see **D. MacArthur**, *Reminiscences*, McGraw Hill, 1964; **W. Sebald**, *With MacArthur in Japan*, Cresset Press, 1967.

4. **S.J. Pharr**, 'A Radical US Experiment: Women's Rights Laws and the Occupation of Japan', in **L.H. Redford** (ed.), *The Occupation of Japan: Impact of Legal Reform*, The Proceedings of a Symposium Sponsored by the MacArthur Memorial, Omni International Hotel, Norfolk, VA, 14, 15 April 1977, pp. 131–2. See: **J. Williams**, *Japan's Political Revolution under MacArthur: A Participant's Account*, University of Georgia Press, *c.* 1979.

5. Fukui, 'Postwar Politics', p. 155; **W.G. Beasley**, *The Rise of Modern Japan: Political, Economic and Social Change since 1850*, Weidenfeld and Nicolson, 1900 (2nd ed., 1995), p. 214; **R.H. Minear**, *Victor's Justice – The Tokyo War Crimes Trial*, Princeton University Press, 1971.

6. According to Storry, the Japanese 'accepted [the trial] as the possibly inevitable punishment meted out by the victors upon the vanquished. . . . On the whole the Japanese reaction to the Tokyo Trial was one of boredom'. Storry, *History of Modern Japan*, p. 249; **International Military Tribunal for the Far East**, *Transcript of Proceedings*, no. 85, p. 7275, 8 October 1946 and no. 416, pp. 48410–12, 16 April 1948 cited in **M. Maruyama**, *Thought and Behaviour in Modern Japanese Politics*, *expanded edition*, **I. Morris** (ed.), Oxford University Press, 1969, first published in 1963, pp. 85, 92. A series of other trials hearing cases against minor war criminals was held at various sites in Japan and abroad. These found over 5,000 guilty and sentenced 900 to be hanged (including Matsui Iwane for his responsibility as Supreme Commander of the Shanghai region during the 'Rape of Nanjin').

7. Ishibashi Tanzan was appointed to the Yoshida cabinet in 1946 as Finance Minister. His economic policies, designed to stimulate recovery, were criticised by SCAP as favouring the *zaibatsu*. See **K. Kimura**, 'Ishibashi Tanzan, the Man and His Policy', *Contemporary Japan*, 15, 1946.

8. See: **T.A. Bisson**, *Zaibatsu Dissolution in Japan*, University of California Press, 1954; **E.F. Hadley**, *Antitrust in Japan*, Princeton University Press, 1970.

9. **E.M. Martin**, *The Allied Occupation of Japan*, Stanford University Press, 1948, pp. 122–50.

10. *Constitution of Japan* cited in **Supreme Commander for the Allied Powers, Civil Information and Education Section**, *Education in the New Japan*, vol. 1, p. 106. See also **D.F. Henderson**, *The Constitution of Japan: Its First Twenty Years, 1947–1967*, University of Washington Press, 1969; **K. Inoue**, *MacArthur's Japanese Constitution: A Linguistic and Cultural Study of its Making*, Chicago University Press, 1991; **R.E. Ward**, 'The Commission on the Constitution and Prospects for Constitutional Change in Japan', *Journal of Asian Studies*, 24, 1965.

11. *Kôdansha Encyclopedia of Japan*, vol. 2, Kôdansha, 1983, pp. 9–12; Storry, *History of Modern Japan*, p. 251.

12. *Constitution of Japan*, pp. 106–7; *Kôdansha Encyclopedia*, pp. 9–12. See also **Supreme Commander for the Allied Powers**, *The Political Reorientation of Japan*, 2 vols, 1949.

13. Beasley, *Rise of Modern Japan*, pp. 216, 221–2; **S.B. Levine**, *Industrial Relations in Postwar Japan*, University of Illinois Press, 1958.

14. **T. Fujita**, 'The Progress of the Emancipation of Japanese Women', *Contemporary Japan*, 16, 1947, pp. 281–2; Pharr, 'A Radical US Experiment', p. 126; **K. Yamakawa**, 'Japanese Women under the New Constitution', *Contemporary Japan*, 17, 1948, pp. 141–4.

15. *Fundamental Law of Education* cited in **General Headquarters**, *Education in the New Japan*, vol. 1, pp. 109–11; Marshall, *Learning to be Modern*, pp. 146–50; 155–60; 161–6.

16. Beasley, *Rise of Modern Japan*, pp. 222–3; **A. Waswo**, 'The Transformation of Rural Society, 1900–1950', in Duus (ed.), *The Cambridge History of Japan*, p. 60. See also **R.P. Dore**, *Land Reform in Japan*, Oxford University Press, 1959.

17. **Y. Morita**, 'The National Income and the Standard of Living of Japan', *Japan Quarterly*, 3, 1956, pp. 105–17; **F. Okazaki**, 'Population Problems of Japan', *Contemporary Japan*, 27, 1948, pp. 248–54; Storry, *History of Modern Japan*, pp. 228, 238–9.

18. **T. Morito**, 'The Task of Youth in Rebuilding Japan', *Contemporary Japan*, 16, 1947, pp. 260–1.

19. **M. Shiozawa** and **T. Shimada**, 'Documentary on Postwar Women Living Alone', *Japan Quarterly*, 23, 1976, pp. 363–5; **K. Tsurumi**, *Social Change and the Individual: Japan Before and After Defeat in World War II*, Princeton University Press, 1970, pp. 258–9.

20. Morito, 'The Task of Youth', pp. 262–3.

21. *Imperial Rescript on Reconstruction* cited in **General Headquarters**, *Education in the New Japan*, vol. 1, pp. 109–11; Marshall, *Learning to be Modern*, pp. 77–8; **R.L. Durgin**, 'Japan's Youth Looks Ahead', *Contemporary Japan*, 17, 1948, p. 234; Beasley, *Rise of Modern Japan*, p. 229.

22. Fukui, 'Postwar Politics', p. 188; **Y. Kosai**, 'The Postwar Japanese Economy, 1945–1973', in Duus (ed.), *The Cambridge History of Japan*, vol. 6, pp. 494–502; Beasley, *Rise of Modern Japan*, pp. 245–7. See **J.B. Cohen**, *Japan's Postwar Economy*, Indiana University Press, 1958; **C. Johnson**, *MITI and the Japanese Miracle: The Growth of Industrial Policy, 1925–1975*, Stanford University Press, 1982; **T. Nakamura**, *The Postwar Japanese Economy – Its Development and Structure*, University of Tokyo Press, 1981.

23. Beasley, *Rise of Modern Japan*, pp. 225–6. On the Self-Defense Force, see **J.E. Auer**, *The Postwar Rearmament of the Japanese Maritime Forces, 1945–1971*, Praeger, 1973; **J.H. Buck**, *The Modern Japanese Military System*, Sage Publications, 1975.

24. Although Japan was allowed to maintain the Ryûkyû and Bonin Islands under US trusteeship, all her other territorial acquisitions and interests in China, Korea, Taiwan and the Kuriles were surrendered. Most importantly, Japanese independence was made conditional upon membership in and adherence to the US–Japan Security Treaty. A number of outstanding issues remained. The USSR, India, Burma and a number of east European nations refused to sign the San Francisco Peace Treaty, while the Chinese had not even been invited due to the 'Two-China Problem'. Within the next five years, bilateral peace treaties were concluded with each of these countries. Reparations took considerably longer to settle. On the San Francisco Peace Treaty, see: **B.C. Cohen**, *The Political Process and Foreign Policy*, Princeton University Press, 1957; **J.W. Dower**, *Empire and Aftermath – Yoshida Shigeru and the Japanese Experience, 1878–1954*, Harvard University Press, 1971; **F.S. Dunn**, *Peacemaking and the Settlement with Japan*, Princeton University Press, 1963. Further readings on the Security Treaty include: **M.E. Weinstein**, *Japan's Postwar Defense Policy, 1947–1968*, Columbia University Press, 1971. **M.T. Bennett** discusses the issue of reparations in his article, 'Japanese Reparations: Fact or Fantasy', *Pacific Affairs*, 21, 1948, pp. 185–94.

25. **S. Yoshida**, *The Yoshida Memoirs: The Story of Japan in Crisis*, **K. Yoshida** (trans.), Heinemann, 1961, p. 288. On the rise of the left in post-war Japan, see **A.B. Cole**,

G.O. **Totten** and **C.H. Uyehara**, *Socialist Parties in Postwar Japan*, Yale University Press, 1966; **R.A. Scalapino**, *The Japanese Communist Movement, 1920–1966*, University of California Press, 1967. Conservative political parties are dealt with in **N.B. Thayer**, *How the Conservatives Rule Japan*, Princeton University Press, 1969.

26. See **S.J. Dowsey** (ed.), *Zengakuren, Japan's Revolutionary Students*, University of California Press, 1970.

27. Pharr, 'A Radical US Experiment', pp. 110–11; **T. Iwai**, '"The Madonna Boom": Women in the Japanese Diet', *Journal of Japanese Studies*, 19, 1993, pp. 103–4; **Prime Minister's Office**, *Fujin no chii ni kansuru yoron chôsa*, 8 April 1950, pp. 14–15; **Prime Minister's Office**, *Fujin no shimin-ishiki ni tsuite no chôsa*, April 1956, p. 27. **R.P. Dore**, *City Life in Japan: A Study of a Tokyo Ward*, University of California Press, 1963, p. 175.

28. **Prime Minister's Office**, *Fujin to shokugyô: Shokugyô fujin no yoron chôsa*, November 1948, pp. 2–3; **T. Koyama**, *The Changing Social Position of Women in Japan*, UNESCO, 1961, p. 68; Prime Minister's Office, *Fujin no chii*, 8 April 1950, p. 12.

29. Beasley, *Rise of Modern Japan*, p. 229. B.K. Marshall, *Learning to be Modern*, pp. 174–92.

30. **R.L. Sims**, interview by Darren Aoki, 22 September 1999; Beasley, *Rise of Modern Japan*, p. 219.

31. Beasley, *Rise of Modern Japan*, p. 230.

8

Conclusion

Japanese history is less well known, and less well understood in the English-speaking world than it deserves to be. There remains a deeply ingrained tendency for those in the West to view Japan and the Japanese with a mixture of fascination, indignation and grudging – often extremely grudging – respect. Japan, it is believed, was – and remains – a world apart, the Japanese by turns unbearably obsequious, inhumanly brutal and ruthlessly efficient. They were a people, it almost seems to be suggested, who inhabited a different, albeit parallel, universe as they set about ending their country's isolation, embarked upon a series of increasingly catastrophic wars, laid the foundations for their post-war economic 'miracle' and endured the humiliation of occupation by an overseas power.

It has been the fundamental purpose of this book to help to clarify such issues by providing readers from the English-speaking world with an accessible, up-to-date and well-informed interpretation of Japanese history between the Restoration of 1868 and the American Occupation of 1945. We believe that the pairing of a Japanese historian and a British historian has forced us to confront the tendency that is inherent in many of us, it seems, to approach the past with a combination of ethnocentric assumptions and 'presentist' preoccupations. We hope therefore that the arguments which we have propounded in the course of the book will command, not of course complete agreement, but at least serious attention and a considerable amount of respect.

It has been our aim, more specifically, to persuade our readers of the truth, and importance, of three major propositions. We have tried to show that, while there is no doubting the uniqueness of nineteenth and early twentieth-century Japanese history, this uniqueness should not be misunderstood. Japan, we have stressed, was not unique in her uniqueness: Japan, like every other country in the world, developed in her own way, with her own character, her own peculiarities and her own sense of national identity.

We have tried to show in particular that late nineteenth and early twentieth-century Japan was by no means the unchanging, homogeneous society that it is so often portrayed. Of course, it is a tribute of sorts to the power of the stereotype that we have been at such pains to show that Japan, like any other country, displayed elements both of homogeneity and of heterogeneity. However, it can surely come as no surprise to discover that the Japanese, like the people of almost any other country, were divided – and sometimes divided very sharply – by politics, occupation, income, ideology, education, religion, class, gender, age and region.

We have gone on to argue that, because Japan was marked neither by 'unique' uniqueness nor by unchanging homogeneity, one must look elsewhere for ways of understanding the developments that took place between the Restoration and the Occupation. We have suggested, it will be recalled, that what was needed was to look to the specific political, economic, social and cultural conditions that pertained during the period under discussion. The way that Japan developed, we believe, depended not only upon the nature of Japanese society and Japanese culture but also upon the particular combinations of circumstances with which the Japanese found themselves confronted between 1868 and 1945.

If may be felt perhaps that this is to substitute one set of platitudes for another. However, there is a great deal more to it than this. When we switch our attention from ahistorical views of Japan's unchanging uniqueness and homogeneity to the detailed historical examination of political, economic, social and cultural developments, Japanese history begins to look very different indeed. A historical focus confirms, not surprisingly, that there was nothing preordained about the course that Japanese history took between 1868 and 1945. It is only with hindsight that we can identify the winners and losers, that we can distinguish the political initiatives, economic changes and cultural shifts that now seem inevitable from those that now appear to have been doomed from the outset.

The adoption of a historical perspective suggests too that the Japanese people were unchanging primarily in their capacity for change. They were distinguished less by their unbending purity, homogeneity and cohesiveness than by their willingness to adapt their behaviour, their institutions and even their beliefs as circumstances appeared to demand. The conventional view of the relationship between Japanese history, Japanese society and Japanese culture is therefore doubly misleading. It not only explains Japanese history in terms of certain immutable national characteristics but identifies as immutable characteristics which seem strangely at variance with the empirical evidence that we have presented during the course of this book. Japan was not the country, and the Japanese were not the people, that those in the English-speaking world have often been led to believe.

Appendix I

Timeline of major events and developments

Main themes in each period	Year	Events
TOKUGAWA PERIOD 1600–1868		
1850s: The Opening of Japan	1853	United States naval squadron under **Commodore Perry** ends Japanese isolation.
	1854	Commodore Perry returns to Japan; conclusion of US–Japan Treaty of Friendship.
	1858	**Unequal Treaties** concluded with United States, Britain, Holland, France and Russia.
Early 1860s: New era in politics – Anti-Bakufu Movement gains strength	1861–64	Various plans to effect emperor-centred feudalism in which many advocate overthrow of the *bakufu* but not the social order.
		National isolation formally dismantled, acceptance of foreign representatives.
		Numerous altercations between Japanese domains and foreigners.
1865–68: Twilight of the Tokugawa shōgunate and the Transformation of Objectives – Development of notion of national strength and wealth based on the idea of 'use the barbarian to subdue the barbarian': strength through Western military technology and systems; reappraisal of the value of foreign trade. Emergence of new leadership including Ōkubo, Kido and Iwakura.	1866	*Satsuma* and *Chōshū* sign secret alliance dedicated to the overthrow of the *shōgun*, giving anti-Tokugawa movement a solid core of leadership.
	1867	Accession of **Meiji emperor.**
MEIJI PERIOD 1868–1912		
1868: Meiji Restoration – Tokugawa overthrown and assumption of power by new leadership of lower-ranked *samurai*. Demise of feudalism not necessarily foreseen. Japan was neither on the verge of social and political collapse nor were its leaders, in seeking to meet the Western challenge, intent on destroying pre-modern arrangements.	1868	Emperor made ruler of Japan; civil war near Kyoto ends in defeat of Tokugawa forces and capitulation of *shōgun*.
		Charter Oath issued.
		Edo renamed Tokyo and designated new capital.

Main themes in each period	Year	Events
MEIJI PERIOD 1868–1912		
1868–77: Abolition of Feudalism – centre gradually asserts its authority over the periphery, and by 1870 moves made to end feudalism. In addition to Ōkubo, Kido and Iwakura, a new generation of leaders emerges including Itô, Yamagata, Mori and Ōkuma.	1869	New governmental system established (until 1885) and dominated by domains of *Satsuma*, *Chôshû*, Tosa and Hizen. Gradual assertion of control over feudal domains.
	1871	Postal system established.
		Burakumin given legal equality although *de facto* discrimination remains.
		Domains abolished and replaced by prefectures.
1870s: 'Civilisation and Enlightenment' – period of reform and intellectual activity advocating widespread adoption of Western ideas and systems as the best means of modernisation. Prominent figures include Fukuzawa and Tokutomi.	1870–74	**Great Promulgation Campaign.**
	1871–73	**Iwakura Mission.**
	1872	**Abolition of feudal status** system replaced with simplified structure generally based on equality.
		Promulgation of Educational Ordinance (**Fundamental Code of Education**)
Early 1870s to mid-1880s: People's Rights Movement – numerous groups around the nation emerge espousing constitutional parliamentary government. 1874 to 1878 seen as a period associated with disenfranchised *samurai* who agitate for the establishment of a national assembly. In the following three years, wealthy peasants and some business interests join the movement. The movement is radicalised in the early to mid-1880s with the inclusion of peasants suffering from government fiscal policy. Main leaders include Itagaki and Ōkuma.	1873	Opening of railway between Tokyo and Yokohama.
		Opening of government model silk factory at Tomioka.
		Conscription Law.
		Persecution against 'hidden Christians' ended and Christian missionaries allowed to enter Japan.
		Land tax introduced making land ownership legal.
	1874	**Taiwan Expedition** and assertion of Japanese control over Ryûkyû Islands.
	1874–75	Itagaki and others form organisations pressing for the establishment of constitutional, parliamentary government.
	1875	Japan receives Kurile islands in exchange for Sakhalin.
		Press and Libel laws introduced with penalties of imprisonment and fines.

Main themes in each period	Year	Events
MEIJI PERIOD 1868–1912		
	1876	**Compulsory commutation of samurai stipends.**
	1877	**Satsuma Rebellion**
		Tokyo University founded.
	1878	Ôkubo assassinated; **Itô** becomes pre-eminent leader.
		Prefectural assemblies established.
	1879	Ryūkyū Islands incorporated into Japan as Okinawa Prefecture.
1880s: Growth of Meiji Conservatism – New ambivalence to West and more selective attitude to Westernisation/modernisation. Political groups opposing Meiji leadership coalesce into first political parties. Dominant leader is Itô.	1879–80	Petitions made to emperor from private groups and individuals calling for establishment of national assembly.
	1881	**Jiyūtô** formed by **Itagaki** and others.
		Imperial Rescript promising establishment of national assembly by 1890.
		Inflation devalues yen; bankruptcies and tenancy soar following government deflationary policies.
	1882	Martial Law published.
		Imperial Rescript to Soldiers demanding absolute loyalty to emperor.
		Itô travels to Europe to study Western constitutions.
		Ôkuma and others form political party.
		Bank of Japan established.
	1882–85	Peasant insurrections.
	1884	Peerage system established.
	1885	Formation of Japan Shipping Company following merger of Mitsubishi and a rival.
		Western style cabinet introduced; **Itô** becomes first prime minister.

Main themes in each period	Year	Events
MEIJI PERIOD 1868–1912		
	1887	Foreign Minister Inoue resigns over treaty revision proposals.
		Peace Preservation Ordinance gives government arbitrary power over political opposition.
	1888	Privy Council established as consultative body.
	1889	**Meiji Constitution** promulgated.
		Assassination attempt on **Ōkuma** over treaty revision proposals.
1890–1905: 'Enrich the Country, Strengthen the Military' – with the consolidation of the Meiji polity, the leadership turned towards securing international respect, recognition and influence. Domestically, this period was characterised by experimentation with parliamentary politics by the 'oligarchs' and the political parties. Main figures include Itō, Yamagata, Katsura and other 'oligarchs', Itagaki and Ōkuma.	1890	First general election.
		Imperial Rescript on Education.
		Imperial Diet opened.
	1893	Introduction of systematic entrance examinations for bureaucracy.
	1894	Renegotiation of **'unequal treaty'** with Britain, concluded with Anglo-Japanese Treaty of Commerce and Navigation (implemented 1899).
	1894–95	**Sino-Japanese War**; concluded with Shimonoseki Treaty.
	1895	**Triple Intervention** by Russia, Germany and France. Liadong returned.
	1897	Japan adopts gold standard.
	1898	**Civil Code.**
		Society for the Study of Socialism established.
	1899	Ainu Protection Law.
	1900	**Peace Police Law** – workers' association and collective bargaining made illegal; and political activity severely restricted.
		Electoral reform: tax qualifications reduced from 15 to 10 yen.
		Boxer Rebellion in China.
		Rikken Seiyūkai formed by **Itō**.

Main themes in each period	Year	Events
MEIJI PERIOD 1868–1912		
	1901	Government-sponsored Yawata Iron Works opened.
		Tanaka Shozô makes protest to emperor over Ashio Copper Mine pollution.
	1902	**Anglo-Japanese Alliance** concluded.
1905–12: **Sense of Social Crisis** – with accelerating industrialisation and urbanisation and the completion of the Meiji mission to secure international respect, it appeared to the authorities that modernisation was undermining the unity of society. The growth of the Seiyûkai, the rise of labour and the left, and greater intellectual and artistic pluralism all contributed to this sense of apprehension. The emperor system and *kokutai* ideology became more rigid. Main leaders included Katsura, Yamagata and Hara.	1904–05	**Russo-Japanese War**; concluded by Portsmouth Treaty.
	1905	**Hibiya Park Riots.**
		Korea becomes Japanese protectorate.
	1906	Japan Socialist Party formed.
		Railways nationalised.
	1907	Compulsory primary education extended to six years.
		Ashio Copper miners' riot.
	1909	**Itô** assassinated.
	1910	Great Treason Incident resulted in execution of prominent socialists and anarchists including Kôtoku and Kanno Sugako in 1911.
		Annexation of Korea.
	1911	**Bluestocking** women's group established by **Hiratsuka Raichô**.
		Japan achieves full tariff autonomy.
		Chinese Nationalist Revolution bringing Qing Dynasty to an end.
	1912	Meiji emperor dies.

Main themes in each period	Year	Events
TAISHÔ PERIOD 1912–26		
1912–31: 'Taishô Democracy' – with the gradual extension of political party power and the decline of *genrô* power, attempts were made to introduce more popular participation and democracy. At the same time, a number of repressive measures were passed. These were aimed at limiting the flourishing of political, social and intellectual pluralism all of which were responses to social change born of modernisation and economic problems in the 1920s. Japan attempted to increase its influence in China through the pursuit of formal and informal imperialism. Main leaders included Yamagata, Hara, Katô, Wakatsuki and Hamaguchi.	1912	Accession of Taishô emperor.
	1912–13	**First Movement for the Protection of Constitutional Government**
	1914–18	**World War I** – Japan declares war on Germany and seizes German possessions in the Pacific and East Asia. Wartime economic boom.
	1915	**Twenty-One Demands** issued to China which is compelled to accept most of them.
	1917	Russian Bolshevik Revolution.
	1918	**Rice Riots.**
	1919	**Paris Peace Conference.**
		Electoral reform – tax qualifications on voting reduced to 3 yen.
	1921	Prime Minister Hara assassinated.
		Washington Naval Conference; Anglo-Japanese Alliance ended.
	1922	**Nine-Power Treaty** – includes China. Official end of 'spheres of influence' in favour of the Open Door Policy.
		Levelling Society formed, calling for equality for **burakumin.**
	1923	**Great Kantô Earthquake**; Korean and Chinese residents massacred in aftermath; anarchists Ôsugi and Itô Noe murdered.
	1924	United States prohibits immigration from Japan.
	1925	Japan recognises USSR.
		Peace Preservation Law.
		Universal manhood suffrage promulgated.
		First radio stations in Tokyo, Osaka and Nagoya commence broadcasting.
	1926	Beijing Tariff Conference.
		Death of Taishô emperor.

Main themes in each period	Year	Events
SHŌWA PERIOD 1926–89		
1926–31: Social and Economic Upheaval – domestic financial crises followed by the Great Depression helped stimulate various social movements. Foreign policy shifts between moderate, internationalist and hard-line, hawkish positions.	1926	**NHK** (Japan Broadcasting Association) established following death of Taishō emperor.
		Accession of Hirohito as **Shōwa emperor.**
	1927	**Tanaka** becomes prime minister.
		Minseitō formed.
		Eastern Conference convened to discuss Japanese foreign policy and involvement in China.
	1928	First election held under universal manhood suffrage.
		Tanaka government clamps down on left and arrests communists.
		Assassination of Chinese warlord **Zhang Zuolin.**
	1929	Tanaka resigns; return to liberal cabinets with appointment of **Hamaguchi** as prime minister.
		Crash of Wall Street stock market and start of Depression.
		Japan returns to gold standard (suspended since 1917).
	1930	**London Naval Conference** pushed through by Hamaguchi; controversy over 'Right of Supreme Command'.
		Hamaguchi shot and later dies.
		Depression hits Japanese economy.

Main themes in each period	Year	Events
SHÔWA PERIOD 1926–89		
1931–36: Domestic and Foreign Policy Crises – with the renegade actions of the Kwantung Army in Manchuria, the increasing influence of the military in politics, economic problems in the first half of the period and increasingly violent acts of terrorism, Japan gradually rejected the international order, and fumbled for a coherent policy in regards to its involvement in China. Domestically, party cabinets were replaced by 'national unity cabinets' which sought to effect political unity among a variety of groups.	1931	Crop failure and famine in the Tôhoku region.
		Manchurian Incident (18 September).
	1932	Puppet state of **Manchukuo** established under rule of Pu Yi who is later installed as emperor.
		Prime Minister Inukai assassinated (May 15 Incident).
		End of party cabinets until 1946 and start of period of **'national unity cabinets'**.
	1933	Japan withdraws from **League of Nations** following its condemnation of the Lytton Report.
	1934	Japan abandons Washington Naval Treaty.
	1935	Increasing army factionalism results in assassination by 'Imperial Way Faction' of a prominent 'Control Faction' major-general who was head of the Military Affairs Bureau.
	1936	**February 26 Incident** – insurrection led by 'Imperial Way' faction intent on effecting direct imperial rule.
1937–41: China War – at war with China, Japan threatens the interests of the Western powers. War with the West, especially the United States, becomes increasingly likely. Foreign policy and domestic politics geared more and more towards preparations for total war. Main leaders include Konoe.	1937	Five-Year Plan introduced to co-ordinate main industries.
		Fundamental Principles of the National Polity published.
		Marco Polo Bridge Incident precipitates war with China.
	1937–38	**Rape of Nanking.**
	1938	National Mobilisation Act promulgated.
		Konoe introduces **New Order in East Asia**.
	1939	US repeals Treaty of Commerce and Navigation.
	1940	Commencement of **New Political Order** including **Tripartite Pact** concluded with Germany and Italy.
		Greater East Asia Co-Prosperity Sphere established.
		Imperial Rule Assistance Association and the voluntary dissolution of the political parties.
		Greater Japan Industrial Patriotic Society founded.

Main themes in each period	Year	Events
SHŌWA PERIOD 1926–89		
	1940–42	Large parts of south-east Asia invaded and captured by Japanese troops.
1941–45: Pacific War – main leaders include Tōjō.	1941	Soviet–Japanese Neutrality Pact.
		Tōjō cabinet formed.
		Attack on **Pearl Harbor** (7 December/8 December – Japanese time) and the Malayan Peninsula.
	1942	Japanese lose naval battle at **Midway** (June).
	1943	Guadalcanal abandoned by Japanese troops (February).
		Assembly of Great East Asian Nations.
	1944	Saipan captured by Americans (July).
		Resignation of **Tōjō** as prime minister (July); replaced by Koiso.
		Air-raids on major Japanese cities
	1945	Okinawa captured by Americans (June).
		Potsdam Declaration (26 July) calls for unconditional surrender.
		Atomic bombing of **Hiroshima** and **Nagasaki** (6 and 9 August).
		USSR breaks Neutrality Pact and declares war on Japan (8 August).
		Japan accepts Potsdam Declaration (14 August).
		Japan surrenders (September 2).
1945–52: Allied Occupation of Japan		**Allied Occupation** of Japan commences.

Appendix II

Glossary of Japanese terms

The glossary lists, and gives a brief description of, the Japanese names and words that occur in the book. Entries in **bold** indicate cross-references within the glossary, while those in *italics* refer to people, groups and/or events which are referred to in the chapters. Family names are followed here by personal names (according to standard Japanese practice – e.g. **Itô** Hirobumi).

Akihito – personal name of current emperor whose reign began in 1989. Reign name is Heisei ('Achieving Peace').

bakufu – military government of the **Tokugawa shogunate** from 1603 to 1868.

Burakumin – people who in the feudal era were regarded as outcastes. Located mainly in urban areas, the burakumin lived in communities segregated from the rest of the population. Although granted full equality in 1871, they continued to suffer extreme social and economic discrimination.

Chôshû – feudal domain on the western tip of Honshû corresponding to the modern prefecture of Yamaguchi. One of the most important domains in the anti-**Tokugawa** movement. Supplied **Meiji** leadership with some of its ablest leaders including **Kido**, **Itô**, **Yamagata** and numerous **genrô**.

daimyô – lords of domains in feudal period.

Edo – the former name of **Tokyo** and seat of the **Tokugawa bakufu**.

Fukuzawa Yukichi (1835–1901) – foremost theorist and advocate of *'civilisation and enlightenment'*-style modernisation and Westernisation in the early **Meiji** period. Prolific writer and author of many influential works including *The Encouragement of Education*. Established Keiô University and the *Jiji Shimpô* newspaper.

genrô – 'elder statesmen', 'oligarchs'. *Genrô* status was accorded unofficially to those whose contributions to the state included anti-**Tokugawa** activity leading to the *Meiji Restoration* and a leadership role in the drafting and implementation of the **Meiji** reforms. Although *genrô* (e.g. **Katsura**) were recognised as late as the 1910s, their influence dwindled in the face of the challenge from the political parties in the 1910s and 1920s. From the 1920s onwards, there was only one *genrô*, Saionji Kinmochi, who attempted to stem the rise of militarism in the 1930s. He died in 1940 and failed in his attempts to establish a successor body to the *genrô*.

Guandong Army – Japanese army with independent status in Guandong Province, Manchuria. Highly politicised, it was responsible for the murder in 1928 of **Zhang Zuolin**, a major Chinese warlord, and the *Manchurian Incident* of 1931. It essentially ruled Manchuria, later **Manchukuo**, and acted as the Japanese Empire's main defence against the USSR. It was disbanded following the Second World War.

Hamaguchi Osachi (1870–1931) – president of **Minseitô** and prime minister from 1929 to 1931. Advocated a conciliatory foreign policy and forced through ratification of *London Naval Treaty* in 1930, arousing military's animosity. He died from injuries sustained during an assassination attempt by a member of a civilian right-wing organisation, effectively bringing to an end the **Minseitô**'s liberal reform agenda.

Hara Takashi (1856–1921) – major figure and behind-the-scenes leader in **Seiyûkai**. Held numerous cabinet posts in 1900s and 1910s and was able to expand party power through moderate reform, compromise and, at times, clashes with the **genrô**. First 'commoner' prime minister (1918–21). He and the **Seiyûkai** were accused of corruption and scandal. Stabbed to death.

Hiranuma Kiichirô (1867–1952) – influential figure in justice and law. Member of the House of Peers and president of the Privy Council. Prime minister in 1939 and tried to water down radical aspects of *New Order* movement. Sentenced to life imprisonment as class 'A' war criminal.

Hiratsuka Raichô (1886–1971) – founder of the *Bluestocking* women's organisation in 1911. One of the founders in 1920 of a women's political group advocating women's rights, the New Women's Society.

Hirohito – Emperor of Japan from 1926 to 1989. Also known as the **Shôwa** emperor.

ie – 'house'. It was the primary patriarchal entity around which family lineage and relationships were structured. Authority over the household was exclusively in the hands of the husband/father, as defined in the Civil Code of 1898.

Inukai Tsuyoshi (1855–1932) – prominent participant and anti-government journalist in *People's Rights Movement*. Lower House representative, cabinet minister, leader in the *First and Second (1922) Movements for the Protection of Constitutional Government*, prime minister 1931 following *Manchurian Incident*. Assassinated.

Ise – **Shinto** religion's premier shrine located near Nagoya. Ise was central to *State Shinto* ideology since it was the main shrine of the sun goddess from whom it was believed the imperial lineage was derived. '*New religion*' cult centre and major pilgrimage destination.

Ishibashi Tanzan (1884–1973) – prominent liberal economist and theorist, and critic of Japanese involvement in China during the **Taishô** period. Nonetheless, he was purged in 1947 because of his economic policies which were said to favour the **zaibatsu**. Later rehabilitated, he was prime minister in 1956 and, throughout his post-war career, was devoted to promoting relations with China.

Itagaki Taisuke (1837–1919) – participant in the anti-**Tokugawa** movement; *People's Rights Movement* leader; **Jiyutô** founder and leader; opposition politician and cabinet minister in the Imperial Diet in the 1890s.

Itô Hirobumi (1841–1909) – descendant of *Chôshû* **samurai** family and anti-**Tokugawa** movement participant. Major architect of the *Meiji Constitution*; prime minister four times between 1885 and 1901; **genrô**. One of the founders of the **Seiyûkai**. Increased Japanese control in Korea though he was not an advocate of annexation. He was assassinated in Korea.

Itô Noe (1895–1923) – member of women's group, *Bluestocking*; radical anarchist; arrested with her partner **Ôsugi** and murdered by police in the aftermath of the *Kantô (Tokyo) Earthquake* of 1923.

Iwakura Tomomi (1825–83) – court noble before the *Meiji Restoration*; influential anti-**Tokugawa** movement leader; leading official in the **Meiji** government. Led a mission of top officials and bureaucrats to Western countries (*Iwakura Mission*) from 1871 to 1873.

Jiyûtô – 'Freedom Party'. Founded in 1881 by *People's Rights Movement* activist **Itagaki**. Became 'Constitutional Freedom Party' in 1890, and in 1900 merged into the **Seiyûkai**.

kami – 'god', 'deity'. Although there was an official **Shinto** pantheon of gods centred around a creation myth, many of the 'gods' were spirits associated with natural phenomena and great people.

Kansai – region around **Ôsaka** and Kyoto in western Japan.

Kantô – region around **Tokyo** in eastern Japan and location of highly destructive 1923 earthquake (*Great Kantô Earthquake*).

Katayama Tetsu (1887–1978) – Christian active in labour and socialist movement. Elected to Imperial Diet. Leading reformer in *Occupation* period and in 1947 became prime minister. Headed a coalition socialist government until 1948 which failed to enact radical reforms.

Katô Takaaki (1860–1926) – leader of **Kenseikai** and prime minister twice between 1924 and 1926. Although he headed a coalition government, he passed *universal manhood suffrage* legislation. He was less successful in reforming the House of Peers, the tax system or introducing labour legislation.

Katô Tomosaburô (1861–1923) – admiral; prime minister from 1922 to 1923, heading non-party cabinet. Supported naval arms limitation but not universal manhood suffrage.

Katsura Tarô (1848–1913) – participant in the anti-**Tokugawa** civil war. Army officer, **genrô** and protégé of **Yamagata**. Prime minister three times between 1901 and 1913. Concluded Anglo-Japanese Alliance and at centre of political scandal which helped bring about *Movement for the Protection of Constitutional Government*.

Kenseikai – 'Constitutional Government Party'. Formed in 1916 out of a political party founded in 1913 by **Katsura**. Led by **Katô** from 1916 to 1926 and major proponent of universal manhood suffrage and other liberal reforms. It became the **Minseitô** in 1927.

Kido Takayoshi (1833–1877) – descendant of **Chôshû samurai** family and leader in anti-**Tokugawa** movement. One of the most important leaders in the *Meiji Restoration*; participant in *Iwakura Mission*; helped draft the *Charter Oath*; advocated state centralisation and modernisation along Western lines.

Koiso Kuniaki (1880–1950) – army general and leading member of *Control Faction*. Prime minister from 1944 to 1945 following the fall of **Tôjô**. Sentenced to life imprisonment as class 'A' war criminal.

kokutai – 'national polity' or 'national essence'. It refers to the entirety of a nation's institutions, character and spirit as informed by its culture and history. In Japan, it came to be rigidly defined in terms of the imperial institution, its relationship to the people and *emperor system*/worship.

Konoe Fumimaro (1891–1945) – court noble and prime minister three times in the late 1930s and early 1940s prior to the Pacific War. Architect of New Order movement; involved in numerous attempts to forge compromise between competing political and military interests and to mobilise and co-ordinate national war effort. Designated a class 'A' war criminal.

Kyoto – ancient capital of Japan and seat of the emperor from 794 to 1868.

Manchukuo – following the occupation of Manchuria by the **Guandong Army** after the 1931 *Manchurian Incident*, it was transmogrified into a puppet state under the rule of Pu Yi, the last Chinese emperor. Despite condemnation by the League of Nations, Japan recognised Manchukuo as an 'independent' nation although, in reality, she controlled its politics, social institutions and economy, linking its economic development to the war needs of the home islands.

Meiji – 'enlightened rule'. Name of the first modern emperor, Mutsuhito, and the name of his reign (1868 to 1912) which was ushered in by the 1868 *Restoration*. Constitution of 1889 named after him. **Shinto** shrine completed in 1920 commemorating his reign and central to emperor worship.

Minobe Tatsukichi (1873–1948) – leading constitutional theorist in the 1910s and 1920s. His ideas were condemned in the 1930s and this led to the publication of the *Fundamental Principles of the National Polity*.

Minseitô – 'Constitutional People's Government Party'. Formed in 1927 following the merger of the **Kenseikai** with other groups. Leading figures included **Wakatsuki** and **Hamaguchi**. Disbanded in 1940.

Mori Arinori (1847–89) – **Satsuma** advocate of Westernisation and architect of educational system. Minister of education twice between 1885 and 1889 when he was assassinated for his pro-Western views.

Mukden – site of the 1931 *Manchurian Incident*.

Nagasaki – port city on southern island of Kyûshû. Prior to the opening of Japan, it was the centre of '*Western learning*' and was the only city in Japan open to foreigners (mainly Dutch and Chinese). Centre of '*hidden Christians*'.

Nanjin (Nanking) – capital of Nationalist China on the banks of the Yangtze River. Captured by Japanese forces in early 1938 and suffered terrible atrocities for two and a half months. This incident became known as the '*Rape of Nanking*' and now, the 'Nanking Atrocities'.

NHK (Nihon Hôsô Kyôkai/Japanese Broadcasting Association) – government-controlled body established in 1926 with monopoly over radio broadcasting. Main vehicle in the dissemination of government propaganda until 1945.

Okada Keisuke (1868–1952) – admiral; navy minister twice in the late 1920s and early 1930s; prime minister in 1934. Despite attempts to re-establish political control over the military, the *February 26* insurrection of 1936 brought about the resignation of his cabinet.

Oku Mumeo (1895–) – women's movement leader, led the New Women's Society from 1922; publisher of the magazine *Working Women*; elected three times to the Upper House of the Diet in the post-war period; founder of a housewives' consumer movement in 1948.

Ôkubo Toshimichi (1830–78) – low-ranking **Satsuma samurai** and leader in anti-**Tokugawa** movement. Participant in the *Iwakura Mission*; leading **Meiji** government figure, and one of the most important figures responsible for the **Meiji** political, economic and social, and military reforms. Responsible for suppressing *Satsuma Rebellion* of 1877.

Ôkuma Shigenobu (1838–1922) – anti-**Tokugawa** movement participant; influential *People's Rights Movement* leader; opposition politician and cabinet minister during the 1890s; prime minister in 1898 and from 1914 to 1916.

Ôsaka – second largest city in Japan and traditional commercial capital.

Ôsugi Sakae (1885–1923) – prominent anarchist, especially after *World War I* when he was actively involved in the labour movement. Murdered by the police in the aftermath of the *Kantô Earthquake*.

Qing – Manchu dynasty ruling China from 1662 to their overthrow in 1911.

Rôyama Masamichi (1895–1980) – prominent pre-war liberal.

Ryûkyû – chain of islands (including Okinawa) south-west of Kyûshû and north of Taiwan.

samurai – 'warrior' (also known as *bushi*). Warriors loyal to **shôgun** or **daimyô** in the feudal period, they subscribed in theory to a strict code of loyalty, honour and chivalry that strongly informed mores and ethics in the modern period. Following the imposition of peace by the **Tokugawa** in the seventeenth century, they served as government officials and bureaucrats as their martial skills were no longer required. Following the *Meiji Restoration*, they lost their previous privileges and rights and were gradually incorporated into society at large.

Sanpô – 'Greater Japan Industrial Patriotic Association'. Following the dissolution of labour unions in 1940, Sanpô was established to mobilise the labour force behind the war effort.

Satsuma – feudal domain corresponding to the modern prefecture of Kagoshima in Kyûshû. One of the most important domains active in the anti-**Tokugawa** movement, it supplied the **Meiji** leadership with some of its ablest leaders including **Ôkubo** and numerous **genrô**.

Seiyûkai – 'Constitutional Political Friends' Society' founded by **genrô** Itô. Leading members included **Hara** and **Tanaka**. Despite internal factionalism, it was one of two main political parties active until 1940 when it dissolved itself.

Shinto – 'Way of the Gods'. Indigenous religion centred around notions of purity, worship at shrines and numerous *kami*. Prior to the **Meiji** *Restoration*, *'national learning'* theorists and Shinto intelligentsia advocated restoration of imperial rule and the doctrine of the divinity of the emperor. **Meiji** authorities developed selected aspects of Shinto into *State Shinto* which became one of the primary ideological underpinnings of **kokutai** ideology and the *emperor system*.

shôgun – 'Barbarian-Quelling Generalissimo'. Title given by the emperor to his highest military leader in the feudal era. *De facto* secular leader of feudal Japan during the **Tokugawa** period.

Shôwa – 'Brilliant Harmony'. Period name and reign name of Emperor **Hirohito** from 1926 to 1989.

Taishô – 'Great Justice'. Period name and reign name of emperor Yoshihito from 1912 to 1926. His name became associated with tentative liberal trends in politics and society (*'Taishô Democracy'*) that occurred between 1912 and the Manchurian Incident of 1931.

Tanaka Giichi (1864–1929) – *Chôshû* **samurai**; general and leader of the *Chôshû* faction in army following death of **Yamagata** in 1922. Prime minister (**Seiyûkai**) from 1927 to 1929. Initiated *Eastern Conference* in which he advocated a strong continental policy to further Japanese interests. Responsible for clamping down on the left wing, especially the Communist Party and, during his premiership, for reintroducing authoritarian-style government.

Tôhoku – largely agricultural region of northern Honshû that suffered famine and economic hardship in the Great Depression.

Tôjô Hideki (1884–1948) – high-ranking military officer and war minister. Prime minister from 1941 to 1944. Assumed increasing, but not total, power by taking on many ministerial posts throughout World War II. Resigned premiership in 1944 due to lack of support and possible rebellion against his leadership. Hanged as class 'A' war criminal in 1948.

Tokugawa – the military dynasty which held the hereditary title of **shôgun** from 1603 to 1867. Tokugawa *Yoshinobu* was the last **shôgun** from 1866 to 1867.

Tokutomi Sohô (1863–1957) – leading journalist. Prior to the *Sino-Japanese War* (1894–95), he was a member of a group that advocated Western parliamentarianism, pacifism and internationalism. He later advocated expansionism and was purged after *World War II*.

Tsuda Umeko (1864–1929) – one of the first women to study in the US and founder of a girls' school in 1900 (now Tsuda Women's University). Played a leading role in the promotion of women's higher education and English education.

ujigami – 'protective deity' in accordance with **Shinto** belief of a hamlet, village or region.

Uno Chiyo (1897–1996) – novelist. Noted for her ability to convey women's psychology, one of her most famous works was *Confessions* (*Irozange*) in the early 1930s.

Wakatsuki Reijirô (1866–1949) – leader of **Kenseikai** from 1926 to 1927 and prominent member of **Minseitô**. Prime minister twice (1926–27; 1931). Introduced unpopular measures to deal with the effects of the Great Depression and unable to prevent further incursions by the **Guandong Army** following the *Manchurian Incident*, he and his cabinet resigned, ushering in a decade of *'national unity cabinets'*.

Yasukuni – **Shinto** shrine established in **Tokyo** in 1869 dedicated to soldiers who died in combat for the emperor. Important site in the ideology of *State* **Shinto** since it was – and sometimes, still is – believed that the spirits of the war dead were protectors of the nation.

Yamagata Aritomo (1838–1922) – descendant of a *Chôshû* **samurai** family; participant in civil war against **Tokugawa** regime; major architect of modern army and conscription; prime minister twice; most influential **genrô** in the 1900s and 1910s.

Yoshida Shigeru (1878–1967) – pre-war diplomat and prime minister from 1946 to 1954 (except for 1947 to 1948) with support of various conservative parties. Despite co-operation with early reformist trend of Occupation, he became a leading figure in the *'Reverse Course'* (including rearmament, rehabilitation of purged conservative figures, government re-centralisation, *'Red Purge'* and conservative educational retrenchment). His governments established and routinised the post-war pattern of one hegemonic party dominating electoral politics.

Yoshino Sakuzô (1878–1933) – foremost political theorist during the **Taishô** period and formulator of Japanese-style democracy (*Taishô Democracy*). Supporter of universal manhood suffrage and liberal reforms to the House of Peers, Privy Council and army.

zaibatsu – 'financial clique'. Conglomerates which dominated Japanese economy until 1945 with strong ties to the major political parties and government. The original four conglomerates were *Mitsui, Mitsubishi, Sumitomo* and *Yasuda*. 'New zaibatsu' including *Nissan* emerged in the 1930s.

Appendix III

Select bibliography

Chapter 1: Introduction

Beasley, **W.G.**, *The Rise of Modern Japan: Political, Economic and Social Change since 1850*, Weidenfeld & Nicolson, 1990.

Dower, **J.**, *Japan in War and Peace: Essays on History, Race and Culture*, HarperCollins, 1995.

Hunter, **J.E.**, *The Emergence of Modern Japan: An Introductory History since 1853*, Longman, 1989.

Jansen, **M.B.** and **P. Duus** (eds), *The Cambridge History of Japan*, vols 5 & 6, Cambridge University Press, 1989.

Morley, **J.W.** (ed.), *Dilemmas of Growth in Pre-War Japan*, Princeton University Press, 1974.

Pyle, **K.B.**, *The Making of Modern Japan*, Heath, 1978.

Silberman, **B.S.** and **H.D. Harootunian** (eds), *Japan in Crisis: Essays in Taishô Democracy*, Princeton University Press, 1974.

Waswo, **A.**, *Modern Japanese Society 1868–1994*, Oxford University Press, 1996.

Chapter 2: Politics and political systems

Akita, **G.**, *Foundations of Constitutional Government in Modern Japan: 1869–1900*, Harvard University Press, 1967.

Beasley, **W.G.**, *The Meiji Restoration*, Stanford University Press, 1973.

Berger, **G.M.**, *Parties out of Power in Japan: 1931–1941*, Princeton University Press, 1977.

Butow, **R.**, *Tôjô and the Coming of the War*, Stanford University Press, 1961.

Dower, **J.**, *Japan in War and Peace: Essays on History, Race and Culture*, HarperCollins, 1995.

Duus, **P.**, *Party Rivalry and Political Change in Taishô Japan*, Harvard University Press, 1968.

Ike, **N.**, *The Beginnings of Political Democracy in Japan*, Johns Hopkins Press, 1950.

Irokawa, **D.**, *The Culture of the Meiji Period*, **M.B. Jansen** (ed. and trans.), Princeton University Press, 1965.

Jansen, **M.B.** (ed.), *The Emergence of Meiji Japan*, Cambridge University Press, 1995.

Jansen, **M.B.** and **G. Rozman** (eds), *Japan in Transition from Tokugawa to Meiji*, Princeton University Press, 1986.

Maruyama, **M.**, *Thought and Behaviour in Modern Japanese Politics*, *Expanded Edition*, **I. Morris** (ed.), Oxford University Press, 1969, first published in 1963.

Najita, T., *Hara Kei in the Politics of Compromise, 1905–1915*, Harvard University Press, 1967.

Norman, E.H., *Japan's Emergence as a Modern State: Political and Economic Problems of the Meiji Period*, Institute of Pacific Relations, 1940.

Pittau, J., *Political Thought in the Early Meiji Period, 1868–1889*, Harvard University Press, 1967.

Scalopino, R.A., *Democracy and the Party Movement in Prewar Japan: The Failure of the First Attempt*, University of California Press, 1953.

Shillony, B.-A., *Politics and Culture in Wartime Japan*, Clarendon Press, 1991.

Totman, C., *The Collapse of the Tokugawa Bakufu, 1862–1868*, University of Hawaii Press, 1980.

Chapter 3: International relations and imperial expansion

Bamba, N., *Japanese Diplomacy in a Dilemma: A New Light on Japan's China Policy, 1924–1929*, University of British Columbia Press, 1972.

Beasley, W.G., *Japanese Imperialism, 1894–1945*, Oxford University Press, 1987.

Buruma, I., *Wages of Guilt: Memories of War in Germany and Japan*, Vintage, 1995.

Conroy, H. (ed.), *Pearl Harbor Re-examined: Prologue to the Pacific War*, University Press of Hawaii, 1990.

Crowley, J.B., *Japan's Quest for Autonomy: National Security and Foreign Policy 1930–1938*, Princeton University Press, 1966.

Dower, J. *War Without Mercy: Race and Power in the Pacific War*, Faber & Faber, 1986.

Duus, P., R.H. Myers and M.R. Peattie (eds), *The Japanese Informal Empire in China, 1895–1937*, Princeton University Press, 1989.

Duus, P., R.H. Myers and M.R. Peattie (eds), *The Japanese Wartime Empire, 1931–1945*, Princeton University Press, 1996.

Ienaga, S., *Japan's Last War: World War II and the Japanese, 1931–1945*, Blackwell, 1979.

Iriye, A., *The Origins of the Second World War in Asia and the Pacific*, Longman, 1987.

Iriye, I., *After Imperialism: The Search for a New Order in the Far East, 1921–1931*, Harvard University Press, 1965.

Mayo, M. (ed.), *The Emergence of Imperial Japan: Self-Defense or Calculated Aggression*, Heath, 1970.

Myers, R.H. and M.R. Peattie (eds), *The Japanese Colonial Empire, 1895–1945*, Princeton University Press, 1984.

Nish, I.H., *Japanese Foreign Policy, 1869–1942: Kasumigaseki to Miyakezaka*, Routledge & Kegan Paul, 1977.

Chapter 4: Economic growth, industrial relations, consumption and saving

Allen, G.C., *A Short Economic History of Modern Japan, 1867–1937*, Allen & Unwin, 1946.

Crawcour, E.S., 'Industrialization and Technological Change, 1885–1920', in P. Duus (ed.), *The Cambridge History of Japan*, vol. 6, *The Twentieth Century*, Cambridge University Press, 1988.

Gordon, A., *The Evolution of Labor Relations in Japan: Heavy Industry, 1853–1955*, Harvard University Press, 1985.

Hirschmeier, J. and T. Yui, *The Development of Japanese Business*, Allen & Unwin, 1975.

Lockwood, W.W., *The Economic Development of Japan: Growth and Structural Change, 1868–1938*, Oxford University Press, 1955.

Macpherson, W.J., *The Economic Development of Japan, 1868–1941*, Cambridge University Press, 1995.

Minami, R., *The Economic Development of Japan: A Quantitative Study*, Macmillan, 1986.

Nakamura, T., 'Depression, Recovery, and War, 1920–1945', in P. Duus (ed.), *The Cambridge History of Japan*, vol. 6, *The Twentieth Century*, Cambridge University Press, 1988.

Nakamura, T., *Economic Growth in Prewar Japan*, Yale University Press, 1983.

Odagiri, H. and A. Gotô, *Technology and Industrial Development in Japan: Building Capabilities by Learning, Innovation and Public Policy*, Clarendon Press, 1996.

Smethurst, R.J., *Agricultural Development and Tenancy Disputes in Japan, 1870–1940*, Princeton University Press, 1986.

Smith, T., *Political Change and Industrial Development in Japan*, Stanford University Press, *c*. 1955.

Taira, K., *Economic Development and the Labor Market in Japan*, Columbia University Press, 1970.

Tsurumi, E.P., *Factory Girls: Women in the Thread Mills of Meiji Japan*, Princeton University Press, 1990.

Chapter 5: Education, religion and the media

Fridell, W.M., *Japanese Shrine Mergers, 1906–1912: State Shinto Moves to the Grassroots*, Sophia University, 1973.

Gluck, C., *Japan's Modern Myths: Ideology in the Late Meiji Period*, Princeton University Press, 1985.

Hardacre, H., *Shinto and the State, 1868–1988*, Princeton University Press, 1989.

Huffman, J.L., *Creating a Public: People and Press in Meiji Japan*, University of Hawaii Press, 1997.

Iritani, T., *Group Psychology of the Japanese in Wartime*, Kegan Paul International, 1991.

Kasza, G.J., *The State and the Mass Media in Japan, 1918–1945*, University of California Press, 1988.

Marshall, B.K., *Learning to be Modern: Japanese Political Discourse on Education*, Westview Press, 1994.

Mitchell, R.H., *Censorship in Imperial Japan*, Princeton University Press, 1983.

Murakami, S., *Japanese Religion in the Modern Century*, H.B. Earhart (trans.), University of Tokyo Press, 1968.

Smethurst, R.J., *A Social Basis for Prewar Japanese Militarism*, University of California Press, 1974.

Chapter 6: Individual, family, class and nation

Bernstein, G.L. (ed.), *Recreating Japanese Women: 1600–1945*, University of California Press, 1991.

Embree, J.F., *Suye Mura*, University of Chicago Press, 1939.

Fujimura-Fanselow, K. and A. Kameda (eds), *Japanese Women: New Feminist Perspectives on the Past, Present, and Future*, The Feminist Press, 1995.

Hane, M., *Reflections on the Way to the Gallows: Rebel Women in Prewar Japan*, University of California Press, 1988.

Kinmôth, E.H., *The Self-Made Man in Meiji Japanese Thought: From Samurai to Salary Man*, University of California Press, 1981.

Large, S., *Organized Workers and Socialist Politics in Interwar Japan*, Cambridge University Press, 1981.

Lebra, J., J. Paulson and E. Powers (eds), *Women in Changing Japan*, Westview Press, 1976.

Lewis, M., *Rioters and Citizens: Mass Protest in Imperial Japan*, University of California Press, 1990.

Najita, T. and J.V. Koschmann (eds), *Conflict in Modern Japanese History*, Princeton University Press, 1982.

Robins Mowry, D., *The Hidden Sun: Women of Modern Japan*, Westview Press, 1983.

Sievers, S.L., *Flowers in Salt: The Beginnings of Feminist Consciousness in Modern Japan*, Stanford University Press, 1983.

Totten, G.O., *The Social Democratic Movement in Prewar Japan*, Yale University Press, 1966.

Tsurumi, K., *Social Change and the Individual: Japan Before and After Defeat in World War II*, Princeton University Press, 1970.

Weiner, M. (ed.), *Japan's Minorities: The Illusion of Homogeneity*, Routledge, 1997.

Chapter 7: Epilogue: the Allied Occupation, 1945–52

Dower, J.W., *Empire and Aftermath – Yoshida Shigeru and the Japanese Experience, 1878–1954*, Harvard University Press, 1971.

Finn, R., *Winners in Peace: MacArthur, Yoshida, and Postwar Japan*, University of California Press, 1992.

Kawai, K., *Japan's American Interlude*, University Press of Chicago, 1960.

Koyama, T., *The Changing Social Position of Women in Japan*, UNESCO, 1961.

Nakamura, T., *The Postwar Japanese Economy – Its Development and Structure*, University of Tokyo Press, 1981.

Schaller, M., *The American Occupation of Japan: The Origins of the Cold War in Asia*, Oxford University Press, 1985.

Supreme Commander for the Allied Powers, *The Political Reorientation of Japan*, 2 vols, 1949.

Ward, R. and Y. Sakamoto (eds), *Democratizing Japan: The Allied Occupation*, University of Hawaii Press, 1987.

Index

abolition of feudal domains *see* feudalism and feudal system
absentee landlords *see* landlords
Agricultural Development and Tenancy Disputes in Japan, 1870–1940 216n
agricultural subsidies *see* farming
Ainu see minorities
air force *see* armed forces
air raids 44, 82, 111, 224
Akihito *see* Heisei emperor
Akita, G. 25
Allied Council for Japan 218
Allied Powers 1, 42, 45
Allied Occupation 1, 7, 8, 9, 12, 21, 178, 179, 198, 206, 218–232 (Chapter 7, Epilogue), 233, 234; Occupation administration and structure 218–219, 229; Occupation forces 218, 222, 227, 229; Occupation reforms 222–224, 229; restoration of sovereignty 227; 'reverse course' 226–228, 229
America *see* United States of America
anarchism 36, 203
Anglo-Japanese Alliance 63–64, 68, 71
anti-Christian proscription 153
Anti-Comintern Pact 78, 79
anti-imperialism 70, 80, 202
anti-monopoly law 220
armed forces: air force 82, 83; imperial army 19, 22, 28, 37, 40, 53, 54, 56, 64, 81, 83, 140, 164; imperial navy 22, 40, 64, 75, 83; *see also* military
arranged marriage *see* marriage
Article 9 222; *see also* Constitution of 1947
artisans 15
'Asian values' 107
Asahi Shinbun 168, 170
Assembly of Greater East Asia Nations 82; *see also* Greater East Asia Co-Prosperity Sphere, 'New Order in East Asia', pan-Asianism

assimilation 210; *see also* minorities
atomic bombing, Hiroshima and Nagasaki 5, 44, 83
Attu 82
Austria-Hungary 35, 66
authoritarianism 1, 2, 3, 38–45, 46, 47, 55, 204
Automobile Manufacturing Industry Law 101

Baelz, Erwin 135, 148
Balkans 57, 61
'bamboo-spear psychology' 225
Bank of Japan 27
Barnhart, M. 24
Barrington Moore, S.D. 46, 102
Beasley, W.G. 62, 229
Beijing 5, 61, 63, 79
Beijing Tariff Conference, 1925 71
Belgian State Bank 27
biological experimentation *see* Unit 731, war atrocities
birth rate 182–183, 184; contraception 183; fertility 182; *see also* population
black market 224
Bluestocking 189, *see also* Hiratsuka Raichô
Bonin Islands 58
Boxer Rebellion 63, 64, 65
Britain *see* United Kingdom
British Commonwealth 219
Buddhism 146, 147, 149, 150–151, 152, 174n, 208; charitable activity 150; institutional reform 150; missionary work in colonies 150; priests 137; separation from Shinto 147
burakumin see minorities
bureaucracy 3, 22, 23, 30, 33, 34, 40, 42, 104, 150, 159, 204
Burma 2, 44, 53, 81, 82, 83, 231n
Buruma, I. 145

cabinet 22, 23, 24, 25, 143
Cabinet Bureau of Statistics 101